KERR COUNTY

TEXAS

Probate Records

1856~2002

Compiled by

Gloria C. Dozier

HERITAGE BOOKS
2008

HERITAGE BOOKS
AN IMPRINT OF HERITAGE BOOKS, INC.

Books, CDs, and more—Worldwide

For our listing of thousands of titles see our website
at
www.HeritageBooks.com

Published 2008 by
HERITAGE BOOKS, INC.
Publishing Division
100 Railroad Ave. #104
Westminster, Maryland 21157

Copyright © 2008 Gloria C. Dozier

Other books by the author:

Kerr County, Texas Birth Records
Kerr County, Texas Death Records, 1903-1960
Kerr County, Texas Divorce Records, 1856-1990
Kerr County, Texas Land Records, 1837-1927, Volume 1, A-K
Kerr County, Texas Land Records, 1837-1927, Volume 2, L-Z
Kerr County, Texas Probate Records, 1856-2002
Kerrville Daily Times *Obituary Books, 1986-2000, Master Index*
Kerrville Daily Times *Obituary Index, 1925-April 30, 1979*
Kerrville Mountain Sun *and* Kerrville Advance *Obituary and
Death Notice Index, 1898-1965*

International Standard Book Number: 978-0-7884-3741-0

INDEX

FORWARD

Kerr County, Texas Probate Records

Apparently Kerr County started numbering
their probate records about 1862, with
Roland Nichols listed as number 1. This
book documents those recorded from that
time through the year 2002.

The Document Number is the order in which
the person's information was recorded.
The approximated date of the recording is
under YEAR. In some cases, the recording
of the document may be several years after
the actual death.

If the number is a CV, it means it was
transferred to a county court.

There were previous probates, but they did
not seem to have anything but a dash
preceding the name. The earliest of these
was Daniel C. Murphy who was killed in
1856 by Indians at the Boneyard Waterhole
near Hunt, Kerr County, Texas. It was
called Boneyard because of the many
bleached animal bones found there.

When enumerating started the first ten
names recorded were:
        1—Roland Nichols   recorded 1862
        2-F. W. Bourner   recorded 1872
        3-Edward Felsing   who died in 1862
        while trying to get away from
        Confederate Troops with a group of
        men who did not want to join the
        Confederacy. The Confederates did

not bury the men they killed, but left them to rot. After the Civil War, the bones were gathered up and brought to Comfort, Texas and buried under a marker that says True to the Union.

4-Gustav C. Steves died about 1862
5-Hiram Nelson --1862
6-Henry Lange --1865
7-Sam Carr—1865
8-Robert Mc Minn —a. 1869
9-W. J. Glenn—1870
10-Edward Brown--1872

There are names on the list that the spelling may not be quite accurate. Early writing was hard to read and that many people could not read or write so the recorders wrote what they heard.

Gloria Clifton Dozier

KERR COUNTY, TEXAS PROBATE RECORDS

File	Deceased	Year

A

File	Deceased	Year
13844	Aaron, Douglas Edward	1993
5248	Abbott, Brian	1973
3086	Abbott, C. G.	1964
11974	Abbott, Edith Sutton	1990
9558	Abbott, Frederick M. Jr.	1985
8203	Abbott, Leah S.	1982
9105	Abbott, Lem Carroll	1984
1284	Abercrombie, Joe Dick	1991
14859	Abernathy, Evelin Johnson	1995
5021	Abernathy, George L.	1973
4816	Abernathy, John R.	1972
5911	Abernathy, Katherine	1976
3640	Ables, Alfreda Gertrude	1966
7480-A	Abraham, Dorothy Lee	1980
7877	Abrahams, Lorena	1981
14080	Abrahams, Otis A.	1993
11584	Abshier, William R.	1989
15510	Aceto, Angelo	1996
16386	Acker, Earl	1997
16458	Acker, Gloria D.	1998
19156	Ackert, Ella Anna	2002
1831	Acklam, Marie	1981
7830	Acklam, Raymond	1981
4809	Adain, John Hugh	1972
15250	Adair, Florence Jennings	1995
10836	Adamik, Franklin	1987
3690	Adams, Arthur E.	1967
4422	Adams, Beatrice B.	1970

File	Deceased	Year
14730	Adams, David Norvell	1994
5641	Adams, Don H. Hoerster	1975
16792	Adams, Dorothy Ray aka	
	Dorothy Rae	1998
13424	Adams, Edna Irene	1992
1953	Adams, Hearne O.	1955
13402	Adams, Joe Ward	1992
12194	Adams, Juanita Bishop	1990
5203	Adams, Lilian Mollerrd	1973
17058	Adams, Lorena H.	1999
14220	Adams, Louis Carrolle	1993
13288	Adams, Mary Ella	
	Redwine	1992
1201	Adams, Sallie L.	1944
1829	Adams, W. C.	1954
15176	Adams, William Ford	1995
2278	Adams, Willie P.	----
15150	Adcock, Dave	
	Everett Sr.	1995
845	Adkins, James L.	1935
13624	Adkins, Hobert D.	1992
9888	Adkins, May Rogers	1986
7681	Adnerski, John	1973
13946	Adolf, Helen	1993
827	Adrain, M. Joe	1934
16198	Agee, James E.	1997
7791	Agee, Mildred V.	1981
2633	Aguero, Domingo E.	1950
18782	Aguero, Lily	2001
13396	Ahern, Ruth S.	1992
15188	Ahern, Ruth S.	1995
5104	Aherns, Hugo	1973
8661	Ahlers, Albert P.	1983
15798	Ahner, David	1996

File	Deceased	Year
14234	Ahr, Rosa Josephine	1994
18944	Ahrens, Gerald	2002
12460	Ahrens, Guenther Hugo	1990
5894	Ahrens, Kenneth	1976
18942	Ahrens, Margaret	2002
8631	Ahrens, Minnie B.	1983
18632	Ahrns, Ann A.	2001
CV960050	Airhart, Lisa Carol	1996
14872	Ajjan, Louis Elias	1995
5839	Akin, Delmer L.	1975
3679	Akin, James Virgil	1967
4710	Akin, Viola Leah	1971
11940	Akowicz, Henry G.	1989
2175	Albaugh, E. R.	1957
8278	Albe, Minnie B.	1982
4290	Albe, Richard H.	1969
11752	Alberthal, Leroy A.	1989
8507	Albrecht, Bruno	1983
18790	Albrecht, Edna Taply	2001
1378	Albrecht, Gustav	1948
12150	Albrecht, Helen M.	1990
11544	Albrecht, Robert A.	1989
14278	Albrecht, Walter J.	1994
14356	Albrecht, Willie O.	1994
1311	Albrecht, William A.	1946
15516	Albright, Raymond William	1996
2708	Alderdice, J. A.	----
14156	Alderdice, Meta	1993
15068	Aldis, Barney	1995
4062	Aldrich, Henry V.	1968
16714	Aldrich, Julia	1998
10766	Aldridge, Lucille Bordagas	1987
12512	Aldridge, William Hal	1991

3

File	Deceased	Year
15220	Alexander, Cy Cameron	1995
15604	Alexander, Dorothy Faye Grant	1996
12344	Alexander, John Everett	1990
17830	Alexander, John Nathan	2000
4448	Alexander, Michael L.	1970
8843	Alexander, Milton	1984
17806	Alexander, Roxy L.	2000
11664	Alexander, Wayne Robert	1989
6479	Alexander, Wayne W.	1977
17748	Alexander, Woodrow E.	2000
15196	Allan, Norma Smith	1995
10194	Allan, Roy Burton	1986
18864	Allcorn, Ernest Taply	----
18986	Allcorn, Hazel Shave	2002
2384	Alleger, William T.	----
19390	Allen, Alvin Douglas	2002
19094	Allen, Alvin W.	2002
12550	Allen, Arline Houghton	1991
SE82	Allen, Betty Key	1982
17910	Allen, Charles Robert	2000
5878	Allen, David W.	1975
4690	Allen, Earl Davis	1971
16578	Allen, Felma	1998
SE66	Allen, Frank Rhodes	1982
SE66	Allen, Frank Rhodes	1982
1690	Allen, J. E.	1953
1735	Allen, J. T.	1953
14514	Allen, James Victor	1994
5715	Allen, Kelso	1975
12670	Allen, Lee Martin	1991
1898	Allen, Lewis Raymond	1955
4322	Allen, Marjorie F.	1969
9574	Allen, Neyland R.	1985
1398	Allen, Thomas H.	1948

File	Deceased	Year
16150	Allen, Virginia Alice	1997
352	Allen, W. W.	1913
6602	Allen, Winfield	1978
13476	Allen, Zoe Marlow	1992
1844	Allerkamp, Elsa	1954
10804	Allerkamp, Esther	1987
17648	Allerkamp, Olga E.	2000
3031	Allerkamp, Rudolf	1962
2364	Allerkamp, William	1959
7011	Alliger, Robbie Tipse	1979
13568	Alison, A. P.	1992
10768	Allison, Caroline Bixler	1987
4556	Allison, Charles N.	1971
18660	Allison, D. Rhea	2001
11758	Allison, Helen Hines	1989
15770	Allison, Irene M.	1996
18756	Allison, Lena Mary	2001
18918	Allman, Tommy J.	2002
12828	Alson, Martin L.	1991
657	Alssn, Sven Orvar	----
7838	Althaus, Margaret	1981
8663	Althaus, Margaret	1983
13016	Althoff, Gerhardt F.	1991
.19170	Alvarado, Lydia A.	2002
841	Alvis, Joseph M.	1934
11782	Aman, Sue P.	1989
18858	Amann, Janice Hensley	2002
14982	Amann, Peggy Bohner	1995
11798	Ambrose, Clarence W. Jr.	1989
15902	Amerman, A. E. Jr.	1997
18526	Amerman, Dorothy Kenyon	2001
4289	Ammons, Jesse H.	1969
5406	Amos, Clovis A.	1973
14326	Amos, Estelle Ford	1994

File	Deceased	Year
19232	Amsbury, David Leonard	2002
7753	Amsler, D. W.	1981
18562	Amsler, Dana	2001
8178	Anderson, Dr. A. G.	1982
16398	Anderson, Andrew	1997
3191	Anderson, Anna K.	1964
9268	Anderson, Aouida Canville	1984
3936	Anderson, Asa Scott	1968
4761	Anderson, Mrs. Asa	1972
10554	Anderson, Autie Mae	1987
16702	Anderson, Billy Don	1998
17512	Anderson, Doris L.	1999
267	Anderson, E. L. (Everett L.)	1909
17530	Anderson, E. M. (Tex)	1999
15546	Anderson, Florrie Cotter	1996
11074	Anderson, Francis	1988
9464	Anderson, Francis W.	1985
2041	Anderson, Frank Elam	1963
11528	Anderson, Frank L.	1989
1914	Anderson, Frank S.	1955
15928	Anderson, George Lynn	1997
1074	Anderson, Geo. R.	1941
2126	Anderson, Harry R.	1957
6038	Anderson, Helen R.	1976
4332	Anderson, Ida Mae	1970
17134	Anderson, Jesse Charles	1999
5743	Anderson, Kate K.	1975
10048	Anderson, Lola B.	1986
16988	Anderson, Lucille Mickey	1998
13454	Anderson, Margaret E.	1992
5591	Anderson, Marjorie T.	1974

File	Deceased	Year
14948	Anderson, Mary E.	1995
16752	Anderson, Oscar Press aka	
	Oscar Press Leslie	1998
18190	Anderson, Robert	2000
494	Anderson, Sarah	1921
18926	Anderson, Shirley	2002
2407	Anderson, Stewart H.	1959
287	Anderson, W. C.	1909
11060	Anderson, William	1988
6501	Andrahe, John C. Sr.	1977
15402	Andres, Carrie	1996
13820	Andrews, Albert L. Jr.	1993
2820	Andrews, Beulah S.	1962
9032	Andrews, Edith Koger	1984
9666	Andrews, Eileen Ann	1985
3171	Andrews, Etta A.	1964
11410	Andrews, Ima Wolfe	1988
16598	Andrews, John William	1998
CV99010	Andrews, John William	1999
10634	Andrews, Mary Aileene	1987
9704	Andrews, Richard M.	1985
6277	Andrews, Roy M.	1977
16728	Andrus, Cleveland	1998
2170	Annis, J. B.	1957
1785	Anthony, J. M.	1954
2041	Anthony, Mary J.	----
12746	Antony, Marie S.	1991
17214	Antony, Trixie Jeanne	1999
1186	Apelt, Chase	1944
4985	Apelt Sr., Kurt C.	1972
1317	Apelt, Martha	----
5572	Apelt, William F.	1974
17782	Apple, Lillian M.	2000
3424	Appleby, A. D.	1965
16316	Appleby, Shirley M.	1997

File	Deceased	Year
16744	Apts, Leonard B.	1998
17332	Apts, Ruth E.	1999
4618	Arbuckle, Miriam E.	1971
6483	Arbuckle, William Barnes	1977
14628	Archer, Cecil L.	1994
17002	Archer, Elizabeth B.	1998
18682	Archer, Marvin C.	2001
17370	Archer, Phillip Raymond	1999
13032	Archibald, Donald L.	1991
17210	Archibald, Edith Ives	1999
10398	Archibald, Fontella B.	1986
15574	Architect, Louis H.	1996
14050	Architect, Mildred W.	1993
18774	Ard, Audrey Norene	2001
16464	Arens, Robert William	1998
16762	Arhelger, Glen A.	1998
15578	Arhelger, John W.	1996
5731	Armour, Elsva Mae	1975
13872	Armstrong, Margaret Lorraine	1993
19026	Armstrong, Paul William	2002
989	Arndt, Otto W.	1938
17102	Arnecke, Bernice L.	1999
SE57	Arnecke, Bessie M.	1981
12032	Arnecke, Charles O. Sr.	1990
10950	Arnecke, Henry L.	1988
1440	Arnold, A. M.	1949
7784	Arnold, Eugene H.	1981
5759	Arntzen, Archer P.	1975
13660	Arredondo, Eugene	1992
5586	Arreola, George R.	1974
2833	Arreola, Gregorio	1962
4547	Arretz, Hedwig	1970
14256	Arsave, Diane Olivarez	1994

File	Deceased	Year
17054	Arto, Martha Walker	1999
8833	Arvin, Patricia	1984
2082	Ash, Ed I.	1965
6423	Ash, Vivian	1977
15668	Ashbrook, George Cleo Sr.	1996
2420	Ashby, A. B.	1959
15550	Ashcroft, Izora	1996
9522	Ashcroft, James M.	1985
12624	Asher, Asa Henry	1991
15606	Ashford, Irene S.	1996
11994	Ashford, Theodore	1990
11928	Ashley, John Edward	1989
753	Ashmore, Thomas	1930
3323	Ashton, Sidney C.	1965
16202	Atkins, Jacqueline Terry	1997
10108	Atkins, Jay E.	1986
5853	Atkins, John S.	1975
5214	Atkins, Melicena B.	1973
13092	Atkinson, Bess	1992
16208	Atkinson, Harriet Hudson	1997
14606	Atkinson, M. B.	1994
5885	Ator, Cora Lois	1975
18344	Ator, Yvonne Joyce	2001
4772	Attaway, Claude	1972
1452	Attaway, E. F.	1949
3051	Attaway, Etta Norcutt	1963
8307	Atwater, Frank Glasgow	1982
15432	Atwater, Madine Ives	1996
13354	Atwell, R. L. Jr.	1992
2472	Aubrey, Gertrude C.	1960
3022	Auld, Aydeen	1963
7292	Auld, Dan Sr.	1980

File	Deceased	Year
2812	Auld, Gussie Mae	1962
16498	Auld, Helen	1998
5959	Auld, J. M.	1976
12849	Ault, Herbert Eugene	1991
1480	Ault, J. P. (John P.)	1950
19202	Aultz, Rose Mary	2002
15618	Austin, Billie C. Jr.	1996
10750	Austin, Maurice Lee	1987
2278	Aven, Estelle L.	1957
6029	Averill, Charlotte	1976
6582	Averill, Hazel M.	1978
5049	Averill, William Mc Faddin	1973
8375	Avery, Betty Key	1982
6225	Avery, Willard C.	1977
2370	Ayala, Ignacio	1958
739	Ayala, Pablo	1933
10352	Ayala, Santana	1986
17294	Ayala, Yolanda	1999
9842	Aycock, Ola M.	1985
4398	Ayers, Elma W.	1970

B

File	Deceased	Year
5481	Babb, Richard Clifford	1974
7611	Babcock, Howard E.	1981
11780	Babecki, Clarence Joseph	1989
18258	Bacen, William F.	2001
1872-55	Bach, J. F.	
2904	Bacon, Delbert	1962
1248	Bacon, Fannie	1945
3714	Bacon, George Wallace	1967

10

File	Deceased	Year
5342	Bacon, Hazel	1973
182	Bacon, Jessie	----
11128	Bacon, Joseph Driver	1988
253	Bacon, C. P	1906
457	Bacon, W. G.	1918
16644	Baccus, Charles Henry	1998
16642	Baccus, Jessie Conklin	1998
19274	Bachman, Jayne M.	2002
201	Bader, Edythe M.	1980
6204	Bader, James L.	1976
4299	Badger, Elaine Carter	----
4302	Badger, Elaine Carter	----
7902	Baethge, Alma	1981
8000	Baethge, Emil H.	1982
17354	Bagby, Donald Edwin	1999
13298	Bailey, Dorothy Ratliff	1992
13436	Bailey, Charliy Everett	1992
10086	Bailey, Elloitt E.	1986
18996	Bailey, Everett N.	2002
3474	Bailey, F. G.	1966
2471	Bailey, Harriet	1960
14554	Bailey, Haskell	1994
5631	Bailey, Jack D.	----
10584	Bailey, Layton Jr.	1987
7641	Bailey, Mamie	1981
9770	Bailey, Mary Elizabeth	1985
18252	Bailey, Mouise D.	2001
359	Bailey, P. R.	
	(Paten R.)	1914
5451	Bailey, Randolph	----
1080	Bailey, Rebecca Ann	1941
15198	Bailey, Robert Lynn	1995
6212	Bailey, Russell Neal	1976
6543	Bailleif, Arthur	1977
14526	Bain, Cecil Lloyd	1994

File	Deceased	Year
14052	Bain, Sarah Frances	1993
19332	Baker, Alvin C.	2002
4986	Baker, Annie A.	1972
3790	Baker, Claude P.	1967
213	Baker, Cora	----
1171/1178	Baker, Elizabeth	1943
508	Baker, Jesse H.	1922
11534	Baker, Kenneth Martin	1989
3654	Baker, Lynne Earle	1966
6300	Baker, Marion L.	1976
9730	Baker, Mary Gleason	1985
2197	Baker, Mattie C.	1958
18835	Baker, Mildred K.	2002
971	Baker, Rosa	1938
14950	Baker, Van Newman	1995
5646	Baker, Vin	1975
8352	Baker, Viola L.	1982
2966	Baker, Virgie	1963
1276	Baker, Virginia C.	1946
1055	Baker, W. C.	1940
5169	Baker, William I.	1973
2333	Baker, Young W.	1959
6171	Bakeman, Ethel	----
4579	Baldridge, E. E.	1971
9552	Baldwin, Effie Dell Toler aka Bonnie Baldwin	1985
5861	Baldwin, Evelyn M.	1975
15280	Baldwin, George W.	1995
2919	Baldwin, Helen Hull	1963
6644	Baldwin, James E.	1978
6276	Baldwin, J. V.	1977
1066	Baldwin, Lew	1941
17838	Baldwin, Nora G.	2000
1578	Baldwin, Owen W.	1996

File	Deceased	Year
16382	Baldwin, Ruth L.	1997
1947	Baldwin, W. H.	1955
8453	Baldwin, Walter E.	1983
5007	Bales, M. K.	1973
5766	Balfe, Ruth Mc Kinstry	1975
1294	Ball, Bertha	1946
4642	Ball, Mary Jean	1971
17432	Ballard, Kermit H.	1999
13238	Ballard, Mary Elizabeth Finucane	1992
16778	Ballard, Mildred Evelyn	1998
14154	Ballard, Nowal Albert	1993
692	Ballard, P. H.	1930
18196	Ballard, Sophie Etta	2000
16936	Ballard, William Delbert	1998
9448	Ballew, Lucile	1985
3809	Bammel, Bobby H.	1967
3807	Bammel, Edwin S.	1967
9954	Bandeleen, Leroy L.	1986
18666	Bandy, Fred R. Sr.	2001
13718	Banister, John R. III	1993
16796	Banks, Dorothy Elizabeth	1998
14144	Banks, James E.	1993
16356	Banks, Mariam K.	1997
17276	Banks, Vincent Allen	1999
11612	Bannon, Frank W.	1989
11612	Bannon, Mildred T.	1989
11134	Banta, Brook Wilson	1988
9043	Banta, Callie Mae	1984
9250	Barber, G. H.	1984
6181	Barber, Herbert O.	1976
14530	Barber, Walter F.	1994
17638	Barclay, T. S.	2000

File	Deceased	Year
14918	Barecky, Dennis Ray	1995
5684	Barfield, Lela A.	1975
16338	Barfoot, Harry Edwin	1997
17736	Barger, Mary Bates	2000
12198	Barham, Guy S. Jr.	1990
758	Barham, John G.	1932
4454	Barker, Alice W.	----
14748	Barker, Bobbie Jean	1994
7693	Barker, Caleb	1981
5671	Barker, David B.	----
8532	Barker, John Preston	1983
1537	Barker, Leta	1951
7576	Barker, William Jewel	1981
6461	Barkley, William Clarence	1977
147	Barleman, Charles	1896
148	Barleman, Charles	1896
149	Barleman, Charles	1902
8840	Barlow, Clyde V.	1984
8388	Barlow, Munroe Otis	1982
6092	Barnes Bernard E.	1976
9048	Barnes, Bryant	1984
5134	Barnes, Cecil W.	1973
5169	Barnes, Dorothy	1973
13548	Barnes, Evelyn H.	1992
278	Barnes, George A.	1909
SE93	Barnes, Hazel J.	1983
14242	Barnes, J. C.	1994
18838	Barnes, Leslie Theodore	2002
6357	Barnes, Louis E.	----
1671	Barnes, Mabel Peters	1998
17392	Barnes, Richard F.	1999
12548	Barnett, Dorothy D.	1991
7725	Barnett, William Joseph	1981

File	Deceased	Year
11328	Barnett, William Woodson Jr.	1988
14020	Barnhart, D. W.	1993
19266	Barnhart, James G.	2002
3082	Baron, Alfredo	1964
3060	Baron, Mary	1963
10360	Barraza, Beatriz	1986
10362	Barraza, Erika	1986
10358	Barraza, Jose Manuel	1986
13266	Barrett, H. E.	1992
13300	Barrett, Howard E.	1993
9976	Barrett, Randolph	1986
SE59	Barron, Andres S.	----
10226	Barron, James F.	1986
1872-112	Barron, William	----
17018	Barrone, Martin J. Jr.	1998
8622	Barrow, Charles L.	1983
8272	Barrow, Corilla S.	1982
15552	Barrow, William Edward	1996
3934	Barry, Eugene	1968
9116	Barry, Ford Eleanor	1984
4017	Barry, Mattie W.	1968
3630	Barry, Robert G.	1966
SE13282	Bartel, Meta	1992
8529	Bartell, Garner Gillis	1983
10174	Barter, W. A.	1986
3545	Bartholomew, William H.	1966
8537	Bartlett, Walter L.	1983
2437	Bartley, Beatrice	1959
4571	Bartley, Walter R.	1970
9282	Barton, Dorothy E.	1984
2778	Barton, Elizabeth	1962
14478	Barton, Lelia	1994
13558	Barton, Rhea G.	1992
8532	Barton, Willis Fisher	1983

File	Deceased	Year
8554	Barton, Willis Fisher	1983
2777	Barton, W. H.	1962
19372	Bass, Willard Otto	2002
5070	Bass, Wesley Sr.	1972
4521	Basse, Fritz C.	1970
1817	Basse, Olga	1954
10666	Bassham, T. C.	1987
8581	Baston, Juanita P.	1983
7106	Baston, Willis H.	1979
14806	Batchelor, Gerald Wilson	1995
4820	Batchelor, Sloan L.	1972
4950	Bates, Ben Bounds	1972
8040	Bates, Russell R.	1982
9792	Batley, Lee Maxwell	1985
10648	Batley, Willie Mae	1987
4264	Baucom, Pearl Nichols	----
17482	Bauer, Emil Hugh	1999
2593	Bauer, Ida	1960
8981	Bauer, John M.	1984
2595	Bauer, Paul A.	1960
4733	Baughan, Walter Thomas	1967
SE73	Bauman, Maxie F.	1982
12912	Bauman, William J.	1990
18112	Baumann, Gwendolyn D.	----
3041	Baxter, Gertrude M.	1963
12330	Bazan, David A Jr.	1990
5865	Beach, Allison Tate	1975
7861	Beach, Deryl E.	1981
7039	Beach, Eleanor C.	1979
4168	Beach, Jean Mc Call	1969
5868	Beach, Robert	1975
4184	Beach, Korna Byrne	1969
2840	Beakley, F. C.	1962
11828	Beall, Daniel Elbert	1989

File	Deceased	Year
19244	Bear, Martha Minerva	2002
1583	Beard, D. D.	1951
16746	Beard, Dearl Lee	1998
19146	Beard, Fred Jr.	2002
14280	Beard, Mable	1994
18006	Bearden, Will Roy	2000
8377	Bearman, Robert C.	1982
15342	Beasley, Anna L.	1995
16606	Beasley, Brownie F.	1998
9832	Beasley, Gabriel Wesley	1985
5078	Beasley, Joseph A.	1972
16816	Beasley, Mary E.	1998
15184	Beasley, Sunshine Violet	1995
SE109	Beaty, Sylvia E.	1986
13900	Beaumont, William	1993
5900	Beaver, Charles F.	1976
10078	Beaver, Charles Henry	1986
4334	Beaver, J. E.	1970
4108	Beaver, James L.	1969
15424	Beavers, Glen Earl	1996
16672	Beavers, Richard Clifton Sr.	1998
13892	Beazley, Doris Nibbitts	1993
6853	Beazley, Edith H.	1979
17406	Beazley, Louella N.	1999
12152	Beck, Harley B.	1990
10870	Beck, Walter E.	1987
9596	Beck, William F. T.	1985
15244	Beckendorff, Deborah Lara	1995
SE91	Becker, Berthe F.	1982
16206	Beddow, Raymond Rees	1997
14958	Bedea, Douglas Dale	1995

File	Deceased	Year
CV750083	Bedea, Douglas Dale	1995
13560	Bedell, Ivan Luther	1992
4664	Bedell, Jessie Elle	1971
12012	Bedfield, William R.	1990
1631	Beecraft, Frances A.	1952
3199	Beeman, Frances S.	1964
19166	Behrendt, Helen Jannie	2002
17956	Behrendt, Roland Gus	2000
5373	Behymer, Charles Loring	----
924	Beitel, Ally Jr.	1937
604	Beitel, Annie	1926
591	Beitel, Charles F.	1925
11342	Belcjer, Magala Gertrud	1988
9372	Bell, Aldelyn J.	1985
9492	Bell, Burie Le Fay	1985
18434	Bell, C. H.	2001
19342	Bell, Elam	2002
3296	Bell, Ernest A.	1965
10262	Bell, Frederick Herbert	1986
18472	Bell, Helen E.	2001
6517	Bell, John James	1977
7986	Bell, Leona Heuer	1981
13788	Bell, Linn Roe	1993
11588	Bell, Marvin Hirsch	1989
4092	Bell, Maybelle R.	1969
14096	Bell, Ruth Louise	1993
5665	Bell, W. C.	1975
11938	Bell, William E.	1989
17174	Bellis, Donald R.	1999
7003	Bellomy, Frank Ray	1979
8615	Bellomy, Grace T.	1983
17202	Bellomy, Joyce Adele	1999
13452	Belluomini, Adolph L.	1992
5446	Belluomini, Josephine	----
6595	Belluomini, Verda	1978

File	Deceased	Year
2150	Bellott, Willard	1957
17344	Bellows, Joseph M.	1999
1136	Below, Lucy W.	1943
776	Belser, Herman G.	1932
14522	Benbow, Robert L.	1994
7432	Benfer, Ann La Rue	1980
16092	Benner, Earl Lee	1997
16318	Benner, Ruby Jouil	1997
SE27	Bennett, Clarence Leslie	1978
17476	Bennett, D. W.	1999
18198	Bennett, George G.	2000
16560	Bennett, Jules Edmund	1998
9256	Bennett, Laverne H.	1984
17632	Benning, Geraldine Howell	2000
12220	Benning, William Charles	1990
4639	Bennison, Henry H.	1971
7686	Benson, Claribel	1981
4184	Benson, Epsy Frances	1971
11794	Benson, Erma	1990
3862	Benson, George	1967
12892	Benson, George Clifton	1991
19138	Benson, Hilda Lena	2002
8040	Benson, J. F.	1982
SE93-2	Benson, James Alexander	1993
1695	Benson, Mildred Whitley Polk	1998
670	Benson, William	1929
12590	Bentley, Ann	1991
18554	Bentley, Jean	2001
6220	Bentley, Spencer Shirer	1976
13760	Berg, John W.	1993
11260	Berg, Raymond	1988

File	Deceased	Year
16528	Berge, Walton A.	1998
7672	Berghoff, Lewis W.	1981
9083	Bergin, David P.	1984
7255	Bergman, Joe A.	1980
11736	Bergman, O. James	1989
14360	Bergmann, Harry	1994
1441	Bernard, Max	1949
2942	Bernard, V. B.	1963
3467	Bernhard, A. S.	1966
4645	Bernhard, Earl P.	----
9169	Bernard, Frances Ann	1984
16908	Bernhard, Helen M.	1998
15718	Bernhard, Lois	1996
18314	Bernhard, Marvin Albert	2001
3757	Berry, B. E.	1967
12710	Berry, Bernice	1991
14376	Berry Everett R.	1994
6432	Berry, James D.	1977
5431	Berry, Lizzie May	----
6979	Berry, Luther L.	1979
178	Berry, Myron	----
14376	Berry, Verna Oleta	1994
6603	Berryman, Charles Vernon	1978
11944	Berryman, Mary W.	1990
17800	Berson, Anita W.	2000
10680	Berthe, Nora Lee	1987
18194	Berthiaume, Harriet Mitchell	2000
19030	Bertram, Bertha Josephine	2002
5618	Berwick, Kathryn E.	----
9121	Besier, Dora E.	1984
12664	Besier, John A. Sr.	1991
16276	Besier, John A. Jr.	1997

File	Deceased	Year
2118	Besse, Annette Barker	1957
4936	Best, Emily J.	1972
2034	Best, Fred E.	1956
15480	Best, Mildred Evdell	1996
14580	Betcher, Edwin	1994
3269	Bettercourt, Edward J.	1965
14148	Betts, Maria Rosaris	1993
15778	Betty, Jennifer Lynne Salenatine	1996
3310	Betty, Lemuel	1965
12274	Betty, Marjorie Rose Lloyd	1990
11082	Bevers, Bill	1988
1482	Bevil, G. P.	1950
19322	Bevis, Muriel June	2002
8331	Bialkowski, Ethel V.	1982
8036	Bibb, Charles Paul	1982
14930	Bible, Dorothy Roy	1995
18970	Biddy, Bruce A.	2002
7324	Bidwell, Delmar E.	1980
6478	Bidwell, Kenneth J.	----
10630	Biediger, Arthur	1987
11602	Biehler, Charles Leroy	1989
5079	Biehler, Ernest	1972
8932	Biehler, John William	1984
11522	Bien, Joyce R.	1989
12878	Bierman, Eddie	1991
11840	Bierman, Hedwig	1989
921	Biermann, Andreas	----
5297	Biermann, Elsie	----
759	Biermann, Fritz	1932
5928	Biermann, Herman	1976
1352	Biermann, Marie	1947
4873	Bierschwale, D. E.	1972
1097	Bierschwale, De Witt	1942

File	Deceased	Year
5128	Bierschwale, Emily	----
15824	Bierschwale, Charles H.	1996
9598	Bierschwale, J. R. Jr.	1985
4874	Bierschwale, R. G.	1972
8079	Bierschwale, T. J.	1982
1674	Bigger, John C.	1953
3247	Bigger, Sara K.	1964
14126	Biggs, Lawrence Eugene	1993
18476	Biggs, Sarah Ann	2001
12676	Bill, Caterina Morin	1991
17158	Billings, Charles M.	1999
13274	Billings, Wesley	1992
9080	Billingsley, Frank H.	1985
9123	Billnetzer, Jo Joyce Brett	1984
6408	Birck, William F.	----
6905	Bird, Doeboy	1979
10150	Bird, Don H.	1986
7666	Bird, Ira E.	1981
4687	Bird, Irene	1971
6926	Bird, Lydia R.	1979
16000	Bird, Nina	1997
637	Bird, Sampson	1972
12726	Birkenfield, Thomas F.	1991
6260	Birotte, Genia Mae	1976
15372	Bischoff, Paul	1996
9800	Bischoff, Shirley	1985
9114	Bishop, Annie N.	1984
12290	Bishop, Elvis O.	1990
10314	Bishop, James Victor	1986
5167	Bissell, Cecil A.	1972
18382	Bittner, Margery G.	2001
6081	Bittner, Rudy	1976
12380	Bixby, Irana Lorue	1990
1779	Black, Axel J.	1954

File	Deceased	Year
8551	Black, Hattie	1983
17136	Black, Mary A.	1999
3094	Black, Q. P.	1964
5644	Black, T. A.	1975
14824	Blackard, Katherine Evelyn Lea	1995
SE87	Blackburn, Erna Sophie Henrietta	1983
9476	Blackburn, Earnest A.	1985
10048	Blackburn, Howard W.	1986
15826	Blackburn, John R.	1996
18604	Blackburn, Kaye G.	2001
10212	Blackburn, Mary Thelma	1986
3873	Blackburn, May E.	1967
17122	Blackburn, Olga M. (Judy)	1999
14742	Blackburn, Tommie Smith	1994
17762	Blackburn, Victor N.	2000
19096	Blackmon, Dorothy Jane	2002
16906	Blackshear, Sarah Neil	1998
3832	Blackwell, Clifford E.	1967
12840	Blackwell, James Frank	1991
11124	Blades, Hazel Irene Schuver	1988
13014	Blair, Edna Piper	1991
16928	Blair, Florence Allen	1998
15364	Blair, James W.	1996
3720	Blair, Walter P.	1967
6027	Blair, Willie H.	1976
16810	Blaha, Annie Mable	1998
1562	Blake, James H.	1951
10598	Blake, Margaret C.	----
2533	Blake, William G.	1960
11712	Blakeley, Billy Jack	1989
5625	Blank, Charles Robert	1978

File	Deceased	Year
SE97	Blankenship, Leslie Velpo	1982
17948	Blanks, Anne Joan	2000
698	Blanks, Burnette	1929
10512	Blanks, John Berry	1987
2743	Blanks, Johnnie	1961
5949	Blanks, Louis	1976
1700	Blanks, Theodore	1953
12104	Blanton, Ethel Frances	1990
18762	Blanton, Jewel O.	2001
17250	Blanton, Pauline M.	1999
7717	Bledsoe, Terrell Marion	1981
3087	Blevins, John Ceaman	1964
15910	Blevins, Loren Winfield	1997
14458	Blevins, Robert Sr.	1994
8066	Blisard, Clara V.	1982
17096	Bliss, Imogene Adkins	1999
1494	Blissinger, Philip J	1950
1739	Block, Herman S.	1953
12140	Blodgett, Cathryn Elizabeth	1990
4746	Blodgett, Vern L.	1972
14546	Bloeser, Rita E.	1994
3510	Blondeau, Anna	1966
2844	Blondeau, E. P.	1962
15156	Bloss, Madaline Sneed	1995
15382	Bloss, Richard R. Jr.	1996
7651	Blount, Alvie E.	1981
1497	Blount, Claude	1950
4295	Blount, Milton D.	1969
13186	Bloys, Herman Ava	1992
11802	Bloys, James Arthur	1989
16448	Bluntzer, Joseph Theodore	1998
3433	Boales, Della	1965

File	Deceased	Year
11302	Boatright, Edna Mae	1988
8162	Boatwright, Alexander C.	1982
12142	Boatwright, Helen R.	1990
8611	Boaz, Frances M.	1983
646	Bobbitt, E. B. (Eric)	1928
19136	Bocan, Jean	2002
8637	Bode, Elgin Paul	1983
7674	Bode, Fred W.	1981
11172	Bode, Maggie Mae	1988
5238	Bockhoff, Harriet L.	1973
5057	Bockhoff, Harry W.	1973
19206	Bocock, Charles William III	2002
5356	Bocock, Jane Nees	----
3426	Bocock, Nell	1965
2466	Boechman, Ernest W. Sr.	1960
7984	Boechman, Lucille	1981
12186	Boechmann, Earnest W.	1990
8746	Boechmann, Nikki Marie	1983
1192	Boechmann, Will	1944
11800	Boedecker, George M.	1989
1234	Boehmer, Henry T.	1945
1194	Boehmer, Mina Louise	1944
2912	Boerkoel, Josie	1962
11488	Boerner, Charlotte K. aka (cv920021) Charlotte Katherin Caldwell	1989
6355	Boerner, Erno	1977
1872-2	Boerner, F. W.	1872
1872-115	Boerner, Otto	1892
3572	Bohanna, Clyde	1966
13222	Bohanna, Lorena	1992
4997	Bohanna, Myrtle	----
CV940082	Bohannab, Ruby C.	1994
14212	Bohannan, Lovie Leta	1993

File	Deceased	Year
15642	Bohart, Donella P.	1996
2662	Bohnert, Gotfried	1961
15154	Bohnert, Louis F.	1995
16696	Boise, Mary Helen	1998
18176	Boldin, Viola	2000
15476	Bollenbach, Edward J.	1996
11538	Bolleter, M. W.	1989
13178	Bollman, Altavine P.	1992
14092	Bollman, William H.	1993
7098	Bolte, Cecelia A.	1979
15088	Bomer, Edwin Truman	1995
16196	Bomer, Irene	1997
1001	Boney, Frank N.	1938
7422	Bonham, Myrtle Mac Nash	1980
7634	Bonn, Ernest A.	1981
1314	Bonn, Henry	1947
4631	Bonn, Julia	1971
1189	Bonnell, Allie H.	
	Frances	1919
16996	Bonner, Eleanor Beth	1998
5662	Bonner, Josephine	----
1804	Bonner, John Miford	1954
11514	Bonner, Marguerite D.	1989
10312	Bonner, S. F.	1986
1972/77	Bonner, W. E.	1955
1456	Booth, Herman	1949
6326	Boothe, James Ross	1977
7700	Boozer, Sallie A.	1981
10872	Borchers, Chester H.	1987
12076	Bordelon, Allen J.	1990
16252	Borden, Edith Frances	1997
1462	Borders, Charles	1950
5854	Bordon, Bessie Byrn	1975
2641	Boren, Leonard E.	1961

File	Deceased	Year
19210	Boren, Linda K.	2002
4140	Boren, Madge B.	1969
858	Bormell, W. H.	1934
16228	Bosio, Patsy D.	1997
17902	Boston, Deloris L. aka Smith-Boston, Delores Lorraine	2000
14064	Bosworth, R. L.	1993
14064-A	Bosworth, R. L.	1995
2332	Bottimer, Mildred S.	1959
SE61	Bottom, Morris E.	1982
9524	Bourschweidt, Alois B.	1985
7517	Boutin, Richard E.	1980
12246	Bouton, John W.	1990
6726	Bowden, George Raymond	1978
523	Bowden, Willard	----
12720	Bowdle, Helen Pauline	1991
14974	Bowdle, Robert Lloyd	1995
8181	Bowers, Imogene Robinson	1982
17434	Bowers, Robert D.	1999
8885	Bowlin, Ray V.	1984
13746	Bowling, Jerry L.	1993
11678	Bowman, Mildred T.	1989
13084	Bowyer, Bennie Mae	1992
8214	Bowyer, Virginia Wills	1982
13902	Bowyer, Wilbur	1993
16478	Boyd, Harry Glen	1998
725	Boyd, Haskell	1931
19274	Boyd, Irene F.	2002
19062	Boyd, Lucile W.	2002
9420	Boyer, Floyd A.	1985
15972	Boyer, Ruth Sitta	1997
SE13582	Boyett, Ruth Eleanor	1992
4414	Boykin, S. R.	----

File	Deceased	Year
19132	Boyle, Euphemia	2002
10420	Brackney, Esther V.	1987
9600	Brackney, Virgil D.	1985
5517	Bradberry, Carl B.	----
8196	Bradbury, Blanche E.	1982
14595	Braden, David P.	1994
6510	Braden, Fay E.	1977
15674	Braden, Thetis	1996
9588	Bradford, Bessie	1985
5328	Bradford, Chlse Belle	----
SE5	Bradford, Guy B.	1970
12164	Bradley, Al Lawton	1990
11072	Bradley, Alice Maude Dennison	1988
4458	Bradley, Bart/Bert	1970
9788	Bradlow, Warren Kenneth	1985
4443	Bradshaw, Philip P.	1970
9956	Bradshaw, William Clifton	1986
4818	Brady, Elizabeth C.	1972
1835	Brailey, Lena Rountree	1954
12964	Bramsch, Edith	1991
4054	Bramsch, Henry L.	1968
5403	Brandon, James Edward	----
15348	Brandon, Florence B.	1995
11232	Breandrup, Clifford K.	1988
SE97-2	Brandt, Alfred J.	1997
18586	Brandt, Esther Mabel	2001
8880	Branstatter, Otha Chandler	1984
9996	Braswell, Alice M.	1986
5006	Braswell, Jane N.	----
11948	Braswell, Max R.	1989
4027	Braswell, W. F.	1969
10898	Bratcher, Cordelia	1987

File	Deceased	Year
8889	Bratcher, Ed	1984
15888	Bratcher, Edward Jr.	1996
1927	Bratton, Laura R.	1955
1366	Brauer, Josephine	1948
8593	Brauer, Walter	1983
6222	Braun, Anthony	1976
3263	Braun, August	1964
10206	Braun, Aurilla	1986
16028	Braune, Ester Jane	1997
16030	Braune, Nelson Milton	1997
1784	Brautigam, August	1954
3895	Bray, H. M.	1968
13762	Brayton, Arnold Earle	1993
16584	Brayton, Pattie Ruth Gebhard	1998
11324	Brazelton, Dorothy Jenkins	1988
6434	Brazie, Louise S.	1977
1109	Breautigun, Nellie	1942
16376	Bredlow, Elizabeth Irene	1997
2052	Breen, Elizabeth A.	1956
17840	Breen, Harry Charles	2000
4747	Breen, Richard A. (Dick)	----
18520	Brehmer, Elvira Schiller	2001
17170	Brehmer, Herbert William	1999
15756	Brehmer, Lucile Mc Coy	1996
4911	Breihan, B. W.	----
15132	Bremseth, Joseph Paul	1995
17896	Brennen, Lorriane L.	2000
220	Brent, Charles	----
15620	Brewer, Paul Leland	1996
2179	Brewer, Wesley Frank	1957

File	Deceased	Year
1613	Brewton, Earle M.	1952
3085	Brewer, Joseph A.	1964
17570	Brice, Mary Harrence Leath	1999
15292	Brice, Richard L.	1995
14374	Brick, Verna Oleta	1994
10672	Bridges, Allen O.	1987
1460	Bridges, Elvin	1949
10716	Bridges, James W.	1987
676	Bridges, Joe	1929
876	Bridges, Joe & Mittie	1934/35
10722	Bridges, Vera E.	1987
17334	Briese, Edward R.	1999
14490	Briese, Jenny Jo	1994
10294	Briese, Lois E.	1986
18648	Briggs-Leighton, Martha Elizabeth Hortin	2001
6273	Briggs, W. C. Jr.	1977
10040	Bright, Evelina L.	1986
5843	Bright, H. C.	1975
10580	Bright, Mary S.	1987
18584	Brightwell, Betty Ruth	2001
5251	Brill, Galdys Una	1973
4541	Brill, Harry Karl	1971
12662	Brineman, John Hower	1991
1693	Brink, Menlo	1953
6122	Brinkley, Albert Eugene	----
9362	Brinkley, Robert D.	1985
16766	Brinkley, Sarah B.	1998
10492	Brinson, Anna L.	1987
7516	Brinson, Thomas E.	1980
14218	Brinstein, Kathryn	1993
728	Briscoe, D. R.	1931
9010	Briscoe, Myrtle B.	1984
2119	Briscoe, Virgil	1957

File	Deceased	Year
14918	Britsch, Elroy C.	1995
4553	Britt, Lillian G.	1971
5001	Brittain, Edna	1973
2715	Brock, Arthur W. Jr.	1961
2158	Brock, Nancy	1957
2291	Brodie, W. H.	1958
4089	Brogden, Lula M.	1969
11380	Brogdon, Donnie E.	1988
15792	Bronstein, Ervin Isaac	1996
17610	Brook, Charles Paige	1999
19352	Brooks, Jack Daniel	2002
18064	Brooks, Jimmie Lee	2000
2591	Brooks, Meryl M.	1960
12258	Brooks, William Calaway	1990
18456	Brooks, Rose Merle Thomas	2001
18340	Brookshier, Juanita	2001
16266	Brosch, Margaret H.	1997
17230	Brough, Lela Geyer	1999
455	Broughton, Dell	----
456	Broughton, Dell	----
2666	Broughton, Florence	1961
14830	Broun, Carletta	1995
3124	Brown, A. P.	1964
4849	Brown, Addie E	1972
5094	Brown, Almos L.	1973
12024	Brown, Anna M.	1990
8089	Brown, Arthelia Lenore	1982
941	Brown, Andrew L.	1937
13770	Brown, Arlie John	1993
11530	Brown, Bannon Joseph	1989
18090	Brown, Ben T.	2000
15860	Brown, Beth N.	1996
18152	Brown, Billie Marion	2000
575	Brown, C. H.	1944

File	Deceased	Year
253	Brown, C. P.	----
1670	Brown, Carl T.	1952
2148	Brown, Charles A.	1957
18074	Brown, Charles Merle	2000
13836	Brown, Clovis A.	1993
12308	Brown, Curtis	1990
8713	Brown, Dorothy Neil Hamblen	1984
9454	Brown, Dorothy Neil	1985
1872-10	Brown, Edward	1872
5805	Brown, Erna Franks	1975
14406	Brown, Ethel Mae	1994
3886	Brown, Fay W.	1968
18012	Brown, Frances J.	2000
18564	Brown, Frank B. Jr.	2001
3057	Brown, George N.	1963
4662	Brown, Gladys E.	1971
2242	Brown, Grace	1958
8236	Brown, Guy J.	1982
18982	Brown, Helen D.	2002
12242	Brown, Henry H.	1990
1411	Brown, Horace	1949
14572	Brown, H. Raymond aka Horace Raymond	1994
8252	Brown, Howard A.	1982
17578	Brown, James C. Jr.	1999
9298	Brown, James Clinton	1984
1872-41	Brown, J. D.	1877
4531	Brown, J. Dee	1970
3735	Brown, James Morgan	1967
SE28	Brown, Jane Fatjo	1979
16136	Brown, Jesse Lloyd aka Jessey Lloyd aka J. Lloyd Brown	1997
18038	Brown, Jennie Ruby	2000

File	Deceased	Year
6229	Brown, J. W.	1955
7735	Brown, Joseph C.	1981
10920	Brown, Kate P. S.	1987
1872-122	Brown, Mrs. L. J.	1892
16960	Brown, Laura A.	1998
8901	Brown, La Verne	1984
15272	Brown, Lourene Schell	1995
19148	Brown, Lydia W.	2002
587	Brown, Maggie	----
13678	Brown, Manuel G.	1993
11278	Brown, Margaret S.	1988
18822	Brown, Marjorie M.	2002
16784	Brown, Mary Lou Self	1998
12628	Brown, Mary Mc Laughlin	1991
215	Brown, O. J.	----
7070	Brown, Paul H.	1979
13356	Brown, Randolph W.	1992
7616	Brown, Sammie Lee	1981
6230	Brown, Viola Louise	1916
11118	Brown, Virgil Bozarth	1988
7987	Brown, W. B. Jr.	1981
8606	Brown, William G.	1983
18538	Brown, William Thomas	2001
7964	Browning, Luther M.	1981
13218	Browning, Margie Leona	1992
10396	Broyles, Grafton W.	1986
9642	Broyles, Lou Nora	1985
14786	Bruce, Robert L. Jr.	1994
13316	Bruce, Sidney Laws	1992
16822	Brueckheimer, Elmer C.	1998
5852	Brumley, Aaron Devon	1975
8561	Brundrett, Hazel Elsie	1983
5887	Brundrett, Herald M.	1976
10868	Brundrett, Herald Mc Elvaney	1987

File	Deceased	Year
18692	Brundrett, John C.	2001
7477	Brundridge, Minnie	1980
13102	Brunner, Mark Craig	1992
19214	Bruno, Earl R.	2002
8617	Bruns, Christian Frank	1983
16384	Brunskill, Leah R.	1997
410	Bruntley, Claude	----
12240	Bruton, Conner Lee	1990
5441	Bruton, D. H.	1974
3174	Bruton, Elma Reed	1964
17238	Bruton, Harry Merrell Jr.	1999
17240	Bruton, Jennie W.	1999
730	Bruton, Mrs. M. E.	1931
10248	Bruton, Mary Elma Lawson	1986
10144	Bruttschell, Martha H.	1986
15316	Bryan, Shayna	1995
16888	Bryant, Docia Hart	1998
14408	Bryant, Samuel Hinsey	1994
18850	Bryant, Vernon Leon	2002
9878	Bryant, William Smith	1986
2346	Bryden, Raymond Starr	1959
10328	Brynes, Bradfrod S.	1986
17316	Buck, L. Causey	1999
1437	Buck, Maude S.	1949
4496	Buck, Walter H.	1971
5310	Buckalew, Susan M.	1973
14810	Buckley, R. M.	1995
16850	Buckner, Johnnie R.	1998
1958	Buelow, Frank H.	1988
SE51	Bugrinovich, Martin	----
2449	Buhler, David K.	1959
6559	Buie, R. C.	1977
9494	Builda, Aberta A.	1985

File	Deceased	Year
16636	Builta, Roy A.	1998
10734	Bull, Lillian M.	1987
15164	Bull, Melvin E.	1995
SE92	Bullard, Alexander	1983
3443	Bullard, John Lovie	1965
18504	Bulles, Steven Thomas	2001
19194	Bullis, Lloyd S.	2002
11726	Bunch, Iva Mae	1989
10568	Bundick, Lois Augusta	1987
1825	Bundick, Louis	1954
3189	Bunn, Fannie Elizabeth	1964
3188	Bunn, Martin Luther	1964
5015	Bunsh, Barney H.	-----
17074	Bunton, Harper M.	1999
6637	Burdett, Susan Elaine	1978
12442	Burdick, Marsh Ann	1990
6745	Burg, Clifton W.	1978
SE02-2	Burgasser, Bernadett Ann	2002
18330	Burger, Cecil Warren	2001
14504	Burger, Ray C.	1994
2191	Burgess, C. Robert	1958
10570	Burgess, Mabel C.	1987
18238	Burgett, Jacqualyn N.	2001
3905	Burgman, Walter	1968
7805	Burk, Effie K.	1981
558	Burke, Emma Lake	1923
10470	Burker, Roman	1987
8405	Burke, Thomas W.	1983
4845	Burke, William Earle	1972
18448	Burkett, Joseph W. Jr.	2001
10236	Burkholder, Champ Clark	1986
8121	Burks, Charlotte L.	1982
7104	Burks, George C.	1979
68	Burks, Isom	1872

File	Deceased	Year
291	Burks, Mrs. Julia	1910
127	Burleman, Jennie	----
7163	Burleson, Elizabeth M.	1979
15884	Burleson, G. D.	1996
6288	Burleson, James E.	1977
11498	Burleson, Lillias Pauline Smith	1989
832	Burleson, William Eddie	1934
SE33	Burner, George W.	----
18282	Burnett, Clinton Clyde	2001
3505	Burnett, Dora Ellen	1966
415	Burnett, J. R.	1917
1468	Burnett, J. R.	1951
2312	Burnett, Lynn J.	1958
3942	Burnett, M. Lee	1968
1284	Burnett, Thomas W.	1946
18886	Burnett, William H.	2002
6299	Burney, Betty G.	1977
2669	Burney, Ella F.	1961
870	Burney, Dee	1934/35
3155	Burney, Ella	1964
2105	Burney, Hattie M.	1957
3025	Burney, Ida A.	1963
16072	Burney, Jewell	1997
1857	Burney, Lee	1955
1168/1172	Burney, Linnie M.	1943
359	Burney, Mattie	1914
7642	Burney, Milton	1981
608	Burney, R. H.	1926
15110	Burney, Victor Douglas	1920
3110	Burney, William	1964
13480	Burns, Dorothy Jane	1992
54	Burns, E. L.	1872
13102	Burns, James Aaron	1992
5993	Burns, John Teasdale	1976

File	Deceased	Year
1377	Burns, Julia C.	1948
6703	Burns, Ralph Nolan	1978
15030	Buron, Grace Rosetta	1995
3119	Burow, Fred	1964
17630	Burrell, John H.	2000
1374	Burrer, Edwin	1948
19366	Burrhus, Betrice P.	2002
18734	Burrhus, Donald V.	2001
10234	Burrough, Robert E. aka R. E. Burrough aka Robert Earl Burrough aka Bob Burrough	1986
2980	Burroughs, Earl H.	1963
8486	Burrow, Emma P.	1983
7772	Burrus, J. T.	1981
10582	Burrus, Zelma M.	1987
6956	Burt, Harold A.	1979
3268	Burt, Mynard T.	1965
4511	Burt, William F. Jr.	1970
1303	Burton, A. B.	1946
7435	Burton, Jeanette	1980
4376	Burton, Leon H.	----
2086	Burton, William	1957
18818	Burton, William L.	2002
12712	Bury, Charles R.	1991
2242	Busby, H. E.	1958
1455	Busby, J. H.	1949
14516	Busch, Pannie Norman	1994
906	Bushart, Brasher	1936
14854	Bushland, Raymond C.	1995
3670	Bushong, J. L.	1967
18474	Bussell, Minnie Lee	2001
SE97-1	Bustin, Thos. N.	1997
1557	Buswell, Calvin	1951
6951	Butcher, Jay S.	1979

File	Deceased	Year
8432	Butcher, Jessie P.	1983
7047	Butler, Charles D.	1979
3172	Butler, E. W	1964
8582	Butler, Frances Alexa Fletcher	1983
18306	Butler, George D.	2001
12182	Butler, Gordon Bentley	1990
1715	Butler, J. R	1953
1587	Butler, John S.	1951
286	Butler, M. F.	1909
299	Butler, M. F.	1910
17090	Butler, Mary Elizabeth	1999
10442	Butler, Nea	1987
6302	Butler, P. P.	1977
1218	Butler, Pattie E.	1944
689	Butt, Charles C.	1915
4306	Butt, E. (Eugene) T.	1969
1783	Butt, Florence	1954
7404	Butt, Juanita	1980
2658	Butt, Kearney	1961
809	Button, Joseph	1934
3552	Buxton, Earl Sr.	1966
4921	Byars, Samuel A.	1972
15238	Byas, Thomas Carroll Jr.	1995
10118	Byerly, Arthur H.	1986
15486	Byerly, Harlan Howard	1996
8111	Bynum, Luther H.	1982
18614	Byrd, Curtis Eugene	2001
17104	Byrd, Elaine H.	1999
5684	Byrd, Elizabeth F.	1948
14584	Byrd, Fannie L.	1994
5820	Byrd, Mildred A.	1978
3098	Byrd, Myrta Lane	1964
16478	Byrd, Robert H.	1998
15226	Byrne, Cletus L.	1995

File	Deceased	Year

C

File	Deceased	Year
4737	Cabiness, Dorothy	1971
14180	Cade, Alfred E.	1993
3420	Cade, G. P.	1965
11564	Cade, Gilford L.	1989
16142	Cade, Robert Bernard (Bobby)	1997
3900	Cade, W. A.	1968
5872	Cage, Dewitt G.	1975
18560	Cagle, Elvis K.	2001
18602	Cagle, Joyce	2001
17234	Cagle, Judith Ann	1997
15938	Cailloux, Floyd A.	1997
9079	Calcott, George H.	1984
11488	Caldwell, Charlotte Katherine aka Charlotte K Boerner	1989
5795	Caldwell, Francis M.	1971
11698	Caldwell, James H.	1989
4886	Caldwell, Thomas Harvey Sr.	1972
14668	Caldwell, Zelma V.	1994
3260	Calentine, Carrie	1964
10700	Calhoun, Gordon M.	1987
9472	Calhoun, Le Verne Pearl	1985
2208	Callahan, Charlie E.	1958
6575	Callahan, Myrtle Mae	1978
9776	Callahan, Wanda Ruth	1985
3976	Callison, Annie Will	1968
2439	Calvert, Joseph Lynch	1959
12286	Calvitt, Robert Charles	1990
17698	Cambridge, Richard William	2000
11564	Cameron, Leroy George	1989

File	Deceased	Year
5908	Camerson, William Frederick	1997
10488	Campbell, Albert Jr.	1987
3321	Campbell, Anna	1965
874	Campbell, C. B.	1935
3800	Campbell, Edna M.	1967
16934	Campbell, Fred W.	1998
18128	Campbell, George Lee	2000
12680	Campbell, Gladys Harper	1991
14964	Campbell, Harshell	1995
15106	Campbell, Isaac N.	1995
13236	Campbell, Jane	1992
8936	Campbell, Lucile Johnson	1984
17874	Campbell, Marguerite Holvey	2000
9178	Campbell, Samuel M.	1984
11378	Campbell, Ted R.	1988
4389	Campbell, Virginia	1970
2024	Canafax, Bess Hammond	1956
566	Canafax, John Taylor	1924
10012	Canniff, Ruby Dobbs	1986
13246	Cannon, D. C.	1992
7022	Cannon, Edith Bray	1979
2540	Cannon, F. B.	1960
4305	Cannon, Flinoy B. Jr.	1969
498	Cannon, Ida (?Ada)	1922
8433	Cannon, William A.	1983
8873	Canon, Frederic Phipps Sr.	1984
17738	Canto, Rilda	2000
4861	Cantrell, George T. Sr.	1972
4256	Cantrell, Nellie Furr	----
4254	Cantrell, Nellie Mae	----
19134	Cantu, Diego Jr.	2002

40

File	Deceased	Year
SE10892	Cantu, Santos A.	1987
17144	Cantwell, Addison Harold	1999
17172	Cantwell, Clara	1999
18058	Cantwell, Opal	2000
18798	Cantwell, Price	2001
19090	Carabajal, Victor	2002
8584	Caras, Martha J.	1983
15362	Carawya, Jack J.	1996
145	Card, Mary A.	?1874?
15572	Cardone, Theresa C.	1996
12558	Cardwell, Walter W. Jr.	1991
7679	Carels, Georgette	1981
1461	Carels, Harold	1950
6466	Carey, Margaret M.	1977
18636	Carey, William H.	2001
9342	Cariker, Lottie S.	1985
9944	Cariker, Mildred	1986
2183	Carleton, William	1957
6333	Carlington, Walter E.	1977
4201	Carlisle, Armet A.	1969
13742	Carlisle, Jack W.	1993
7833	Carlisle, Opal Ray Walters	1981
4080	Carlisle, W. E. Sr.	1969
12646	Carlson, Harvey A.	1991
18920	Carlson, Mildred R. O.	2002
7875	Carlson, T. Cedric	1981
10968	Carlton, Rachel M.	1988
12826	Carlton, Richard J.	1991
637	Carmach, Samuel V.	1927
5777	Carman, Henrie Dell	1975
5109	Carman, John J.	1973
8569	Carmichael, Esther	1983
16288	Carmichael, Dorothy E.	1997

File	Deceased	Year
3198	Carmichael, J. D.	1964
5458	Carnahan, Edna	1974
17932	Carnahan, Thelma C.	2000
7837	Carnes, Olline C.	1981
6628	Carney, Donald A.	1978
2206	Carnish, Mary L.	1958
15648	Carpenter, Catherine Graham	1996
2025	Carpenter, Ethel Ford	1956
12860	Carpenter, Fred R.	1991
1028	Carpenter, J. William	1939
18066	Carpenter, James W. Jr.	2000
16974	Carpenter, Lydia Rawlings	1998
8704	Carpenter, Margaret J.	1983
12940	Carpenter, Neil Lance	1991
1879	Carr, Annabel Peterson	1954
11932	Carr, Betty Jo	1989
12394	Carr, Joseph Wayne Sr.	1990
724	Carr, Nell Marie	1931
7	Carr, Sam	1865
17490	Carr, Wayne	1999
CV990197	Carr, Wayne	1999
9364	Carroll, James Nichols	1985
14924	Carroll, Marion Ward	1995
12934	Carroll, Paul L.	1991
15846	Carroon, Lena C.	1996
2409	Carruth, E. B. Jr.	1959
3590	Carruth, Mae Louise	1966
16348	Carruthers, Cynthia Ann	1997
999	Carson, David H.	1938
2815	Carson, Herman S.	1962
4455	Carson, Jesse F.	1970
10300	Carson, W. F.	1986
13112	Carter, Barbara Noel	1992

File	Deceased	Year
8741	Carter, Byron Lowry	1983
1797	Carter, James H.	1954
15336	Carter, James Hawley	1995
16918	Carter, Julia	1998
1908	Cartwright, Cecil R.	1954
15702	Caruthers, Lola M.	1996
10132	Caruthers, Roy	1986
9542	Carver, J. B.	1985
4028	Casanova, Fannie	1968
18500	Cash, Eva Idell	2001
5614	Cash, James H. II	1974
7446	Cash, Warren P.	1980
9706	Caskey, Kitty Belle	1985
12984	Caskey, W. K. Homan	1991
372	Cass, Julia Frances Mosty	1974
3001	Cassity, David E.	1963
9294	Cassity, Gertrude S.	1984
4826	Casterline, Mary A.	----
7199	Castillo, Emilea	1980
4956	Castillo, Esther H.	----
18272	Castillo, Manuel G.	2001
3253	Castillo, Ramon J.	1964
18912	Caswell, Leonard Dean	2002
631	Cathcart, Daniel	1927
4886	Caudle, Irene	1972
4765	Caudle, L. T.	1972
14002	Cauley, Edwin Roy	1993
7419	Cavener, Dr. Jessie	1980
371	Cawling, Marthana	----
7506	Cayton, Marjorie A.	1980
13190	Caywood, Jennie Ruth	1992
13192	Caywood, Thomas Lee	1992
13348	Cearley, Paul Lee	1992
9328	Cellum, Jack Travis	1985

File	Deceased	Year
6845	Cervantes, Frances E.	1979
10998	Cervantes, Sotero	1988
13450	Chabyek, Katherine R.	1992
8766	Chacon, Juan Roses	1983
14162	Cadderdon, Mary Frances	1993
4167	Chalk, Dr. D. J.	1969
4163	Chalk, Dulaney Joe (Dr.)	1969
4591	Chamberlain, Carl W.	1971
2872	Chamberlain, Earl S.	1962
2968	Chamberlain, Ray Miller	1963
1834	Chamberlin, J. W.	1954
4784	Chambliss, R. L.	1972
1781	Chambers, H. L.	1954
11184	Champion, Charles O.	1988
3252	Chance, Cornelia	1964
7785	Chandler, Berniece	1981
2482	Chandler, Bertha	1960
15070	Chandler, Faye Cornelius	1995
16170	Chandler, Ora Williser	1997
1577	Chaney, Edna	1951
5213	Chaney, Harold	1973
14118	Chaney, Ida Dell	1993
14410	Chaney, John H.	1994
13724	Chaney, Mary Harriett	1993
3924	Chapelas, G. A.	1968
16108	Chapman, Adelaide Caroline	1997
17206	Chapman, Angeline L.	1999
3282	Chapman, Charles M.	1965
4717	Chapman, Eddie George	1971
10154	Chapman, H. L.	1986
2664	Chapman, Mary Nell Taylor	1961
18104	Chapman, Pauline Doss	1999

File	Deceased	Year
10220	Chapman, Victor Eugene	1986
18102	Chapman, Victor Lewis	1999
1106	Charlier, Rosalie	1942
5787	Charters, Samuel Mark	1975
18674	Chase, Carl Cline	2001
15256	Chase, Russell E.	1995
9836	Chastain, Clair D.	1985
11212	Chastain, Clarence C.	1988
13990	Chauvette, Adelard E.	1993
15918	Chavez, Mary Aguilar	1997
8405	Chenault, Theo Robert	1982
16330	Cherry, Scott T.	1997
18600	Chesky, Victor	
	Ernest III	2001
9778	Chestnutt, Arthur	1985
5785	Cheves, Margaret Louise	----
16056	Chew, Marie E.	1997
16430	Chicouske, Albertt M.	1998
10790	Chidsey, Evelyn S.	1987
12184	Child, Robert William	1990
15730	Childers, Eric	1996
851	Childs, Ed	1935
8392	Childs, James Guy	1982
7213	Childs, Sterry Hunt	1980
5224	Chiles, J. E.	1973
12398	Chiles, Nova	1990
8596	Chills, Dollie M.	1983
18608	Chiodo, Cleatis M.	2001
3823	Chipman, C. C.	1967
10060	Chipman, C. Ernest	1986
8962	Chipman, Doris H.	1984
10104	Chipman, Eddie George	1986
14284	Chipman, Nora Belle	1994
16532	Chisholm, Marjorie Sue	1998

File	Deceased	Year
10128	Chisum, Jewel Lorene	
	Pelton	1986
8472	Chlebak, George	1983
11810	Chmelik, Theodore F.	1989
7154	Chomout, Frank Anatone	1979
15042	Christensen,	
	Constance M.	1995
10848	Christensen, Laurence	
	M. S.	1987
14474	Christensen, Wilbert R.	1994
12538	Christenson, Arthur Roy	1991
3729	Christenson, Florida	1967
2857	Christenson, Francisco	1962
15180	Christley, Paul A.	1995
4702	Chuck, Victoria Mabel	1971
4780	Cieaiora, Dorothy June	1972
746	Cinnamon, J. D.	----
11852	Claborn, Houston V.	1989
3835	Clampitt, Dewey E.	1967
9075	Clancy, Geraldine M.	1984
7801	Clanton, James C.	1981
10712	Clanton, Mary E.	1987
353	Clapp, H. B.	1914
17938	Clarey, Leslie Ray	2000
18832	Clark, Bertha A.	2002
18288	Clark, Betty Jean	
	Talley	2001
17560	Clark, Brooks Gary	1999
12896	Clark, Elsa Bea	1991
8712	Clark, Florence E.	1983
SE69	Clark, Francis X.	1982
2337	Clark, Harry J.	1959
622	Clark, J. B.	1926
14494	Clark, John M. Jr.	1994
9370	Clark, John Taylor	1984

File	Deceased	Year
9370	Clark, John Taylor	1985
15242	Clark, Leslie B.	1995
4782	Clark, Lillian B.	1972
14260	Clark, Lois A.	1994
7462	Clark, Marie	1980
14102	Clark, Oscar	1993
18758	Clark, Raymond Lee	2001
713	Clark, Theo E.	1930
11284	Clark, Tilford E.	1988
13196	Clark, Virgil William	1992
16234	Clark, Virginia B.	1997
18004	Clark, Weldon L.	2000
9736	Clark, William A.	1985
16118	Clark, William Wesley	1997
SE01-3	Clauss, Frederick H.	2001
3659	Clawson, Josh S.	1966
15286	Clay, Albert A.	1995
1453	Clay, Ida Lee	1949
10162	Claypool, Lillian Deadman	1986
4375	Clayton, John B.	1970
8727	Clegg, Elmer I.	1983
SE02-1	Clelland, Robert Emmitt	2002
4355	Clement, Franklin C.	1940
1286	Clement, Jerome B.	1946
10456	Clements, Dreher Robert	1987
9085	Clements, Lee	1984
11812	Clements, Leona S.	1989
2380	Clements, W. D.	1957
13574	Clemmer, Mattie J.	1992
12604	Clemmer, William B.	1991
9300	Cleveland, Nemis J.	1984
10120	Cleveland, Royce S	1986
13494	Clifton, Erma Brown	1996

File	Deceased	Year
704	Clifton, Tim J.	1930
711	Clifton, Tim J. F.	1930
11300	Clinkscales, Thomas Ross	1988
17198	Cloeter, John Julius	1999
9564	Clompitt, Lester J.	1985
6809	Cloud, Myrtle A.	1978
1281	Cloudt, Walter O. Sr.	1946
13200	Clubb, Dennie Kyle	1992
9584	Clynes, Wellsworth Knight Jr.	1985
6411	Coad, Opal W.	1971
5237	Coats, Odas Arthur	1973
2320	Cobb, Emma	1958
5535	Cobb, Ira M.	1974
12020	Coburn, Maudie A.	1990
10880	Cochran, Lawrence H.	1987
5544	Cochrane, Earl A. Sr.	1974
11848	Cocke, Sadie L.	1989
5548	Cockrell, Elva J.	1974
5437	Cockrell, Elva Loraine	1974
17166	Coday, James Dewey Jr.	1999
8511	Codrington, Agnes Holekamp	1983
12416	Codrington, Charles E.	1990
6534	Codrington, Margaret M.	1978
14960	Codrington, Thomas Phillip Jr.	1995
10388	Cody, Patsy Ross	1986
17534	Coen, Philip R. Jr.	1999
10828	Coffey, L. N.	1987
14796	Coffey, Margaret	1995
5018	Coffman, William Jefferson	----
13748	Cofield, Ruth Adora W.	1993

48

File	Deceased	Year
6611	Cogburn, Charles C.	1978
17714	Coggin, Bessie Elva	2000
SE65	Cohoe, George R.	1982
6061	Colbath, Alfred J.	1976
9912	Colbath, Colene June	1986
9616	Colbath, Cora Anna Olga	1985
16128	Colbath, Irene Lohoma	1997
15234	Colbath, Jack J.	1995
15008	Colbeth, James Edward aka James E. Colbath	1995
1437	Colbath, Mrs. John	1949
1068	Colbath, John H.	1941
9179	Colbath, Patricia Ann	1984
5210	Colbath, Roger Q.	1973
17222	Colbath, Walter L.	1999
697	Colbert, Hiram J.	1930
110	Colby, B.	1891?
904	Coldwell, Carrie	1936
6088	Coldwell, Lula	1976
4091	Coldwell, Mabel	1969
616	Coldwell, Neal	1925
15044	Coldwell, William M.	1995
10844	Cole, Cullen E.	1987
3631	Cole, E. W.	1966
18256	Cole, Jack W. Sr.	2001
4592	Cole, John W.	----
12340	Cole, Karen Clark (Newman)	1990
7010	Cole, Lena Lucille	1979
6530	Cole, Leonard C.	1977
12868	Cole, Ralph C.	1991
13546	Coleman, Adah Leonard	1992
19014	Coleman, Charles Wayne	2002
3014	Coleman, Edward H.	1963

File	Deceased	Year
16336	Coleman, Elizabeth Anne Pullman	1997
13612	Coleman, Eva Dora	1992
7622	Coleman, Isla	1981
18134	Coleman, Margaret Ann	2000
5456	Coleman, Ralph M.	1974
8874	Collens, Paul Icor	1984
10076	Collazo, Margaret	1986
4336	Collazo, Mrs. T. J.	1970
309	Colles, Mary Eva	1911
11620	Collett, Grant Lewis	1989
11004	Colley, Agnes	1988
6658	Colley, James S.	1978
14480	Colley, Roland Lee	1994
19382	Colley, Thomas	2002
2159	Collier, Elbert H.	1957
9314	Collier, John Lee	1985
3619	Collier, William J.	1966
14706	Collins, Bessie F.	1994
10544	Collins, Earl B.	1987
9346	Collins, Elmer Leroy	1985
5678	Collins, Finis C.	1974
7709	Collins, Jack R.	1981
4684	Collins, John H.	1969
332/333	Collins, L. G.	----
14756	Collins, Lois G.	1994
9288	Collins, Lyonell	1984
9590	Collins, Robert Eugene	1985
9348	Collins, Shirley Jean	1985
2165	Collison, Clarence P.	1957
17126	Collum, Charles Lewis Jr.	1999
15990	Columbia, Dorothy Irene Bunca	1997
8730	Colvin, Amy J.	1983

File	Deceased	Year
18092	Colvin, Clara D.	2000
4143	Colvin, Elizabeth B.	1969
4163	Colvin, Elizabeth B.	1969
13732	Colvin, Emiline Kindorf	1993
8810	Colvin, J. W.	1984
15944	Colwell, William Austin	1987
10524	Comer, Jane White	1987
9432	Commander, Billy Joe	1985
16006	Comogys, Duke aka Jewell A.	1997
4385	Comparette, Beatrice	1970
1643	Comparette, D. H.	1952
14794	Comparette, D. H. Jr.	1994
789	Comparette, L. M.	1933
658	Comparette, Laula M.	1925
9834	Comparette, Lena	1985
7095	Compton, Bessie	1979
10818	Compton, Bess C.	1987
8332	Compton, Henry N.	1982
11430	Compton, Ruble Herschel	1989
13138	Condon, Barbara L.	1992
6839	Condon, James L.	1979
2358	Cone, George Sealy	1959
2581	Cone, Odessa Ludwig	1960
4029	Conklin, Fred V.	1968
14682	Conklin, Ryamond Sr.	1994
11226	Connally, Herschel Frank Jr.	1989
17600	Connell, George B.	1999
15438	Connelly, James C.	1996
3618	Conner, Mayo D.	1966
12094	Conner, Walter Clyde	1990
5236	Constanza, Frank D.	1973
8018	Converse, Julian Langston	1982

File	Deceased	Year
12520	Converse, Marion F.	1991
12392	Converse, Roger L.	1990
12264	Conway, Caudle Waddell	1990
12700	Cook, Alma M. aka	
	Lily Alma M.	1991
9394	Cook, Basil P.	1985
15562	Cook, Chilton A.	1996
2345	Cook, Henry Allan	1959
17858	Cook, James W.	2000
1350	Cook, Joseph	1947
18200	Cook, L. Clifford	2001
348	Cook, Mrs. M. A.	?1913
14556	Cook, Marguerite	1994
7189	Cook, Marie C.	1980
17994	Cook, Norma Reagen	2000
7283	Cook, Rena B.	1980
9428	Cook, Vera F.	1985
13998	Cook, Verna M.	1993
843	Cooksey, Jeff	1934
574	Cooksey, Mahala	1925
19036	Cooley, Kenneth Charles	2002
2958	Coombe, Winfred I.	1963
16436	Cooper, Barbara H.	1998
5800	Cooper, Cecelia A.	1975
16048	Cooper, Dorothy May	1997
13464	Cooper, Edward H.	1992
5923	Cooper, H. G.	1976
3316	Cooper, Manly W.	1964
13492	Cooper, Mary Joan aka	
	Mary J. & M. J.	1992
11996	Cooper, Robert E.	1990
13094	Cooper, Wallace Ray	1992
4632	Coose, John N.	1971
5267	Coots, Wynona T.	----
12346	Copeland, James R.	1990

File	Deceased	Year
6427	Copeland, Mary A.	1977
1572	Coppedge, James F.	1951
7676	Copple, Earl Harold	1981
15214	Copple, Lucille Rydberg	1995
11028	Corbell, Hill H.	1988
19006	Corbell, Lucy Manly	2002
61	Corbell, Mary A.	?1886?
66	Corbell, Mary A.	?1885?
2696	Corbett, Pauline H.	1961
15822	Corey, Abbie E.	1996
394	Corkill, Ed	1915
8103	Cormier, Eloi	1982
5392	Cormier, Felix	1974
14602	Cornelius, Martha Virginia Taylor	1994
12382	Cornels, Frederick Brown	1990
6158	Cornish, John J.	1976
9786	Cortez, Carmen Torres	1985
3808	Cortez, Roman	1967
10526	Cory, Obed Iley Jr.	1987
13754	Cosand, Carl Elmer	1993
10152	Costin, William Berry	1986
7993	Cottle, Benjamin Sievely	1981
6218	Couch, Jewel F.	1976
12060	Coulthard, Guy E.	1990
5026	Council, E. V.	1973
7197	Council, Eleanor S.	1980
6089	Council, Goda Henry	----
10140	Council, Hattie	1986
3811	Council, Lillian	1967
998	Council, Lora	1938
1467	Council, W. L.	1950
5621	Coutant, Chester Arthur	1974

File	Deceased	Year
18746	Covert, Amer Lois	2001
1761	Covert, C.	1954
15700	Covert, Henry	1996
10448	Covert, L. Hazel	1987
10548	Covey, Jerry	1987
6624	Cowan, Bohard P.	1978
16998	Cowan, Violet U.	1998
5934	Cowart, Jennie M.	1976
2047	Cowart, T. J.	1956
8009	Cowden, George E.	1982
15170	Cowden, Harry J.	1995
15688	Cowden, Helen C.	1996
1492	Cowden, Jerry Eugene Sr.	1950
8566	Cowden, Lorene Edwards	1983
6393	Cowden, Tommie Jean	1977
15148	Cowell, Loy L.	1995
19116	Cowen, Hazel Lorriaine	2002
2112	Cowen, Mrs. M. L.	1957
17968	Cowin, Velma Marie	2000
18214	Cox, Charles G. Jr.	2000
4403	Cox, Charlie Guilford	1970
17108	Cox, Clara Mae	1999
4978	Cox, Dorothy E.	----
10746	Cox, Edna May	1987
16204	Cox, Elna S.	1997
18125	Cox, Frank Robert Jr.	2000
4734	Cox, George Albert	1971
10954	Cox, George W.	1987
16152	Cox, Howard W.	1997
4339	Cox, Ida Belle	1970
19186	Cox, J. D.	2002
2375	Cox, J. G.	1959
10866	Cox, Lee Alice	1987
5691	Cox, Leonard T.	1974
16318	Cox, Lillian M.	1997

File	Deceased	Year
18208	Cox, Margaret L.	2001
7645	Cox, Mary Catherine	1981
SE6	Cox, Nora Townsend	1971
19316	Cox, Richard Bruce Sr.	2002
2335	Cox, Robert Earl	1959
11070	Cox, Russ L.	1988
9436	Cox, Ruth L.	1985
16132	Cox, Samuel B.	1997
1527	Cox, W. F.	1951
4296	Craft, Mary Ivory	----
15026	Craft, Marie Mosty	1995
15194	Craft, Oma Jean	1995
12568	Craft, William C.	1991
18630	Craig, Alma A.	2001
6986	Craig, Ann	1979
7792	Craig, Charles C.	1981
15768	Craig, Lee E.	1996
15564	Craig, Robert I. Sr.	1996
14994	Craig, Wayne	1995
7528	Craig, Wayne D.	1980
11042	Craighead, Charles Dickenson	1988
11580	Craigie, Hugh M.	1989
15878	Crain, Fred A.	1996
15588	Crain, Joseph R.	1996
10930	Cramer, Fay F.	1987
11356	Cramer, Harry T.	1988
5108	Cramford, Esther M	----
5303	Crane, Phyllis B.	----
6639	Crate, Willa Schmidt	1978
270	Cravey, Eva L.	----
3983	Crawford, George Ross	1968
19060	Crawford, Jimmie Earl	2002
6116	Crawford, Lonnie Leroy	1976
8553	Crawford, Margaret J.	1983

File	Deceased	Year
3184	Crawford, W. C.	1964
10776	Crawley, Marguerite Medor	1987
3015	Cray, Robert	1963
2714	Creager, Beth Mae	1961
9266	Creamer, Barney G.	1984
7618	Creech, Violet Wray	1981
5905	Creel, Andrew Dye	1976
7871	Creel, Helen W.	1981
7969	Creel, Mary Bond	1981
17752	Creiglow, Evelyn Carroon	2000
807	Crenshaw, Earl	1934
320	Crenshaw, M. A.	----
13272	Crenshaw, P. A.	1992
844	Crenshaw, Pleas A.	1935
3620	Crenshaw, Y. L.	1966
7381	Crews, Percy L.	1980
18400	Cribbs, Jackie J.	2001
3213	Crick, A. D.	1964
8539	Crider, Audrey E.	1983
14484	Crider, Juanita Mae	1994
16622	Crider, Ollie Bell	1998
15224	Crider, Syretta Eugenia	1995
1821	Crider, Walter H.	1954
13798	Crist, Virgil W.	1993
10440	Crites, Charles F.	1986
12418	Crites, Floye E.	1990
13830	Critton, Charley	1993
12040	Crocker, Alfred	1990
43	Crockett, A. M.	1882
122	Crockett, O. J.	1874?
7353	Crom, Joe D.	1980
12122	Cromer, Charles J.	1990
7486	Crook, Edwin R.	1980

File	Deceased	Year
10326	Crook, Warren J.	1986
14460	Crooks, Raymond A.	1994
1629	Crooks, W. A.	1952
980	Croom, Jesse	1938
17658	Crosby, Helen R.	2000
16848	Crosland, Lorraine Sellin	1998
17856	Cross, Dorothy Louise	2000
17532	Cross, Joseph L.	1999
3608	Cross, Julian Buckingham Sr.	1966
12400	Crosthwait, Gladys Blanch	1990
1676	Crotty, Charles	1953
542	Crotty, James	1923
17246	Crow, Clarence Dennis	1999
3602	Crow, Jim	1966
12852	Crow, Kate Lucille	1991
13462	Crow, Le Rue Mc Murry	1992
3344	Crow, R. N.	1965
17244	Crow, Viola	1999
10440	Crowl, Joe J.	1987
16300	Crowl, Mary L.	1997
17684	Crowley, George Richard	2000
1184	Cruikshank, Elizabeth	1944
3887	Cruikshank, W. S.	1968
15576	Crumpton, David J.	1996
9220	Crumpton, Hallie Mae	1884
12404	Crutchfield, Jody B.	1990
17886	Crutchfield, Mary Olive	2000
14182	Cull, John W.	1993
7658	Cullum, Alfred E.	1981
3599	Cullum, Frank P. Sr.	1966
11100	Culver, Anna L.	1988
10980	Culver, Ava	1988

File	Deceased	Year
10136	Culver, Jesse E.	1986
15236	Culwell, Edith W.	1995
14712	Culwell, W. J.	1994
18686	Cummings, D. Malcolm	2001
3146	Cummings, Irene W.	1964
6438	Cummings, James C.	1977
19064	Cummings, Virginia B.	----
14342	Cummings, Walter Bound	1994
17514	Crumpton, Vivienne M.	1999
702	Cunniff, William	1930
11816	Cunningham, Andy Ray	1989
1711	Cunningham, L. B.	1953
1403	Cunningham, Robert L.	1948
8397	Cunningham, Rose B.	1982
1771	Cunshaw, Rose D.	1954
4658	Curl, Robert Floyd	1971
16990	Curlee, Rosa E.	1998
19298	Currie, Sylvia Elizabeth May	2002
11034	Curry, Alpha Mildred	1988
11280	Curry, Burnard A.	1988
7545	Curry, Gladys Mc Ginnis	1980
10094	Curtin, Catherine M.	1986
9073	Curtin, Stanley J.	1984
2609	Curtis, L. H.	1961
19102	Curtis, Susie E.	2002
2138	Curtis, Sylvia B.	1957
4585	Curtis, Wilbert A.	1971
SE100	Custer, James Henry	1982
6419	Custer, Viola Gladys	1971
5798	Cutsinger, Ida Neely	1975

File	Deceased	Year
	D	
8867	Dabney, Mary Lee	1984
8719	Daendliker, Emilie	1983
9898	Daendliker, Louis	1986
13248	Dahse, Norwin G.	1992
SE11	Dailey, Aimee L.	1974
12946	Dailey, Lawrence T.	1991
2625	Dale, Robert O.	1961
14724	Dalrymple, Byron W.	1994
3314	Dalsin, Charels A.	1965
2113	Daly, John S. Jr.	1957
4546	Dambach, John I.(?J)	1969
16637	Dancy, Ellen C.	1997
721	Danforth, T. H.	----
4340	D'Angelo, Anthony	1970
10084	Daniel, Aena Martin	1986
10816	Daniel, Beatrice D.	1987
18250	Daniel, Marguerite D.	2001
12348	Daniel, Mildred M.	1990
4902	Daniel, Ruby G.	1972
6818	Daniel, Thomas M.	1978
1930	Daniel, Walton S.	1955
4934	Daniel, Warwick N.	1972
1668	Daniels, Ed	1952
12396	Daniels, Harry E.	1990
15616	Daniels, Lucille B.	1996
6345	Daniels, Tom F.	1976
17462	Danna, Wanda Earle	1999
12468	Dansby, John Wingo	1990
6068	Dantzler, Henry Augusta	1976
8195	Danz, Margaret	1982
1615	Darby, John W.	1952
1867	Darby, Margaret Estella	1954
3929	Darrow, James R.	1968

File	Deceased	Year
12206	Dasch, Edward Clifton	1990
5984	Darst, Albert Otto	1976
6400	Darst, Jarmila Viola	1977
6338	Dart, Grace Ellen	----
3586	Daugherty, Aloysius	1966
2359	Daugherty, Jackson	1959
15208	Davenport, Edwin Jouett	1995
846	Davenport, J. E.	1935
2901	Davenport, Joe E.	1962
5061	Davenport, Josephine	1973
2519	Davenport, Mary B.	1960
18512	David, Sylvia Matlat	2001
308	Davidson, J. J.	1911
14904	Davidson Lala B.	1995
12674	Davidson, Lawrence L.	1991
4532	Davidson, Lois O.	1970
12688	Davies, David Owen Sr.	1991
SE02-3	Davila, Lorenzo	2002
SE99-2	Davis, Anna/Annie B.	1999
2305	Davis, A. E.	1958
19370	Davis, Catherine A.	2002
14532	Davis, Doris	1994
13794	Davis, Dorothy A.	1993
11748	Davis, Dorothy M.	1989
18966	Davis, Elmer Dee	2002
15536	Davis, Emily Z.	1996
15934	Davis, Ernestine M.	1997
16174	Davis (Consolidation)	1997
16180	Davis, Estha Cartwright	1997
16176-A	Davis, Estha Cart- wright aka Estha H. Davis	1998
2306	Davis, Ethel	1958
15626	Davis, Florence Marie	1996
7096	Davis, Fort	1979

File	Deceased	Year
10814	Davis, George Henry	1987
14164	Davis, Harold L.	1993
17442	Davis, Ithama Irene	1999
7934	Davis, Jack	1981
8751	Davis, Jack Ryan	1983
15528	Davis, Jacksie Bradley	1996
2167	Davis, James J.	1957
1397	Davis, John C. (Jack)	1948
16148	Davis, John D. Jr.	1997
4257	Davis, L. C.	1969
3328	Davis, L. L.	1965
3044	Davis, L. T.	1963
SE101	Davis, Lester R.	1984
15448	Davis, Lorena Hood	1996
8048	Davis, Mamie B.	1982
7782	Davis, Martha E.	1981
15998	Davis, Marynell	1997
11524	Davis, Mildred N.	1989
248	Davis, N. F.	1906
5762	Davis, Norman S.	1975
18966	Davis, Pearl E.	2002
13210	Davis, Pearl Sutton	1921
SE7	Davis, Perry C.	1972
17550	Davis, Raymond C.	1999
17866	Davis, Rosemary Pool	2000
13398	Davis, Stella B.	1992
6139	Davis, Stella Lawhon	----
14714	Davis, Stuart Russell Turner	1994
7272	Davis, Velia	1980
65	Davis, W.	----
67	Davis, W. L.	1952
5634	Davis, William H.	1975
5433	Davis, Willie	----
9212	Davis, Winifred Freeman	1984

File	Deceased	Year
12454	Davison, Elizabeth H.	1990
8724	Davison, Estle Harold	1983
17978	Davison, Forbes I.	2000
19144	Davisson, Frances T.	2002
10304	Davoren, William Thomas	1986
791	Daw, W. H.	1933
4678	Dawe, Harold Louis	1971
8163	Dawson, Alvin Marshall	1982
7759	Dawson, Robert E.	1981
5144	Dawson, Zula I.	1973
17918	Day, Ellis Marvin Jr.	2000
3089	Day, Jeff	1964
17204	Dayton, Mary Alice	1999
6917	Deadman, Ernest Lindsey	1979
5572	Deal, Garland Andrew	1974
17794	Deal, James Alfred Sr.	2000
9924	Deam, Andrew Taylor	1986
12404	Deam, Esther Lena	1990
8964	Dean, Guy W. Jr.	1984
15706	Dean, Weldon Custer	1996
5766	Dearing, Evelyn B.	1975
19290	Dearing, Herman A.	2002
9538	Dearing, W. B.	1985
10274	Deaton, Vernell	1986
16102	Dechert, Clayton Walter	1997
2245	Decker, Hattie M.	1958
3637	Decker, James L.	1966
13412	Decker, Robert Porter	1992
9674	De Cosmo, Peter A.	1985
6077	Dedeaux, Caroline L.	1976
19278	Dedeker, Sherman Doc	2002
17320	Deere, Ave Beatrice Ard	1999
4492	Deere, I. C.	1970
2048	Deering, Charles	1956
15152	Deering, Clarabel G.	1995

File	Deceased	Year
629	Deering, John T.	1927
3499	Deering, Mabel M.	1966
195	Defriece, Harriet	----
1765	De Geurin, Virginia C.	1981
9876	Degner, Forest E.	1986
19362	Deidloff, Edward W.	2002
14258	Deidloff, Eleanor	1994
6811	Deike, Max F.	1978
17300	Deily, Fredric Harry	1999
5877	Deisman, Ethan Landymore	1975
12678	De La Fuente, Mirella	1991
1939	Delaney, Stella V.	1955
9034	Delay, George Joseph	1984
18598	Delery, Mary Margaret	2001
18510	Delesandri, Mary Ellen	2001
16856	Delesandri, Pete	1998
18278	Delesdernier, Sophie	2001
SE93-3	Delgadillo, Charles Roderiguez	1993
3822	Delgadillo, Esteban	1967
7715	Delgadillo, Juanita	1981
12448	Delgado, Leo	1990
16838	Del Papa, Omero L. Jr.	1998
2235	Delroi, Jack Delquiste	1958
----	Delp, F.	----
18322	Demaever, Adeline Serfina Vogels	2001
18060	Demarovich, Barbara A.	2000
13182	Dempsey, Charles Rudolph	1992
5162	Dempsey, Ellen	1973
8168A	Dempsey, Ellen Dorothy	1982
16708	Dempsey, Ruth Leavell	1998
18000	Demske, Sheldon E.	2000

File	Deceased	Year
8598	Denbow, Clarence R.	1983
9872	Denbow, Ella M.	1986
4863	Dendy, Velma H.	1972
5992	Dendy, W. C.	1976
17634	Denham, William Dean	2000
15426	Dennis, Glenn F.	1996
18796	Dennis, Joe	2001
11650	Dennison, Alvin H.	1989
1826	Dent, J. J.	1954
1091	Denton, Ethel A.	1941
13950	Denton, Jesse V.	1993
7075	Denton, Leslie P.	1979
1292	Denton, Mary	1946
8148	Denton, Ruth I.	1982
8842	Denton, Troy	1984
8739	Derden, Charles V.	1983
4869	Derden, Francis L.	1972
14956	De Rouen, Alicia P.	1995
16874	De Rusha, George Washington	1998
17260	Deveny, James Albert	1999
7632	De Ville, Herman	1981
11830	De Villiers, Hubert Enright	1989
12028	Devitt, Margaret H.	1990
6207	Devitt, W. G. S.	1976
15634	Devold, Opal F.	1996
8862	Devold, Robert B.	1984
15676	Devoll, Isaac Horten Jr.	1996
12238	Devolt, John I.	1990
17704	Devon, Ruby Lea	2000
15084	Devore, Elsie Witt	1995
1836	De Vore, James H.	1954
15744	De Vore, Phyllis Ann	1996
11040	Dew, George Marion	1988

File	Deceased	Year
17310	Dew, Robby Lee	1999
5610	Dewees, Kate Graves	----
293	Dewry, B. F.	----
5970	Dial, Delmar J.	1976
18302	Diaz, Carlos	2000
2269	Dibrell, John L. Sr.	1958
11576	Dick, Fred	1989
15408	Dicken, George D.	1996
2861	Dicken, Margaret (Molly)	1962
4374	Dickens, Hortense Margaret Elinore	1970
18480	Dickerson, Arthur P.	2001
8835	Dickey, Flora Elizabeth	1984
3850	Dickey, Lucinda H.	1967
11904	Dickey, Lucinda Hillman	1989
5628	Dickey, Myrtle	1974
2444	Dickey, Robert Clement	1959
4913	Dickey, Walter A. Jr.	1971
14394	Dickey, Walter Arthur	1994
10432	Dickey, Wilbur N.	1987
14392	Dickey, Winnie F.	1994
17428	Dickhoff, Kathryn Bernice Hall	1999
14276	Dicks, Bessie J.	1994
5378	Dickson, Charles M.	----
7728	Dickson, Harry E.	1981
10304	Dickson, John L.	1986
32	Dickson, Robert	----
6261	Dickson, Wilma Nell	1977
2774	Diehl, Charles	1962
6908	Diehl, Edith	1979
3530	Dies, Florence Whipple	1966
507	Dies, Martin	----
6218	Dietert, Alex C.	1976
12144	Dietert, Alma D.	1990

File	Deceased	Year
294	Dietert, Annie	1908
12722	Dietert, Cecil F.	1991
203	Dietert, Christian	1902
829	Dietert, Clara	1934
2347	Dietert, Clara Real	1959
13320	Dietert, Eddie	1992
2427	Dietert, Edward	1959
6857	Dietert, Eleanora P.	1979
1986	Dietert, Elizabeth	1956
890	Dietert, Emil E.	1936
120	Dietert, F.	1892
6714	Dietert, Harry W.	1978
1200	Dietert, Henry	1944
8769	Dietert, Hetta Seebe	1983
12144	Dietert, Margaret H.	1990
338	Dietert, Paula	1912
18354	Dietert, Raymond William	2001
2091	Dietert, Richard	1959
667	Dietert, Rosalie	1929
2499	Dietert, Thekla	1960
550	Dietrich, Ben E.	----
9632	Di Giacinto, Virginia Joann	1985
7256	Di Ginder, William F.	1980
6797	Dikemann, Fary Burge	1978
9808	Dimery, Aaron Clyde	1985
10228	Dimery, Samuel A.	1986
10022	Dimery, Thelma L.	1986
8477	Dinier, Erna	1983
11582	Dinkel, Kate M.	1989
13038	Dinkfeld, August M.	1991
2967	Dinwiddie, Elizabeth W.	1963
10984	Dion, Francis	1988
10484	Discher, Arno Ewald	1987

File	Deceased	Year
15892	Disheroon, Ennis R.	1996
13854	Disheroon, Johnnie Juanita	1993
8343	Dishongh, Alton	1982
1900	Dismukes, Addie Lucy	1955
18444	Dismukes, Dorothy Auld	2001
2592	Dismukes, Edna West	1960
19188	Dismukes, Francis Tipton	2002
6684	Dismukes, Charles M.	1978
16828	Dix, Joyce Marion	1998
2249	Dixon, Bertha L.	1958
4388	Dixon, G. O.	1970
14702	Dixon, Grace A.	1994
1072	Dixon, H. E.	1939
2220	Dixon, R. M	1958
14306	Dixon, Wilma Ada	1994
17500	Doades, Thomas Wendel	1999
16278	Dobie, Martha	1997
7678	Dobyns, Rollie Paul	1981
10628	Dockus, Harold J.	1987
6993	Dodd, Floyd T.	1979
16878	Dodd, George Emmet	1998
11492	Dodd, William G.	1988
6828	Dodson, Francis F.	1978
5042	Dodson, J. L.	----
4418	Dodson, Mary Louise	1970
7172	Dodson, Myetta Mae	1979
12412	Dodt, Harry A.	1990
521	Doebbler, Louis	1922
14066	Doebbler, Rubin	1993
4793	Doering, Fred J.	1972
14804	Doering, Lucia J.	1995
9796	Doerr, Carl F. Jr.	1985

File	Deceased	Year
9658	De Geurin, Pirtle Jefferson	1985
15350	Doherty, Francis Kinard	1995
7133	Dolby, Maurine Evelyn	1979
7179	Dolby, Thomas P.	1980
SE53	Dolezal, Eddie	1981
13082	Dolezal, Ora	1992
17566	Dombeck, Clarence J.	1999
SE39	Domengaux, Warren L.	----
7239	Domengaux, Warren L.	1980
1312	Domingues, Evelyn B.	1946
14608	Domingues, Louis	1994
15906	Domingues, Margaret H.	1997
1811	Domingues, P. J.	1954
1063	Donald, Dell	1941
13664	Donald, Clarence Sr.	1992
7187	Donald, Frances B.	1980
16508	Donaldson, Dayul Wilson	1998
19042	Donaldson, Lois R.	2002
9478	Donalson, Anna Belle	1985
9532	Donavan, Tolivr Lee	1985
17614	Donihoo, Ruby Jenkins	1999
15964	Donnelly, Edmund H.	1997
10618	Donnelly, Fannie Josephine	1987
1128	Donnelly, George A.	1942
1457	Donnelly, Jack W.	1949
17110	Donnelly, Mary Jane	1999
7232	Donoho, Mildred Moore	1980
4275	Dooley, Edwin Clifford	1969
3528	Dooley, Francis Wiseman	1966
3315	Doose, William	1965
11906	Doran, Michael Patrick	1989
2852	Doran, W. H.	1962
SE01-4	Dorety, Wade L.	2001

File	Deceased	Year
10474	Dorrill, Abbie Jo Scarborough	1987
13506	Dorrill, George Truitt	1992
11894	Dorris, Hayes H.	1989
16474	Dorris, Le Ora	1998
13650	Dosdall, George E.	1992
17208	Dosdall, Rose A.	1999
8550	Doss, Emmett	1983
13738	Dotson, Obern K.	1993
14658	Doty, William G.	1994
1216	Doudlinger, Ida	1944
8545	Doughty, Jewel M.	1983
8195	Douglas, Lyle	1982
10516	Douglas, Richard H.	1987
7149	Douglas, William Edward	1979
9336	Dove, Frank P.	1985
266	Dowd, J.	1915
1450	Dowd, Particia Suse	1949
6831	Dowd, Queen A.	1978
19292	Dowdey,Edna Earle	2002
6884	Dowding, Bill B.	1979
3414	Dowding, Eva	1965
18792	Dowdy, Carlton Leroy	2001
979	Dowdy, G. E.	1938
10862	Dowdy, Gene W.	1987
12918	Dowdy, George A.	1991
2587	Dowdy, Georgie	1960
12368	Dowdy, James Clyde	1990
15774	Dowdy, Juanita R.	1996
9910	Dowdy, Kyle	1986
5538	Dowdy, Sarah Berniece	1974
3230	Dowdy, Tarleton Leo	1964
445	Dowdy, Thomas	1919
14190	Dowdy, Thomas Leo	1993
4728	Dowell, Edgar Adis	----

File	Deceased	Year
2792	Dowling, Edward John	1962
14104	Downey, Alice R.	1993
14476	Downey, Harry L.	1994
6306	Downey, Mineola Moore	1977
16358	Downum, K. B. aka Kenneth B. aka Kenneth Berry	1997
16870	Downum, Virginia B.	1998
949	Doyle, Albion	1937
944	Doyle, Annie W.	1937
9380	Doyle, Catherine Bannerman	1985
9980	Doyle, Charles Edgar Sr.	1986
3305	Doyle, Clella	1965
1575	Doyle, George M.	1951
1459	Doyle, Lyle J.	1949
7306	Doyle, Merrill	1980
490	Doyle, Walker	----
13774	Draeger, Soledad R.	1993
8996	Drake, Bernard Edgar	1984
6132	Drake, J. D.	1976
17270	Drake, Jack J.	1999
14952	Drake, Willie Ruth	1995
14930	Draper, Elsie Davis	1995
15740	Dreau, Blanche Louise	1996
11210	Dreau, Roger Joseph	1988
12438	Dreier, Sue Thomas	1990
1278	Dreiss, E. A.	1946
17770	Dresser, Margaret Ruth	2000
4050	Dreves, Harry Emil	1968
17046	Drew, Timothy Owen	1998
11952	Driskell, Luther	1990
15114	Driver, Corrine G.	1995
18220	Drozd, Adolph Henry	2001
2056	Drucker, Edna Dixon	1956

File	Deceased	Year
5712	Drucker, Harry	1975
9726	Drucker, Maria	1985
16912	Druebert, Evelyn G.	1998
13536	Drummond, Harold	1992
3047	Drury, Cooper C.	1963
17792	Drury, Janice G.	2000
14248	Dryden, Joseph Samuel	1994
15496	Drysdale, Ardis	1996
15004	Drysdale, George Lee	1995
11234	Dube, Jacquelin R.	1988
15414	Dube, Walter Albert	1996
10510	Dubois, Barbara L.	1987
10678	Dubois, Christopher G.	1987
10508	Dubois, Gerald L.	1987
584	Dubose, J. E.	1925
16124	Duby, Elva Mildred	1997
13258	Duchow, Wallace Gregory Jr.	1992
17582	Duckett, Frank D.	1999
11456	Duckworth, Mary Joan	1988
10478	Duckworth, William Harrill	1987
12686	Duddy, Eleanora B.	1991
10158	Duddy, James T.	1986
985	Duderstadt, F.	1938
19254	Duderstadt, Mildred M.	2002
11030	Duderstadt, Temple J.	1988
17980	Duderstadt, Yvonne Yvette	2000
5407	Duesing, George W.	----
16134	Duesterberg, Gerhard Joseph	1997
18712	Dudgeon, Robert H.	2002
729	Duff, Charles A.	1931/2
9896	Duffy, Mary Ruth	1986

File	Deceased	Year
8965	Dugosh, Florence E.	1984
3573	Duke, James F.	1966
3502	Duke, Henry O.	1966
16260	Duke, Jimmy F.	1997
12584	Duke, Lemma D.	1991
4205	Duke, Noah	1969
7207	Dulin, Harry Lewis	1980
7978	Dulin, Helen Sue	1981
18098	Du Menil, Frances Louise Mc Mullin	2000
9080	Dunaway, George N.	1984
6796	Duncan, Ernest G.	1978
10510	Duncan, Gordon Lester	1987
5624	Duncan, James L.	1975
8449	Duncan, Kenneth E.	1983
17304	Duncan, Maxine G.	1999
6412	Duncan, Othella Blanche	1977
5642	Duncan, Ruth H.	----
10754	Dunham, Perry W.	1987
12010	Duncan, Willie N.	1990
14846	Dunker, Albert W.	1995
5166	Dunks, Herman	----
1937	Dunks, Ira J.	1955
6392	Dunks, Katie	1977
5513	Dunks, Robert Alton	1974
19142	Dunn, Doris	2002
18070	Dunn, Drue Alonzo	2000
9155	Dunn, Florence Lillian	1984
6691	Dunn, Haskell Joseph Sr.	1978
14502	Dunn, Linda Stroud	1994
11206	Dunn, Mary Magdalene	1988
9040	Dunn, Omega Stewart	1984
16404	Dunning, Ida Ruth Blair	1997
15054	Dunning, John Alton	1995
13578	Dunwoody, J. Francis	1992

File	Deceased	Year
13712	Duran, Floripes C.	1993
3205	Durant, Anna	1964
1027	Durant, S. S.	1939
6404	Durham, Lora H.	1977
16286	Durham, Tolford H.	1997
8191	Durrell, John C.	1982
7184	Durrenberger, Edward Beall	1980
12366	Durrenberger, Laura Danford	1990
18156	Durrenberger, Mazo Y. T.	2000
2486	Durrin, Charles S. Sr.	1960
15866	Durrin, Charles S.	1996
6802	Durrin, Elva Ella	1978
7237	Durst, Marvin F.	1980
8629	Durst, Roy W.	1983
6608	Durston, Irene MacKensie	1978
1071	Durwin, H. S.	1939
13842	Dwyer, Ailene Osburn	1993
6096	Dwyer, Edward James	1976
8878	Dwyer, Nora Mae	1984
7583	Dyas, Lorraine L.	1981
17338	Dye, J. R.	1999
10288	Dyer, T. H.	1986
7456	Dyess, Homer	1980
8701	Dyess, Wilbert Cleo	1983
14552	Dyke, Marshall Richard	1994
274	Dykes, Katie	1908
3078	Dyson, Jeff A.	1964

E

11014	Eager, Alvin Thomas	1988

File	Deceased	Year
9540	Eakin, Lena Lois	1985
10540	Eakin, W. E. Sr.	1987
11338	Earl, Anna Mae	1988
4597	Earley, Moy G.	1971
13714	Earley, Pearl Elizabeth	1993
6456	Eastland, Annie Mae	1977
4529	Eastland, Seaborn	1970
16164	Eastman, Paul Rose	1997
13036	Eastridge, Emmitt Clifford	1991
18328	Eastridge, Johnye L.	2001
10422	Eastridge, Milam C.	1987
21	Eastwood, J. Frank	1873
18014	Easton, Sue Vivion	2000
15456	Eaton, Annie Lillian aka Lillian Aaton	1996
3712	Eaton, Courtlandt	1967
8187	Eaton, Frances B.	1982
8373	Eaton, Frank S.	1982
10974	Eaton, Fremont M.	1988
5741	Eaton, Leavy	1975
2103	Eaton, Martel	1957
16550	Eaton, William Carroll	1998
10302	Ebert, Mary Teresa	1986
8160	Eckert, Helen Katherine	1982
10600	Eckerle, Elnora Burge	1987
11966	Eckerle, Elnora B.aka Elnora Burge Eckerle, Mrs. E. B. Echerle	1991
8883	Eckler, Oscar A.	1984
16894	Ecklund, Loren Arvid	1998
16360	Eckstein, Charles Henry	1997
1642	Eckstein, Henry	1952
1162	Eckstein, Lena	1943
11846	Eddins, Gerald L.	1989

File	Deceased	Year
4048	Eddins, Charles R.	1968
3789	Edelstein, Morris	1967
10748	Edens, Curtis EW.	1987
15142	Edens, Lucille J.	1995
18494	Edgar, Rosa Lee	2001
3398	Edge, James F.	1965
16620	Edington, Andrew	1998
16618	Edington, Matguertie Haas	1998
2442	Edmonds, Helen Sinclair	1959
10020	Edmonds, James Enos	1986
5390	Edmonds, Kenneth E.	1974
18320	Edmonds, Lora Mildred Crider	2001
2954	Edmundson, E. B.	1963
8261	Edmundson, E. Mildred	1982
3891	Edson, A. B.	1968
9216	Edson, Amy Eleanor	1984
16218	Edson, Harris E.	1997
17826	Edward, Donald E.	2000
10028	Edward, Frances	1986
2233	Edwards, Arthur	1958
3655	Edwards, C. P.	1966
1310	Edwards, Callie	1943
18852	Edwards,Daniel Marshall	2002
168	Edwards, Dee	1964
12968	Edwards, Jerra Wessa	1991
7417	Edwards, Lillian D.	1980
12228	Edwards, Myrtle M.	1990
10884	Edwards, Robert A.	1987
2745	Edwards, William Knox	1961
7186	Efner, Frank R.	1980
7946	Eggleston, Herbert L.	1981
3169	Ehler, F. E.	1964
6193	Ehlers, Hilda	1976

File	Deceased	Year
12254	Ehlers, La Verne	1990
4258	Ehlers, Paul	1969
9262	Ehlert, Bessie	1984
13044	Eichblatt, Jewel Mae	1991
14676	Eichblatt, Marvin L.	1994
7524	Eickenrot, Edmund	1980
16346	Eilers, Nita May Story	1997
3374	Elam, Kelly	1965
6899	Elder, Hattie A.	1979
6852	Elder, R. B.	1978
3901	Eldred, Margaret E.	1968
4663	Eldridge, Everett Brooke	1971
1611	Eldridge, L. W.	1952
5130/31	Eldridge, Lucile Smith	1973
9280	Eldridge, William Randle	1984
7271	Elhers, Gus Jr.	1980
7121	Elizardi, Frank Pace	1979
16346	Elizardi, Lilly Ann	1997
1719	Elkins, Frank R.	1953
12820	Elkins, Nannie B.	1991
4719	Elkins, W. B.	1971
2522	Ellebracht, Alfred	1960
8645	Ellebracht, Edgar H.	1983
12490	Ellebracht, Leona	1990
18106	Ellebracht, Olivia Emilie	2000
264	Elledge, J. M.	1907
5202	Ellingboe, C. G.	1973
11252	Ellingboe, Olga M.	1988
15118	Ellington, John A.	1995
3058	Ellington, William Q.	1964
18576	Elliott, Al Charles	2001
18878	Elliott, Edward Leroy	2002

File	Deceased	Year
10402	Elliott, Frederick C.	1987
6046	Elliott, Grace J.	1976
12736	Elliott, Joel Allen Sr.	1991
4439	Elliott, Newman Voyne	1970
12580	Elliott, Ora L.	1991
14736	Elliott, Phrania Anna	1994
6032	Elliott, Will	1976
8310	Elliott, William N.	1982
6026	Ellis, C. H.	1976
18854	Ellis, Carl E.	2002
17588	Ellis, Ercell J.	1999
11208	Ellis, Jack William	1988
18770	Ellis, Lenore Y.	2001
14598	Ellis, Lucy T.	1994
7364	Ellis, Mable V.	1980
17318	Ellis, Marion Ramsey	1999
17656	Ellis, Mary Louise	2000
14262	Ellis, Ollie Mc Laurin	1994
10692	Ellis, Thelma H.	1987
3968	Ellis, Willis H.	1966
18786	Ellis, Winifred M.	2001
1973	Ellison, Mrs. C. D.	1955
7418	Elmore, Annie L.	1980
15014	Elmore, Geraldine	1995
12652	Elmore, John A.	1991
1595	Elrick, Fred T.	1951?
15794	Elrod, Ike Leard	1996
7941	Elton, Ashley Edwin	1981
14898	Elton, Edward	1995
15568	Elverd, Mary Elizabeth	1996
8043	Emberton, Erna	1982
10134	Emberton, Jon	1986
4783	Emberton, Oran	1972
19222	Embretsen, Florence	2002
4384	Emerson, Maurine	1970

File	Deceased	Year
18664	Emig, Dorothy B.	2001
18662	Emig, Marion A.	2001
1865	Emmerick, George H.	1954
1313	Emsley, H. C.	1947
1361	Emsley, Jessie E.	1948
1737	Emsley, W. R.	1953
7174	Ender, Gilbert Carl	1979
16676	Ender, Merilyn J.	1998
1795	Endres, Frank	1954
14632	Engle, Albert	1994
1661	Engel, Albert F.	1952
10070	England, Clifford	1986
8717	England, Helen M.	1983
18296	England, Margaret Elizabeth	2001
4862	Engleman, Susie	1972
5836	Engleman, Henry B.	1975
10142	English, Dudley M.	1986
8754	Enloe, F. Genevieve	1983
6440	Epp, Alma	1977
4217	Epple, George L.	1969
2786	Epperson, Fred	1962
8425	Epperson, Virginia Sue	1983
2843	Epperson, Woodrow	1962
7121	Erickson, Clarrisa W.	1978
19112	Ernst, Arvilla, Dell	2002
1500	Ernst, C. Haug	1950
1672	Ernst, Edwin	1952
2875	Ernst, G. W.	1962
4410	Ernst, Patricia	1970
12560	Ersch, Estella E.	1991
2217	Erwin, Arthur Clarence	1958
16638	Erwin, Arthur Elliott	1998
2299	Erwin, Harriette Evans	1958
10270	Erwin, William A.	1986

File	Deceased	Year
11364	Eskew, Bessiemae F.	1988
18118	Espinoza, Aurora Lopez	2000
18838	Espinoza, Eva Salinas	2002
17842	Espinoza, Jose Medina	2000
3903	Espinoza, Juan	1965
16896	Espinoza, Luis	1998
9218	Estes, Cecil Lewis	1984
9844	Estes, Gwendolyn Ellen	1986
15302	Estes, John H.	1995
18862	Estes, Leta	2002
15290	Estes, Ned B.	1995
4313	Etchison, Teresa	1969
12544	Ethridge, George W.	1991
2253	Ethridge, Pearl	1958
1247	Ethridge, Travis	1945
18740	Etring, Elfrieda Erna	2001
17408	Eudaley, Steven Wayne	1999
19318	Euering, Leonard F.	2002
2614	Evans, Alda B.	1961
7347	Evans, Almer Myrth	1980
15900	Evans, Arthur Lewis	1997
15064	Evans, David Wesley Jr.	1995
4510	Evans, Edith E.	1970
7532	Evans, Herbert	1980
2507	Evans, J. Wiley	1960
601	Evans, John W.	1926
2201	Evans, L. M.	1958
6653	Evans, Lawrence S.	1978
19088	Evans, Lemuel Samuel	2002
2709	Evans, Maud Curtis	1961
13106	Evens, Roy Chester	1991
12018	Evans, Roy Joseph	1990
15484	Evans, Thomas J.	1996
9835	Evans, Vera Alline	1972

File	Deceased	Year
6429	Evarts, Helen Valborg	1977
5837	Evertson, Hazel S.	1975
6157	Evertson, James C.	1976
628	Everett, E. F.	1926
5122/59	Ewing, Effie	1973
6341	Ezernack, Joseph Jefferson	1977

F

File	Deceased	Year
6850	Faber, George	1979
18266	Fabro, Santana Galvan	2001
4260	Fair, Eula L.	1969
8165	Fair, John B.	1982
12050	Fairchild, A. C. (Jack)	1990
5958	Faires, Knox F.	1976
3445	Fairies, Lillian E.	1965
7769	Fallis, John C.	1981
693	Fanneieg, Ira S.	1930
17400	Fannin, Cecile M.	1999
9790	Fanning, Albert Thomas	1985
1880	Fant, Joseph D.	1955
4288	Farley, Arthur W.	1969
12134	Farmer, James Warren	1990
8193	Farr, Jennie Mae	1982
20	Farr, R. J.	1892
5471	Farr, Roy C.	1974
12080	Farrar, Fletcher Worth	1992
12718	Farrell, Wilma	1991
11352	Farren, Velam Mae	1988
8003	Farris, Arlie Mathew	1982
SE01-8	Farris, Helen Elizabeth	2001
11808	Farris, Ira Owen	1989

File	Deceased	Year
4749	Farris, Lillie Mae	1971
13802	Fatjo, Amy Elizabeth	1993
11190	Fats, George G.	1988
1190	Faulkner, Anne	1944
11930	Fausnacht, Vivian F.	1989
14134	Faust, Hugo Mirus	1993
17498	Faust, Kathryne O.	1999
6007	Faust, Louis A.	1976
16596	Faust, Mary Elizabeth	1998
17714	Faust, Robert E.	1999
4070	Fawcett, Cornelia	1968
5108	Fawcett, Fred E.	1976
4667	Fawcett, F. Scott	1971
8277	Fawcett, Gladys S.	1982
18946	Fawcett, Norma Walther	2002
13728	Fawcett, Ralph B.	1993
1545	Fawcett, Willis A.	1951
2923	Fawcett, W. C.	1961
7493	Feagen, John A.	1980
8378	Fealey, James J.	1982
14214	Feather, Effied A.	1993
8085	Feather, Lincoln A.	1982
16166	Featherston, Fae Marie	1997
1776	Featherstone, Emily	1954
8058	Feece, Elmer L.	1982
5982	Feeney, Jack F.	1976
1404	Felay, Gustave F.	1948
18492	Felderman, Lucille M.	2001
17754	Felfe, Dorothy Ross	2000
10798	Feller, Marion C.	1987
14678	Fellers, Richard	1994
3	Felsing, Edward	1862?
13938	Felton, C. Stanley	1993
4462	Feltner, Oscar G. Sr.	1870
4938	Feltro, Martha Marie	1972

File	Deceased	Year
1877	Feltro, Verner	1955
16022	Felts, Beulah	1997
6437	Felts, Emmett	1977
1597	Fenlon, Hattie	1951
2221	Fenlon, Thomas	1958
2251	Fenton, Edgar Reeves	1958
10238	Fennett, Gene H.	1986
840	Fergason, Sallie B.	1934
18218	Fergen, Loren Joseph	2001
2455	Ferguson, Benjamin D.	1959
12220	Ferguson, Bobbie Ruth	1990
19246	Ferguson, Carolyn/	
	Caroline Cook	2002
6237	Ferguson, David F.	1977
11588	Ferguson, Fred Henry	1989
11998	Ferguson, Harvey Otis	1990
8961	Ferguson, Henry N.	1984
1175	Ferguson, Katherine	1943
17882	Ferguson, Mattie Sue	
	Carroll	2000
14424	Ferguson, Monta Byars	1994
856	Ferguson, Saur	
	(?Sam) B.	1933
9758	Ferguson, William A.	1985
16558	Ferrell, Charlie G.	1998
15728	Ferrell, Tom Ford	1996
19106	Ferrell, Vera Nell	2002
12296	Ferrin, Helen Boehm	1990
18352	Ferrin, Henry N.	2001
13110	Ferris, Edith M.	1992
13498	Ferris, Eversley S.	1992
13896	Ferris, Martha B.	1993
16734	Ferriss, Erika Anna	1998
1535	Fessenden, L. R.	1951
6844	Fertsch, Hilmer A.	1978

File	Deceased	Year
12100	Fetkovich, Connie Marie	1990
18486	Feuge, Lorenz W.	2001
972	Fiedler, Edward	1937
1588	Field, Barbara Banta	1996
6891	Fielding, John	1979
17446	Fields, Annetta F.	1999
6064	Fields, Jack S.	1976
12214	Fields, John Blecher	1990
15600	Fife, Rowland Williams	1996
13212	Fifer, Clifton	1992
12534	Fifer, Hilda Louise	1991
12938	Fifer, Melvin	1991
SE95-4	Fifield, James Cecil	1995
14310	Fikes, Robert B.	1994
5635	Finch, Gary L.	1974
12668	Finch, Geri Lynn	1991
13270	Finch, Lillian Elizabeth	1992
6463	Finck, Edmond H.	1977
3432	Findlater, Frank	1965
4542	Findley, Laura Armstrong	1970
2336	Fine, Minnie Mosley	1959
10724	Fink, Loyd Kenneth	1987
9716	Finley, Margaret C.	1985
11158	First, Carol Gowan	1988
1684	Fisch, J. A.	1953
3024	Fisch, Katherine	1963
10756	Fischer, Erwin W.	1987
17192	Fischer, Hazel D. aka Hazel Dufault Fischer	1999
14722	Fischer, Lulu Alberta	1994
11784	Fischer, Oscar F.	1989
15212	Fischer, Richard Elwood	1995

File	Deceased	Year
13800	Fisher, Claude Derk	1993
16852	Fisher, Edna	1998
18130	Fisher, Felix F.	2000
5862	Fisher, Frank	1975
17218	Fisher, James Vernon Sr.	1999
8293	Fisher, John O.	1982
6953	Fisher, Katie Merck	1979
2515	Fisher, Leslie J.	1960
11174	Fisher, Mary Dollie	1988
4703	Fisher, Mary Ellen Carson	1971
13410	Fisher, Robert Wiley Jr.	1992
4857	Fisk, Alma L.	1972
15482	Fitzgerald, H. E. Sr.	1996
14940	Fitzgerald, John L.	1995
12446	Fitzgerald, Malcom Orville	1990
9042	Fitzgerald, Marjorie Young	1984
14980	Fitzgerald, Tambea G.	1995
14868	Fitzgerald, Wilma M.	1995
4160	Fitzharris, Cyril B. Sr.	1969
12054	Fitzpatrick, Edwin R.	1990
1412	Fixer, Addie Ragland	1949
3737	Flach, Christopher E.	1967
13570	Flach, Clarence G.	1992
5520	Flach, Elizabeth	1974
552	Flach, Frank	1923
11372	Flach, Laura	1988
3703	Flach, Max A.	1967
5455	Flach, Paul	1974
6070	Flach, Richard D.	1976
SE12046	Flachbart, Honor (Nora) Donohoe	1990
7266	Flagg, Francis F.	1980

File	Deceased	Year
6037	Flagg, H. M.	1976
13326	Fleet, George Hector	1992
6610	Fleissner, Louis Frank	1978
16184	Fleming, Donald C.	1997
10176	Fleming, Dorris D.	1986
18394	Fleming, Velma W.	2001
15772	Flenniken, William M.	1996
9470	Flessler, Arnold J.	1985
7434	Flessler, Lillian B.	1980
4413	Fletcher, Bertram H.	1970
4103	Fletcher, Mary E.	1969
12002	Flewharty, Margaret H. aka Margaret Hicks Flewharty	1990
12004	Flewharty, James R. aka J. R. & J. Ralph Flewharty	1990
7217	Florence, Cecilia	1980
16730	Florence, Mary Jane	1998
15376	Flores, Ann G.	1996
17014	Florez, Maria D.	1998
16730	Flowers, Virginia Daveland Mosty	1998
374	Floyd, G. W.	1912
762	Floyd, James W.	1932
1115	Floyd, Mrs. M. E.	1942
14172	Floyd, Vesta	1993
2475	Flynn, Charles B.	1960
5744	Flynn, Edward	1975
5234	Flynn, Freddie Mae	1973
14304	Flynn, Maude H.	1994
6721	Foley, James M.	1978
5790	Foley, Josephine M.	1975
9426	Folks, Thomas Lee	1985
18930	Follmar, Isabel M.	2002

File	Deceased	Year
16656	Follmar, Robert Garth Sr.	1998
12900	Fondren, Paul Turnerky	1991
11472	Fontaine, Eda Mae Eggleston	1989
16660	Fontaine, John Brooks Jr.	1998
5450	Fontaine, Louine T.	1974
7803	Fontaine, Sally L.	1981
8354	Foote, Cloe	1982
17274	Forbes, Charles A. Jr.	1999
5977	Forbest, William H.	1976
13924	Forbus, James Douglass	1993
11484	Forbus, Ruth Irene	1989
18624	Ford, Annie D.	2001
16736	Ford, Barbara Blakeney	1998
11352	Ford, Charles L. Sr.	1988
8469	Ford, Lockie Mae	1983
9130	Ford, Russell E.	1984
8358	Fordtran, George L.	1982
18352	Foreman, Kenneth A.	2001
15082	Forest, Dorothy M.	1995
4800	Forister, John Eberle	1972
5288	Forman, Attie L.	1973
3386	Forman, E. M.	1965
5229	Forque, E. G.	1973
5376	Forque, Lorriane	1973
5483	Forrest, Ada Williams	1974
8570	Forrest, E. J.	1983
6234	Forrester, Drew	1977
SE12	Forrester, Mary Ruth	----
12926	Forrester, Ray	1991
8466	Forsgren, Rosalie Z.	1983
2369	Fortenberry, Pattye	1959

File	Deceased	Year
4638	Fortenberry, Suma B.	1971
2556	Fortenberry, Tom Levi	1960
5793	Fortin, Melodia F.	1975
13002	Foskett, Gertrude M.	1991
13474	Fossler, Bonnie Lea	1992
18828	Fossler, Douglas Earl	2002
1277	Foster, Charles C.	1946
4155	Foster, Clyde E.	1969
13680	Foster, Eldon R.	1983
17266	Foster, Helen Lucille	1999
5895	Foster, Jessie B.	1975
11496	Foster, Reginald	1989
4329	Fouquette, Martin John Jr.	1970
11844	Fourmy, Ted N.	1989
3670	Fouty, Frances	1961
7195	Fouty, Grant	1980
5819	Fouty, Nellie Brennan Ault	1975
15680	Fowler, Barbara Kay	1996
17326	Fowler, Doris	1999
15518	Fowler, Eva G.	1996
1702	Fowler, J. L.	1953
16044	Fowler, Leora	1997
2178	Fowler, Mattie E.	1957
16984	Fowler, Thomas William	1998
64	Fowley, John	----
7867	Fox, Alice C.	1981
15474	Fox, Dorothy Bergwell	1996
3916	Fox, Harvey C.	1968
13056	Fox, John Van Liew	1991
8627	Fox, Marion Elwood	1983
10258	Fragua, Joseph Servano	1986
10724	Fragua, Ruth Moore	1987
1204	Francis, Tappan E.	----

File	Deceased	Year
5150	Frank, Charles Jr.	1972
7918	Frank, Ruth Agnes	1981
18430	Frank, Otto F.	2001
17426	Frank, William F.	1999
885	Franke, Ruth H.	1936
4273	Franke, William J.	1969
10638	Franklin, Robert J.	1987
5376	Franks, Margaret P.	1974
16608	Franks, Mona S.	1998
5514	Franzen, Henry A.	1974
6709	Fraser, Adeline Culbertson	1978
16938	Frasier, Lee Carrol Jr.	1998
3570	Fraunecker, Emil	1966
681	Frayne, Thomas	1929
7112	Frazer, E. D.	1979
18236	Frazier, Bill S. aka Billy Seburn	2001
13204	Frazier, Frances Maha	1992
17186	Frazier, Russell E.	2000
SE1	Fredspiel, John J.	1956
17916	Freeman, Edgar B.	2000
17036	Freeman, Helen Marie	1999
15078	Freeman, William Y. Jr.	1995
9654	Freeno, Donniece Cubelle	1985
2508	French, Minnie	1960
1235	Friedman, Mary S.	1945
990	Friedmann, S.	1938
19216	Friedman, S. Thomas	2002
18876	Frisk, Leslie Lincoln	2002
19004	Fritter, Harvey E.	2002
19074	Fritter, Mary M.	2002
2162	Fritz, Blanche	1957
2538	Fritz, William E.	1960

File	Deceased	Year
8534	Frizzell, Ray	1984
106	Froener, Walter L.	1985
SE11386	Fronczak, Daniel Richard	1988
11504	Frost, Helen E.	1989
9570	Frost, T. C.	1985
3837	Fuesler, J. P.	1967
14576	Fuglaar, Velma	1994
10378	Fulbright, Rosa Mae	1986
4955	Fulbright, V. D.	1972
12744	Fulenwider, Gladys	1991
5946	Fulkerson, Charles Clifton	1976
11244	Fullenwider, Edith Marie	1988
6490	Fullenwider, Fred J.	1978
SE43	Fullenwider, William Glen	----
19346	Fuller, John Arthur	2002
13910	Fuller, Julia	1993
15158	Fuller, Mabel Bates	1995
323	Fullerton, C. T.	1912
17696	Fullwood, Buna K.	2000
3479	Fullwood, Jennie E.	1966
12038	Fullwood, Walter S	1990
SE34	Fulton, Blanche E.	----
SE13938	Fulton, C. Stanley	1993
3128	Fultz, Willie S.	1963
2062	Fur, W. H.	1957
11792	Furr, Calvin	1989
14776	Furman, Elizabeth Eastland	1994
4445	Furman, John R.	1970
9406	Furman, John Richard Jr.	1985
15628	Furman, Thomas B.	1996

File	Deceased	Year
13132	Furman, W. A.	1992
16942	Fusilier, Robert J.	1998

G

9814	Gabriel, Robbie H.	1985
16340	Gabriel, Robert M.	1997
9468	Gacke, George A.	1985
2390	Gaddy, Mary	1959
3962	Gaddy, Maurice R.	1968
4377	Gafford, Charles W.	1970
17610	Gafford, Marvin William	1999
12658	Gagnard, Frank	1991
12656	Gagnard, Leona Jo	1991
1416	Gaines, C. I.	1949
18592	Gaines, Flora Dietert	2001
2173	Galbraith, Edward	1957
599	Galbraith, Emma	1926
2193	Galbraith, Florence	1958
3903	Gallagher, Cora C.	1968
19100	Gallagher, William J.	2002
1430	Gallat, E.	1949
2307	Gallatin, Dr. H. H.	1958
2814	Gallatin, Stella Mae	1962
16274	Galley, John E.	1997
2702	Gallihan, Floss	1961
4006	Gallihar, Thomas Edward	1968
8564	Galloway, Hazel Blanche	1983
678	Galloway, James H.	1929
12176	Gambrell, William Mooney Jr.	1990
837	Game, Fred	1934
16236	Gamel, Bill L.	1997
1485	Gammon, J. F. S.	1950

File	Deceased	Year
5341	Gandy, Elmo	----
7007	Gandy, Lannie Elvin	1976
16344	Ganoung, Donald Wayne	1997
11076	Garcia, Benjamin	1988
18772	Garcia, Candelario	2001
16036	Garcia, Fred C.	1997
11556	Garcia, Genaro	1989
9424	Garcia, Isaias Hernandez	1985
9097	Garcia, Marjory Lee Hoffa	1 984
17436	Garcia, Mary Valero aka Maria Garcia	1999
480	Garcia, Modesto	----
485	Garcia, Modesto	----
527	Garcia, Modesto	----
7171	Garcia, Paulina	1979
SE24	Garcis, Ricardo	----
SE98-3	Gardner, Alford Ray	1998
16862	Gardner, Alford Ray	1998
14626	Gardner, Jimmie S.	1994
8997	Gardner, Joe R.	1984
12478	Gardner, John L.	1990
1240	Gardner, Leland Everett	1945
15838	Gardner, Lynn C.	1996
8784	Gardner, Maurice L.	1983
15336	Gardner, Olive Mc Cauley	1995
11862	Gardner, Sam Wood	1989
10506	Gardner, Thelma L. Masters	1987
18334	Garlock, Patrick A.	2001
6756	Garner, Damon Alford	1978
9824	Garner, James Kern	1985
13166	Garner, Marie	1992

File	Deceased	Year
18498	Garrett, Adam James	2001
2788	Garrett, Bill	1962
17388	Garrett, Beulah W. aka Beulah Waldrip Garrett	1999
14548	Garrett, Carl E. aka Carl Garrett & Carl Eugene Garrett	1994
11982	Garrett, Edna M.	1990
6755	Garrett, Ethel	1979
1787	Garrett, George H.	1954
5721	Garrett, Harriet Scott	1975
1229	Garrett, James T.	1945
6688	Garrett, Jessmyr F.	1978
7646	Garrett, Julian Oliver	1981
7933	Garrett, L. D.	1981
1644	Garrett, Laura B.	1952
12888	Garrett, Letha M.	1991
7820	Garrett, Mary J.	1981
5814	Garrett, Othello F.	1975
16710	Garrett, Victor Earl	1998
853	Garrett, W. G.	1935
3401	Garrett, W. G. Jr.	1965
9688	Garrison, Eugene Pete	1985
14770	Garrison, Roberta Dee	1994
11332	Garson, John	1988
12874	Garven, Francois Ginette	1991
18050	Garven, Talbot Bell	2000
CV000222	Garven, Talbot Bell	2000
12528	Garver, Gerald Hughes	1991
14698	Garvin, Clarence I.	1994
CV590137	Garvin, Clarence I.	1995
11796	Garvin, Freddie Vernon	1989
6422	Garvin, Naida T.	1977
17062	Garza, Concepcion R.	1999

File	Deceased	Year
7652a	Garza, Israel R.	1981
4518	Garza, Jesus	1972
12770	Garza, Joseph	1991
11560	Garza, Juanita P.	1989
18582	Garza, Pablo Albert Sr.	2001
SE26	Garza, Reynaldo	1978
10320	Gass, Rowland H.	1986
18744	Gaston, Leona M.	2001
14114	Gates, Bess W.	1993
13996	Gates, Olin N.	1993
7115	Gatz, Lula	1979
11144	Gaura, Louis Joseph	1988
15554	Gayer, Wallace Edwin	1996
16518	Gayler, Noel Truman	1998
246	Gedney, Harry	1906
16872	Gee, Moody Moore	1998
14418	Gee, Myrtis Lowry	1994
4525	Geib, Horace Valentine	1970
4183	Geibel, Dorothy King	1969
13104	Geiger, Anne K.	1992
13172	Geiger, Francis C.	1992
8918	Geischeichter, Charles	1984
17872	Geisen, Marguerite S.	2000
929	Geisler, Heinrich F.	1937
16082	Gentz, Virginia	1997
7515	George, Alice Jean	1980
472	George, Rosa	1920
2416	Gerder, Lucy B.	1959
6888	Gerdes, Frankie Lee	1979
2684	Gerdes, W. A.	1961
2473	Gerdes, William A.	1961
15468	Gerhart, Richard D.	1996
2365	Gerloff, Alain	1959
2759	Gerner, Dorothy	1962
893	Geron, H. R.	1934

File	Deceased	Year
15932	Gessell, Thelma Jeanne	1997
5869	Gholson, Joe Ann	1975
14962	Giano, William David	1995
2076	Gibbens, Mary L.	1957
442	Gibbons, John D.	----
SE7344	Gibbons, Lorita	----
834	Gibbs, Andrew J.	1933
17788	Gibbs, Charles M.	2000
18210	Gibbs, Helen Lee	2000
4530	Gibbs, J. Marion	1970
8895	Gibbs, Lida Jane	1984
2707	Gibson, Amanda	1961
7082	Gibson, George B.	1979
9386	Gibson, Gober	1985
3216	Gibson, John H.	1964
11196	Gibson, Lucille W.	1988
993	Giesebrecht, Carl	1938
932	Gifford, Carl	1937
3556	Gigstead, William N.	1966
13108	Gilbert, Dove Early	1992
13076	Gilbert, Philip Osborne	1992
2920	Gilbert, P. S.	1963
8329	Gilbreath, Gertrude M.	1982
11114	Gilbreth, Zula Mae	1988
6627	Gilgenbach, Earl S.	1978
9692	Gill, John R.	1985
1855	Gill, Loren B.	1954
7169	Gillen, Mirian Blanche	1979
7169	Gillentine, Margaret	1979
2317	Gillentine, Sam	1958
3922	Gilliam, B. L.	1968
12694	Gilliland, Daisy W.	1991
15060	Gilliland, Francis S.	1995
3709	Gillis, C. E.	1967
5717	Gillis, Martha A.	1975

File	Deceased	Year
84	Gilmer, A. M.	1899
12618	Gilmore, Fretwell	1991
5792	Gilmore, Lesa	1975
4471	Gilmore, S. D.	1970?
6390	Gilmore, Stephen F.	1977
12304	Gilson, William F.	1990
889	Giltner, Paul H.	1936
11180	Gimmeson, Dwight Paul	1988
6387	Gingrich, Earl L.	1977
4931	Gingrich, Hazel I.	1972
4795	Ginter, Bertha	1971/72
3728	Gipson, Harold Edward	1967
8368	Gipson, Yvonne Mavis	1982
17396	Girard, Eloise I.	1999
11222	Girard, Leonard Francis	1988
5318	Girard, Shirley M.	1973
18830	Gits, Telespore F.	2002
16302	Gitz, Lila M.	1997
10486	Given, Herschel R.	1987
11160	Givens, Grace C.	1988
15980	Givens, John L.	1997
10232	Givonetti, Paul D.	1986
14318	Glamann, Henry Wm. Jr.	1994
14018	Glanton, Eunice Mae	1993
13408	Glanton, Hermon Printis	1992
4723	Glantzberg, Claire Jackson	1971
4416	Glantzberg, Frederich	1970
15312	Glascock, Joan Pfeiffer	1995
19086	Glaser, Victor Joseph	2002
380	Glause, Fritz	1915
SE50	Glenn, Joseph J.	1979
6301	Glenn, Samuel	1975/77
9	Glenn, W. J.	1870
2724	Gloeshiner, Alma	1961

File	Deceased	Year
7261	Goddard, Joseph M.	1980
12942	Godwin, Francis W.	1991
6683	Goembel, Roy	1978
14412	Goetzel, Laverne Charles	1994
8644	Goff, Eva E.	1983
5626	Goff, Lester D.	1974
834	Goff, R. B.	1934
6441	Gohmert, Pearce D. V.	1977
6002	Gohmert, Roland L. Jr.	1976
1842	Gold, Emil	1954
484	Gold, Leroy	----
2453	Gold, Rose E.	1959
6518	Gold, Will F.	1977/78
15206	Golden, Hazel Marie	1995
17000	Goldman, Irene Broughton	1998
14354	Goldman, Marian	1994
9802	Goldman, Theodore	1985
10542	Gollehon, Charles W.	1987
15526	Gollehon, Mary B.	1996
7041	Gonzales, Antonio	1979
9444	Gonzales, Emilio	1987
10843	Gonzales, Magdaleno	1987
13818	Gonzales, Manuela Deluma	1993
18460	Gonzalez, Emilio D.	2001
17928	Gonzalez, Mario Jesus	2000
11038	Good, Frances Elizabeth	1988
17478	Good, Hildreth Lorraine	1999
12802	Goodall, Felton Ray	1991
2999	Goode, Crawford J.	1963
SE00-3	Goodloe, Sergio Deshawn	2000
12816	Goodman, Malcolm Julius	1991
11832	Goodman, Virginia Jo	1989

File	Deceased	Year
14954	Goodrich, Orville G.	1995
7907	Goodson, Wanda	1981
3319	Goodwin, Jules Payne	1965
SE103	Goodwin, Mona Margaret Elizabeth	1985
14780	Goodwyn, James T.	1994
17056	Gordon, Dale L.	1999
7628	Gordon, Walter Camp	1981
18264	Gordon, Jessie B.	2001
669	Gore, Frank H.	1929
672	Gore, Frank	1929
10808	Gorelick, John	1987
SE38	Gorman, Nell Pationer Carver	----
2697	Gorrell, Vera H.	1961
4661	Gorrell, William Edgar	1971
19080	Goss, Bessie Estell	2002
275	Goss, J. Lee	1908
7525	Goss, J. O.	1980
11434	Goss, James B.	1989
517	Goss, John	----
1856	Goss, O. W.	1954
SE45	Goss, Thelma	1980
5593	Gosselink, Urban Gerald	1974
6998	Gosser, Franklin T.	1977
6240	Gotcher, C. W.	1977
CV980054	Gotcher, Jeanette Bennett aka Jeanette G. Hall	1998
5706	Gotcher, Twila	1974
2915	Gotthard, Alvin T.	1963
4948	Gotthard, Mabel	1972
17598	Gough, Rudy Harold	1999
9816	Gould, Nancy	1985
5888	Gould, Nina S.	1975

File	Deceased	Year
11896	Courley, Mary Ellen	1989
6164	Gourley, Rozell	1976
1646	Gowan, May	1941
7192	Gower, E. Irene	1980
7726	Grace, Bonita	1981
4174	Gracey, May Verble	1969
12582	Graham, Agatha	1991
8824	Graham, Albert Hezekiah	1984
18652	Graham, Arnold F.	2001
14334	Graham, Blanche	1994
13812	Graham, Carl Raymond	1993
10024	Graham, Catherine A.	1986
2841	Graham, E. A.	1962
5975	Graham, Frank W.	1976
14650	Grahma, Gary Ray	1994
2069	Graham, Howard H.	1957
11020	Graham, Italia N.	1988
5598	Graham, J. L.	1974
14790	Graham, Lee Roy	1994
17004	Graham, Margaret Prince	1998
17790	Graham, Maurice Dale	2000
12170	Graham, Millie Venita	1990
13026	Graham, Pearl Baker	1991
16468	Graham, Robert Reid	1998
12654	Graham, Robert Ripley	1991
8785	Graham, Theodore S.	1983
14238	Graham, V. J.	1994
9352	Graham, Vlara	1985
6105	Grammier, Joseph E. Sr.	1976
489	Grant, Alfred	----
6060	Grant, Ella Mae	1976
387	Grant, Fred	----
5004	Grant, Oliver	1972
7348	Grant, Stuart A.	1980
283	Granville, Richard	----

File	Deceased	Year
1876	Grasty, J. Milton	1955
19082	Grasty, Margaret Eunice	2002
6270	Graves, Marie A.	----
19300	Grawburg, Raymond A.	2002
7351	Gray, Claude H.	1980
13790	Gray, Darrel Dean	1993
5509	Gray, Edna D.	1974
8831	Gray, Eli L.	1984
8496	Gray, Herbert S.	1983
11336	Gray, Hugh Jefferson	1988
19226	Gray, James A.	2002
5317	Gray, Joe Hannah	1973
13448	Gray, Joseph A.	1992
SE13088	Gray, Katherine C.	1992
8047	Gray, Lloyd L.	1982
SE13090	Gray, Mattie E.	1992
SE11876	Gray, Sarah Sam	1989
17726	Gray, Thomas G. Jr.	2000
SE71	Green, Addie B.	1982
11788	Green, Alexa Marie	1989
4117	Green, Claude	1969
8869	Green, Donald Robert	1984
882	Green, Edward H.	1936
7695	Green, Forrest A.	1981
16472	Green, Freda Reichardt	1998
2240	Green, John	1958
5447	Green, Johnie James	1974
14644	Green, Lila Dee	1994
13564	Green, Loel Owen	1992
1800	Green, Mara C.	1954
11296	Green, Ray Charles	1988
10446	Green, Rebecca	1987
12088	Green, Ruth Brown	1990
13346	Green, Vivian Rhoads	1992
17708	Greene, Bernice M.	2000

File	Deceased	Year
5319	Greene, Edythe Bennett	1973
2825	Greene, Elmer Andrew	1962
13972	Greene, Theodore S.	1993
6397	Greenwald, Frank	1977
6133	Greer, James A.	1976
17964	Greeson, Effie A.	2000
19034	Gregg, Ralph B.	2002
9226	Gregory, Aleatha Elizabeth	1984
16975	Gregory, Ella B.	1998
14120	Gregory, Ervin A.	1993
7224	Gregory, Halfrie	1979/80
10924	Gregory, Leona M.	1987
5899	Gregory, Leonard A.	1976
720	Gregory, W. V.	1931
6233	Gresham, Bert R.	1976
16138	Gresovitch, Dess D.	1997
15598	Grief, Edith Lovejoy	1996
6492	Grier, Frank Oliver	1977
8377	Grier, Jefferson B.	1982
12792	Grier, Verla M.	1991
6169	Griesbach, Josephine	1976
SE90	Griesenbeck, Bertha F.	1983
6000	Griffin, B. E.	1976
14196	Griffin, C. J.	1993
4588	Griffin, Carroll Riggs	1971
16526	Griffin, Elaine B.	1998
8016	Griffin, Emmanuel L.	1982
SE96-3	Griffin, James L.	1996
14122	Griffin, Harvey C.	1993
18470	Griffin, Henry	2001
17770	Griffin, Iva Louise Creech	2000
13932	Griffin, Jean B.	1993
4446	Griffin, Spencer Lloyd	1970

File	Deceased	Year
3778	Griffith, Claud P.	1967
1772	Griffith, Emma G.	1954
6965	Griffith, Melvin S. Jr.	1979
3524	Griffith, W. V. Jr.	1966
17282	Griggs, Edna Saenger	1999
7540	Griggs, Guy G.	1981
5600	Grigsby, Willis	1974
9962	Grimes, Billie E.	1986
2211	Grimes, Helen P.	1958
9866	Grimm, Henry C.	1986
10810	Grimm, Laurence F.	1987
899	Grinder, Mitchel	----
12594	Grinrod, Harry Charles	1991
18384	Grinrod, Sylvia E.	2001
1367	Grinstead, Jessie E.	1948
5467	Grinstead, Pam D.	1974
3847	Grisson, Anna H.	1967
16314	Grochoske, Shirley I.	1997
16230	Groh, Earl C.	1997
8714	Grona, Fritz Max	1983
7282	Grona, Lydia K.	1980
1666	Grona, Will	1952
12498	Grosenbacher, Lucille Selma	1990
18700	Gross, Katherine L.	2001
9486	Grosser, Everett Ernest	1985
10356	Grothous, Edward B.	1986
9139	Grove, Dorris Mc Intosh	1984
9097	Grove, Henry David	1984
17676	Gorve, Willaim Barry	2000
17152	Guardiola, Mary	1999
5052	Guenther, Dora	1973
16432	Guenther Howard W.	1997
5093	Guerrero, Jovita V.	1973
14330	Guest, Hulda Mosel	1994

File	Deceased	Year
5259	Guidry, Curtis J.	1973
767	Guidry, Luke F.	1932
6488	Guidry, Melanie R.	1977
12970	Guiheneuf, Louis J.	1991
15828	Guilden, Ethel R.	1996
4107	Guill, A. C.	1969
6734	Guill, Millie M.	1978
4444	Guill, Russell E.	1970
13040	Guilzon, Edward Jerry	1991
9882	Guin, Maude Lankfeld	1986
16910	Guin, Walter Carl	1998
4701	Guinn, Portia Ethel	1971
15710	Guldmann, Hans	1996
3396	Gumbert, H. H.	1965
14866	Gunn, Joe M.	1995
18626	Gunning, John J.	2001
4037	Gunter, Billie Sunday	1969
7139	Gunter, Hattie B.	1979
8807	Gunter, Thomas Lee	1984
11854	Gust, David	1989
13022	Gustafson, La Vaughn	1991
12864	Gustafson, Victor E.	1991
11416	Gutherie, Billy Joe Sr.	1988
5002	Gutherie, L. M.	1972
9882	Guthrey, Gordon M.	1986
1056	Guthrie, Clarence	1941
SE96	Gutierrez, Gregoria Lopes	1982
16114	Gutierrez, Noe Flores	1997
SE26	Gwyn, H. S. Jr.	1978
2870	Gydeson, Marietta	1962
2886	Gydeson, Marietta	1962

File	Deceased	Year
	H	
7990	Haag, Mary Louise	1981
8578	Haan, Robert E.	1983
3710	Haarman, Donald W.	1967
6253	Habecker, Edward B.	1977
4506	Habermon, A. C.	1971
2077	Habesher, Edward	1957
4763	Hackley, Hope H. B.	1972
3626	Hackley, Oscar	1966
7407	Hackworth, Rubelle	1980
4651	Hackworth, Victor W.	1971
4085	Hagens, Nick	1969
1417	Hagood, Penney A.	1949
16364	Hahn, Sarah S.	1997
10210	Hahn, W. E.	1986
11776	Hail, Marvin P.	1989
11454	Haines, Andrew Joseph	1989
11576	Haines, Lester H.	1989
8848	Haines, Louise Peace	1984
19130	Hainey, Shirlie V.	2002
15116	Hainey, William V.	1995
15182	Hairrold, Birdie E.	1995
11310	Hainlen, Gwendolyn	1988
8440	Halbardier, Eugene Albert	1983
11006	Hale, Alice Mae Thomas	1988
17378	Hale, Elizabeth Martin	1999
7931	Hale, Thomas Clifton	1981
8124	Halek, Betty Lou	1982
7487	Halek, Walter	1980
16460	Haley, Wilbur	1998
11080	Hall, Betty Burney Mosty	1988
SE86	Hall, Blanch Self	1983
5936	Hall, Carl W.	1976

103

File	Deceased	Year
3961	Hall, Chloe Warre	1968
7120	Hall, Clarence	1979
1748	Hall, D. C.	1953
15428	Hall, Edward C. Jr.	1996
17722	Hall, Flora B.	2000
8215	Hall, G. H.	1982
16788	Hall, George W.	1998
1468	Hall, H. L.	1950
19350	Hall, Hattie Lyle	2002
16860	Hall, Hazel	1998
11966	Hall, J. C.	1990
10110	Hall, James C.	1986
16366	Hall, Jimmie D.	1997
14292	Hall, Jane Mears	1994
CV980054	Hall, Jeanette Gardner aka Jeanette Bennet Gotcher	1998
3681	Hall, John C.	1967
10546	Hall, Judith L.	1987
13520	Hall, Laura B.	----
13340	Hall, Mary S.	1992
SE48	Hall, Mearl William	1981
6321	Hall, T. C.	1977
9484	Hall, Thoedore	1985
10914	Hall, William George	1987
500	Hall, Winnifred	1922
2984	Hallenbeck, Henry W.	1963
17602	Halliburton, Dolores Kaemmerer	1999
11344	Halliburton, John H.	1988
17460	Hallmark, Joan Auld	1999
4320	Halloway, Floyd S.	----
13292	Halpin, Roy Fred	1992
1114812	Halstead, Elizabeth V.	1995
6512	Halstead, Harold S.	1977

File	Deceased	Year
2626	Hamill, Eva	1961
15006	Hamilton, Daniel Lee	1995
10662	Hamilton, Darrell Glenn	1987
18179	Hamilton, Grace	2000
7554	Hamilton, Jerrell G.	1980
4885	Hamilton, Jessie	1972
113	Hamilton, L.	----
1896	Hamilton, Mauline	1955
15066	Hamilton, Stella O.	1995
14900	Hamilton, Warren L.	1995
5138	Hammac, Althela	1973
18650	Hammack, Eloise	2001
7449	Hammack, Leon	1980
4068	Hammar, Earl	1968
4036	Hammar, Earl	1969
2554	Hammit, A. L.	1960
10004	Hamlitt, Elnora Pauline aka Elnora Pauline Herron	1986
13656	Hamlyn, Robert E.	1992
16248	Hamman, Lillian E.	1997
7594	Hammond, Alvin M.	1981
19238	Hammond, Billy George	2002
766	Hammond, Elizabeth C.	1931
8250	Hammond, John S.	1982
7721	Hammond, Leslie S.	1981
6597	Hammond, Mildred B.	1978
261	Hammond, S. O.	----
8402	Hammond, Thomas Morgan	1982
8251	Hammond, Ventura S.	1982
8890	Hammonds, Sadie L.	1984
1847	Hampson, Jack	1954
14838	Hampton, Binnie	1995
139	Hampton, Joel	----
4786	Hamquist, Dolores H.	1972

File	Deceased	Year
13194	Hamrick, Hoyt Harold	1992
14510	Hamrick, Laverne G.	1994
18752	Hanauer, Donald	2001
16658	Hanauer, Walter	1998
5995	Hanchey, Gordon B.	1974/76
17650	Hanchey, Ray B.	2000
17502	Hanchey, Rebecca Stuart	1999
12620	Hancock, Herbert	1991
4606	Hancock, Jesse I.	1971
4999	Hancock, Julia N.	1973
11328	Hancock, Marie Hazel	1990
8792	Hander, William W.	1983
1435	Hankamer, Harold M.	1949
9504	Hankinson, Kathryn Jane	1985
14100	Hankinson, Mary E. S.	1993
19208	Hankinson, Maurice Whitlow	2002
5910	Hanks, Otis J.	1975
7420	Hanks, Tom H.	1980
SE60	Hanna, Alice Brannen/ Brannon	1981
2250	Hanna, Frances Lucille	1958
2070	Hanna, J. D.	1957
16270	Hanna, Mary E.	1997
11312	Hanna, Parker P.	1988
1863	Hanse, Hazel Stone	1954
3755	Hansen, Lydia B.	1967
10018	Hanson, Alice Tatum	1986
4730	Hanson, Clifford H.	----
11008	Hanson, Kenneth Lewis	1988
1959	Happel, James H.	1955
18976	Harbison, Robert R.	2002
9147	Harbour, B. E.	1984
3589	Harbour, H. A.	1966
5192	Harbour, Marguerite	1973

File	Deceased	Year
19256	Harbour, Wilma C.	2002
12322	Hard, Beryl Janet	1990
17716	Hardaway, Audrey Evelyn	2000
15760	Hardee, Lottie Mae	1996
6238	Hardemon, Henry	1977
16930	Hardin, Betty Thomas	1998
1297	Hardin, H. D.	1946
2354	Hardin, Myrel	1959
1662	Hardin, Rosa	1952
13868	Harding, David M.	1993
10846	Harding, Harry J.	1987
9400	Harding, Helen H.	1985
17884	Hardison, Lewis M.	2000
10490	Hardison, Mabel T.	1987
18022	Hardon, Richard H.	2000
12912	Hardt, E. F.	1991
19076	Hardwick, Robert V.	2002
10702	Hardy, George C.	1987
2019	Hardy, Robert L.	1956
16086	Hardy, William Doyle	1997
16500	Hargraves, Susan A.	1998
7930	Hargreaves, Effie Anna	1981
13782	Hargreaves, William Henry	1993
15326	Hargrove, George Greer	1995
15420	Hargrove, Kathryn	1996
6489	Hargrove, L. F.	1977
2134	Harley, George Foster	1957
2401	Harlin, H. W. Sr.	1959
19314	Harling, Reginald	2002
2700	Harless, L. D.	1961
6587	Harlow, George J.	1978
6782	Harlow, Lorita M.	1978
4063	Harlow, W. D. Sr.	1968
10520	Harman, Virgil Eugene	1987

File	Deceased	Year
16332	Harmel, Donnie E.	1997
14774	Harmon, Ralph M.	1994
14724	Harmon, Roberta H.	1989
18936	Harmon, William C.	2000
10606	Harner, Martha O.	1987
3187	Haron, Joseph H.	1963
1931	Harper, Herman	1955
11648	Harper, Mary Louise	1989
7143	Harper, Willie B.	1979
3730	Harrell, Emma Florence	1967
3246	Harrell, Frank C.	1964
18910	Harrell, Myrna Elaine	2002
3092	Harrell, Ray W.	1963
1990	Harris, B. B.	1956
129	Harris, B. F.	1892
18716	Harris Dott Harlan	2002
1928	Harris, Elizabeth	1955
4298	Harris, Elva Jane	----
699	Harris, F.	----
12310	Harris, George Napier	1990
14946	Harris, Harvey W.	1995
310	Harris, J. M.	----
3444	Harris, Joe A.	1965
18716	Harris, Joe Randolph	2001
70	Harris, Johanna	----
4297	Harris, John A.	----
4308	Harris, John A.	1969
869	Harris, John M.	1935
10874	Harris, Mary	1987
15682	Harris, Morris V.	1996
3759	Harris, Myrtle Louise	1967
272	Harris, O. E.	----
16388	Harris, Phyllis E.	1997
19126	Harris, Rayford William	2002
6557	Harris, Ruth Bryant	1978

File	Deceased	Year
17384	Harris, Sidney Epps	1999
8679	Harris, Wallace E.	1983
12732	Harris, William G.	1991
16026	Harris, William Henry	1997
6144	Harris, William T.	1976
3228	Harrison, Archie L.	1964
3234	Harrison, Archie L.	1964
14292	Harison, Frank C.	1994
6015	Harrison, Gertrude F.	1976
16868	Harrison, James R.	1998
12508	Harrison, Jesse	1991
18136	Harrison, Joe M.	2000
1630	Harrison, John M.	1952
SE01-1	Harrison, Joyce	2001
1640	Harrison, Leta D.	1952
3235	Harrison, Mildred S.	1964
3229	Harrison, Mildred Saucier	1964
2348	Harrison, Minnie Nash	1959
7130	Harrison, Ruth A.	1979
9544	Harrison, Thomas G.	1985
3159	Hart, A. Glea	1963
2856	Hart, Alice Mary	1962
14886	Hart, Dawn W. aka Lanelle Dawn Whitworth	1995
1372	Hart, Eva Mae	1948
1103	Hart, James H.	1942
18698	Hart, James R. Jr.	2001
4474	Hart, Joseph N.	1971
2325	Hart, J. R.	1959
4474	Hart, Samuel Ewing	1970
3855	Hart, Thomas A.	1967
4647	Hartel, Elmer D.	1971
10800	Hartel, Paul Warren	1987
17178	Harthcock, Louie M.	1999

File	Deceased	Year
9968	Harthcock, Noma	1986
19066	Harting, Hiram W.	2002
17992	Hartmen, Dimple Marie	2000
1267	Hartong, R. C.	1945
5983	Hartung, H. W. Sr.	1976
16074	Hartwell, Virginia L. Spenrath	1997
11288	Hartzel, Naomi Pomeroy	1990
14320	Harvelle, Alma Bedreaux	1994
14322	Harvelle, Benjamin Horace	1994
18124	Harward, Don William	2000
548	Harwell, James Arthur	----
6931	Harwood, Alfred E.	1979
714	Harwood, Mrs. Clair L.	1931
6874	Harwood, Emma	1979
2977	Harwood, J. R.	1963
16724	Harwood, Mary Agnes (Nina)	1998
9344	Harwood, Wallace Baker Jr.	1985
8587	Haselden, Caswell S.	1983
11366	Haskin, John Francis	1988
10148	Hass, Edmnd J	1986
5240	Hassler, Leona	1973
2040	Hassmann, John	1956
15830	Hastings, Murray M.	1996
11720	Hastings, Murray Mc Calmont Jr.	1989
19296	Hatch, C. L.	2002
13496	Hatch, Lewis S.	1992
5806	Hatch, Mary B.	1975
12866	Hatch, Mary Hardin	1991
13476	Hatch, Lewis S.	1992
13136	Hatch, Orin Wakler	1992

110

File	Deceased	Year
15216	Hatch, Truman Lee	1995
4044	Hatch, W. N.	1968
10658	Hatfield, Elizabeth Jeanne	1987
7952	Hatfield, Theodore	1981
13632	Hatfield, Thomas Edward	1992
15524	Hattox, Dennis Newman	1996
4133	Hauck, Anna Dauch	1969
5464	Haufler, August	1974
6125	Haufler, Elsie A.	1976
14178	Haufler, Esther	1993
11168	Haufler, Alvina	1988
14908	Haufler, Louis H.	1995
18174	Haufler, Myrtha Allerkamp	2000
2018	Haufler, William	1956
6044	Hauser, Mildred	1973
14879	Hauser, William J.	1995
3910	Hausler, Edna S.	1968
1667	Havck, Frank Joseph	1952
6090	Havens, Wlater F.	1976
13886	Havas, Theodore W.	1993
17504	Hawkins, Bettie C.	1999
7152	Hawkins, Carl C.	1979
1016	Hawkins, D. G.	1939
4074	Hawkins, Henry Oscar	1969
5110	Hawkins, J. Lahatha	1973
6579	Hawkins, Hosa Roy	1978
17814	Hawthorne, Hugh Montgomery III	2000
CV000111	Hawthorne, Hugh Montgomery III	2000
17372	Hawthorne, James Polk	1999
11608	Hay, Gessner Lane	1989
SE11298	Hay, Sam R. Jr.	1988

File	Deceased	Year
12452	Haygood, Leo Presley	1990
5699	Hayes, Emealie Akers	1975
12386	Hayes, John Ward	1990
7891	Hayes, Mary Frances	1981
4755	Hayes, Robert E.	1971/2
17832	Hayes, Wilford J.	2000
2168	Haynes, A. B. Sr.	1957
12844	Haynes, Edith Shacklette	1991
14372	Haynes, Evelyn Doris	1994
16496	Haynes, Joe Zeigler	1998
16494	Haynes, Mable F.	1998
13804	Haynes, Mabel Fussell	1993
12208	Haynes, Robert M.	1990
18262	Hays, Dorothy M.	2001
1813	Hays, T. M.	1954
9113	Hazelhurst, Mary T.	1984
7519	Heap, Frances	1980
17506	Heap, George A.	1999
4255	Heard, John Jesse	1969
1195	Heard, John J. Jr.	1944
9764	Heard, Mary Kate	1985
3451	Hearne, Meta Kirsch	1966
12424	Hearne, Warren J.	1990
8685	Heartfield, Thomas Brooke	1983
6660	Heath, Garis W.	1978
8819	Heather, William Jerome	1984
19068	Heaton, Frances K.	2002
9274	Heck, Valera M.	1984
15222	Hecker, Jean V.	1995
13162	Heckel, Edmund P. Jr.	1992
5212	Heckler, Charles E.	1973
2898	Heckler, Clara	1962
13384	Heckler, Laura J.	1992

File	Deceased	Year
463	Hedeck, Preston	----
6356	Hedrick, Lawton C.	1977
6124	Hedrick, Leonard L.	1976
6274	Hedrick, Louis L.	1977
397	Hefferman, W. E.	1916
10464	Heffernan, Billy K.	1987
3232	Heide, Helen M.	1964
17030	Heiligmann, Erven	1998
1507	Heimann, Addie Belle	1950
5009	Heimann, Alma	1973
5077	Heimann, Clarence R.	1969/73
3518	Heimann, George	1966
3902	Heimann, John Jr.	1968
3784	Heimann, Lillian	1967
3516	Heimann, Theresa	1966
17162	Heimann, Verda Afton	1999
13244	Heinberger, Robert D.	1992
4895	Heine, Albert W.	1972
7976	Heine, Eunice D.	1981
1469	Heinen, Arthur	1950
5029	Heinen, August	1973
636	Heinen, H. J.	----
4715	Heinen, Ida	----
1903	Heinen, Otto	1955
429	Heinen, Pauline	----
15816	Heinen, Ruth M.	1995
8237	Heinen, Walter	1982
14592	Heiser, Cortus E.	1994
8652	Heldt, Carl Diederich	1983
3256	Helm, Gettie Baker	1964
3021	Helman, Olga M.	1963
6930	Helmer, Albert J.	1979
1420	Helmke, A. W. (Bob)	1942
6442	Hempel, James A.	1977
13074	Hemsell, D. C.	1992

File	Deceased	Year
11978	Hemsell, Marie Landrey	1990
12522	Hencerling, Aderon	
	Laverne	1991
17974	Hencerling, Betty Lou	2000
737	Henderson, Callie	1931
7922	Henderson, E. Roy	1981
946	Henderson, Irvin	1937
1941	Henderson, J. E.	1955
16440	Henderson, Joe G.	1998
701	Henderson, John F.	1930
3292	Henderson, M. D.	1965
6289	Henderson, Martha B.	1977
8478	Henderson, Robert J.	1983
16438	Henderson, Thelma Mary	1998
17864	Henderson, Welton	2000
7077	Hendricks, Anita G.	1979
17072	Hendricks, Laddie J.	1999
3118	Henke, August W.	1964
2084	Henke, Chester W.	1957
8502	Henke, Ed C.	1983
8524	Henke, Edna M.	1983
12044	Henke, Emma	1990
1508	Henke, Emma P.	1950
5910	Henke, Emmett	1976
1226	Henke, Henry	1945
1118	Henke, Louisa	1942
7687	Henke, Thelma B.	1981
6103	Henke, W. R.	1976
12902	Henley, Pearl Marie	1991
7140	Henley, Walter J.	1979
5016	Henning, F. W.	1973
11086	Henninger, Frederick W.	1988
16540	Henninger, Marie	
	Florence	1998
6815	Henry, Charles W.	1978

File	Deceased	Year
6933	Henry, Charles William Jr.	1979
1549	Henry, Emerson B.	1951
18350	Henry, Horace C. Jr.	2001
4507	Henry, Jessie Lynn	1970
18348	Henry, Viola Marie	2001
17508	Hensley, Earl Jr.	1999
16429	Henson, Helen Zoe	1997
8832	Hentze, Alan	1984
252	Heollwig, William	----
4151	Heosey, Marguerite	1969
16152	Hepburn, Bobby C.	1997
14652	Hepler, Mina G.	1994
14024	Hepler, Thaine E.	1993
495	Herbst, Katherine E.	----
920	Herbst, Louise	1937
839	Herbst, Rudolf	1934
15938	Herden, Elaine D.	1995
1504	Hermann, Mary A.	1950
16900	Hermida, Hipolito Fuente	1998
17574	Hernandez, Mary Alice	1999
16658	Hernandez, Raul	1998
9063	Herndon, Agnes P.	1984
7731	Herndon, John R.	1981
16476	Herntz, Harold W.	1998
10004	Herron, Elnora Pauline aka Elnora Pauline Hamlett	1986
14674	Hertel, Elmer N.	1994
8112	Herzik, Lou Dahlin	1982
3142	Herzog, Floydina Kuhlman	1964
842	Herzog, Nathan	1934
16110	Herzog, Oswald Aaron	1997

File	Deceased	Year
8243	Hess, John Wilson	1982
14255	Hesskew, D. Donald	1994
SE84	Hesskew, Leonard J.	1983
17584	Heston, Walter R.	1999
10444	Hetrick, Dorothy Lee	1987
14054	Hetrick, Lyal W.	1993
15120	Hetrick, Paul R.	1995
6578	Heusinger, Iva Lee	1978
8126	Hewitt, Jesse P.	1982
10482	Hewitt, Mabel E.	1987
15890	Hey, Wilson Smith Jr.	1996
18338	Heye, Evva I.	2001
8461	Hiatt, Opal Baum	1983
6826	Hiatt, Robert Franklin	1978
16018	Hibler, Calvin Douglas	1997
5278	Hickey, Catherine H.	1973
3583	Hickey, James J.	1966
19020	Hickey, Mary Jane	2002
18704	Hickman, Annie Muriel	2001
6018	Hickman, Mildred Harrison	1976
9092	Hicks, Frank Marion	1984
5391	Hicks, James C.	1974
1488	Hicks, J. D.	1950
6987	Hicks, Virginia Theresa	1979
7013	Higbee, Adline B.	1979
5235	Higbee, Fred E.	1973
19284	Highbarger, Countess S.	2002
6184	Highsmith, Effa L.	1976
13152	Highsmith, Meldene	1992
1049	Hight, Joe D.	1940
8902	Hightower, erskine W.	1984
656	Hightower, James I.	1927
663	Hightower, James I.	1927
18414	Hilburn, Alice Kott	2001

File	Deceased	Year
11668	Hilburn, Ida Belle Stelzer	1989
1392	Hill, Armentia M.	1948
16888	Hill, Carolyn Hammersmith	1998
19230	Hill, Clifton P.	2002
13514	Hill, Deressa Ruth	1992
2256	Hill, Ella Thraves	1958
18706	Hill, Elmer Jr.	2000
8431	Hill, Frank Y.	1983
284	Hill, Flora E.	----
978	Hill, Grady L.	1938
14836	Hill, Homer Sidney	1995
6459	Hill, John Wade	1977
10466	Hill, Judith C.	1987
17984	Hill, Lenora Palmer	2000
11138	Hill, Maurice F.	1988
17890	Hill, Mildred Harrison	2000
11308	Hill, Nancy F.	1988
13948	Hill, Odette S.	1993
2223	Hill, P. B.	1958
4901	Hill, Pearcy O.	1972
2964	Hill, Pearl	1963
10834	Hill, Robert Judson	1987
14800	Hill, Sam B.	1995
7453	Hill, Sam C.	1980
SE10494	Hill, Stanley Ray	1987
4928	Hill, Tannie K.	1972
14936	Hill, Winston G.	1995
3279	Hilburn, H. H. Sr.	1965
18898	Hillin, Jean	2002
2035	Hillman, Laura E.	1956
14344	Hilton, Burrel Elgin	1994
6056	Hilton, D. A.	1976
11010	Hilton, Myrtle B.	1988

File	Deceased	Year
5155	Hilty, Robert D.	1973
5183	Hilty, Tommie M. T.	1973
3027	Hine, Frederick R.	1963
1015	Hines, Julie E.	1939
3949	Hines, Norman G.	1968
6825	Hinrichs, Edward J.	1979
6135	Hinrichs, Helen S.	1976
7430	Hinrichs, Jack F.	1980
3665	Hinsch, Friedrich Rudolf	1966
4814	Hinsey, Charles Bryant	1972
17236	Hinte, John O.	1999
664	Hintze, Louis	----
3881	Hirth, Raymond G.	1968
7741	Hislar, Everett L.	1981
11018	Hitch, Daniel Robert	1988
16740	Hitch, Helen Churchward	1998
15996	Hitch, Robert Lee	1997
1227	Hitzfeld, Lelia	1945
3133	Hixon, B. M.	1963
5005	Hixon, Julia N.	1973
260	Hixon, Louise A.	1907
8480	Hneidy, Ernest R. Sr.	1983
8481	Hneidy, Ernest R. Jr.	1983
17768	Hoard, Beverly J.	2000
3390	Hobbs, Leland	1965
11640	Hoblet, Betty Rose	1989
16672	Hobson, Leo	1998
19084	Hobson, Mamie C.	2002
13522	Hodge, Austin Franklin	1992
14562	Hodges, E. Joleen L.	1994
SE22	Hodges, Ernst B.	1977
13686	Hodges, Frank R.	1993
10272	Hodges, John Hendrick	1986
16158	Hodges, Noble H.	1997

File	Deceased	Year
17780	Hodges, Ralph L.	2000
15548	Hodges, Robert M.	1996
14402	Hofer, Clair Wellington	1994
1716	Hoffman, Mayme	1953
17678	Hoffmann, Thomas I.	2000
12570	Hoffmeyer, Catherine Portwood	1991
5898	Hoffpauer, Lula Mae	1976
10990	Hoffpauir, Guarry Ford	1988
6128	Hogan, Charles C.	1976
14046	Hogan, John R.	1993
9918	Hogan, Richard C.	1986
15512	Hogan, Ruth Elizabeth	1996
12356	Hohenberger, Cleo Childs	1990
17616	Hohenberger, Leonard W.	1999
10560	Hohlefelder, Robert Anthony	1987
4590	Hoidale, Del S. (?Hordale)	1971
15732	Hoke, Cecil Thomas	1996
15870	Hoke, Pauline K.	1996
8186	Holbrook, Clara Freeborn	1982
9390	Holbrook, L. R.	1985
16920	Holbrook, Mary Louise	1998
1816	Holcomb, Afton Eli	1954
16212	Hold, Joe Columbus	1997
18192	Holden, Dorothy F.	2000
4880	Holder, Earl R.	1972
4549	Holderman, A. C.	1971
5266	Holderman, Flora J.	1973
10858	Holdsworth, Bessie	1987
2764	Holdsworth, Kirk	1962
11850	Holdsworth, Lucile	1989

File	Deceased	Year
915	Holdsworth, Nellie	1936
1464	Holdsworth, Richard	1950
9780	Holdsworth, Robert O.	1985
1395	Holdsworth, Rosa Ross	1948
2330	Holdsworth, Thomas Kirk	1959
969	Hole, John E.	1938
11652	Holekamp, Alex M.	1989
2577	Holekamp, Glenn D.	1960
2501	Holekamp, Grace McBryde	1960
46	Holekamp, H.	----
315	Holekamp, Helen	1911
2712	Holekamp, Jennie McBryde	1961
5283	Holekamp, Kurt A.	1973
6094	Holekamp, Lottie	1976
1883	Holekamp, Moritz	1955
112738	Holland, George Carl	1991
1098	Holland, J. N.	1940
3614	Hollar, Roy	1966
18108	Hollar, Rosita H.	2000
17022	Hollocher, Ann A.	1998
18658	Hollocher, William S.	2001
8947	Holleday, Mary T.	1984
17148	Holliday, James W.	1999
1648	Hollier, A. D.	1952
1596	Hollier, Mabel	1951
8949	Holliman, Ida	1984
17554	Holliman, Linda Sue Scott	1999
17970	Hollimon, Bessie Laura	2000
7029	Hollimon, Frederick Joseph	1979
804	Hollimon, James H.	1933
12752	Hollingshead, Jervis L.	1991
SE67	Hollingsworth, Cecil G.	1982

File	Deceased	Year
6880	Hollingsworth, Jacob Oscar	1979
10608	Hollis, Asai B.	1987
15098	Hollman, Kathryn M.	1995
716	Hollomon, Grover K.	1918
7074	Hollomon, Minnie Lee	1979
313	Hollomon, W. W.	1907
12086	Holloway, Mamie B.	1990
225	Holloway, Pharabee	1904
5384	Holloway, R. R.	1974
SE8	Holmdahl, Edwin J.	1972
14968	Holmen, G. Robert	1995
17494	Holmes, Clyde Francis	1999
15764	Holmes, Coley E. Jr.	1996
10906	Holmes, Joe Blanks	1987
5098	Holmes, Joel J.	1973
17804	Holmes, Julia Bernice Mc Dowell	2000
18290	Holmon, Maria G.	2001
2760	Holomon, George Guy	1962
894	Holt, Connie E.	1936
17048	Holt, Elizabeth C.	1998
18928	Holt, Thomas Ray	2002
4320	Holton, Floyd S.	1970
10336	Holton, James A.	1986
3077	Holtz, John W.	1964
4013	Holtz, Myra M.	1968
17848	Holtzendorf, Harold L. Jr.	2000
15994	Homilius, Bernhard	1997
6598	Homilius, Eddie	1978
16100	Homilius, Ida B.	1997
2639	Homilius, Marie Elizabeth	1961
19356	Honea, Richard G.	2002

File Number	Deceased	Lawyer	Year
7550	Lorenz, Walter	Prohl	1980
-----	Losee, Henry D.	-----	
10796	Lossen, Warren A.	Mc Neil	1987
13586	Lotspeich, Thelma G.	Morriss III	1992
3699	Lott, Arthur	Wilson	1967
4573	Lott, Emilie E.	-----	1971
8793	Lott, Gilbert Hilmer	Schroeder	1983
3812	Lott, L. C.	Burkett	1967
15854	Lott, Lewis J.	Oehler	1996
2016	Lott, Margaret & Clark	Wilson	1956
2793	Lott, William A.	Allison	1962
13072	Loubet, Gertrude W.	Terrell	1992
11240	Loubet, Mac	Terrell	1988
1599	Louy, F. A.	O'Conner	1952
9066	Love, Bessye C.	Tinley	1984
5503	Love, E. B.	Leonard	1974
113654	Love, Elvira	Lochte	1992
18158	Love, Gewndolyn	Dolce	2000
17012	Love, Robert Ernest Sr.	Dolce	1998
4112	Love, W. E.	-----	1969
2656	Loveland, Howard C.	Lochte	1961
18138	Loveless, B. G.	Terrell	2000
14192	Lovett, Gordon H.	Leslie	1993
5279	Lovett, Sam C.	-----	1973
356	Lowrance, Amanda	Garrett	1914
1079	Lowrance, B. B.	Petsch	1941
347	Lowrance, J. S.	Garrett	1913
685	Lowrance, Leah Ann	Baker	1930
3965	Lowrance, Maggie	Burkett	1963
612	Lowrance, P. O.	Garrett	1926
194	Lowrance, William	-----	1902
10026	Lowry, Donald R.	Wallace	1986
4992	Lowry, Dorothy K.	-----	1973
491	Lowry, J. M.	Garrett	
12904	Lozano, Felipe Solis	LeMeilleur	1991
12230	Luby, Donald V.	Hopper	1990
12898	Luby, Mary D.	Hooper	1991
15742	Luby, Mary Jeanette Carr	Dolce	1996
9806	Luby, Robert Edwin	Nagle	1985
11148	Lucas, Corynne, Hill	Wallace	1988
2043	Lucas, Joseph B.	Leonard	1956
7572	Lucas, Mattie	Lucas	1981
4610	Lucas, Nell I.	-----	1971
12546	Luckemeyer, Lawrence William	Lochte	1991

File	Deceased	Year
7450	Horlyk, Rowena O.	1980
3015	Horn, F. N.	1963
8055	Horton, George W.	1982
8825	Horton, Robert	1984
19252	Horsman, A. N.	2002
5289	Horsman, Hubert L.	1973
16414	Hosford, James W.	1997
18544	Hosford, Mildred C.	2001
14620	Hosler, Margaret L.	1994
9278	Hospy, Joseph Frank	1984
7467	Houchins, Robert N.	1980
10912	Houdek, Rossie M.	1987
11910	Hough, Elsie D.	1989
10770	House, Charles M.	1987
16444	House, Jonnie Fortenberry	1998
7511	House, Neil B.	1980
18208	House, Nettie A.	2000
7061	House, Xeda A.	1979
13862	Houser, Bemos C.	1993
10686	Housman, Charles S.	1987
14338	Houston, Tom Harris	1994
10726	Hovan, Albert M.	1987
10534	Hovde, Olga	1987
SE31	Hoven, Alice L.	----
7194	Hoverson, Helen	1980
10323	Hovey, Gene D.	1986
12586	Howard, Charles O. Jr.	1991
SE55	Howard, Hattie	1981
17606	Howard, Jimmie H.	1999
10676	Howard, John L.	1987
10202	Howard, Joe	1986
18688	Howard, Robert George	2001
15686	Howard, Thelma Martin	1996
12008	Howard, Willie C.	1990

File	Deceased	Year
10428	Howe, Fred E.	1987
6343	Howell, Aleilda D.	1977
13046	Howell, B. F.	1991
3438	Howell, Carol Ross	1965
13484	Howell, Clarence Edward	1992
9738	Howell, Claud Walker	1985
7748	Howell, Earl E.	1981
6564	Howell, Inez	1978
2823	Howell, James Edgar	1962
16688	Howell, James Edward	1998
14132	Howell, Leta Belle	1993
6724	Howell, Millie Eliza	1978
15738	Howell, Rose Kathryn	1996
16844	Howell, Susan Flowers	1998
7539	Howlett, Hazeldene P.	1980
17268	Hoy, Judith M.	1999
4119	Hoyt, Abraham	1969
18848	Huang, Lin Y	2002
16836	Hubbard, William C.	1998
422	Hubble, Garland	----
2106	Huber, George Walter	1957
7144	Hudeck, Ann Adeline	1979
10414	Hudeck, Joe J.	1987
16700	Hudek, John J.	1998
9858	Hudek, Olga Helen	1986
9914	Hudson, Charles E. Sr.	1986
302	Hudson, E. M.	1911
17402	Hudson, Joyce Fay	1999
11926	Hudson, Lewis E.	1989
SE97-3	Hudson, Lois A.	1997
2563	Hudson, Nellie	1960
14428	Hudson, Nora L.	1994
14910	Huffaker, Jimmie	1995
10862	Huffman, Ruth Annette	1987
13366	Huggins, Blanch B.	1992

File	Deceased	Year
17788	Huggins, Richard Lewis	2000
2557	Hughes, Bessie	1960
17946	Hughes, Charles F.	2000
2341	Hughes, D. H.	1959
17184	Hughes, Eara Carlos	1999
2143	Hughes, Elzora	1957
3748	Hughes, Helen Louise	1967
19288	Hughes, Mary Virginia	2002
17404	Hughes, Peggy E.	1999
17818	Hughes, Robert Holloway	2000
421	Hughes, Verdie Alama	----
9534	Hughes, Zach A.	1985
255	Hughs, George	1906
4855	Huitt, James L.	1972
18780	Huitt, Louise F.	2001
SE40	Hulett, Ruby Marie/Mae	1980
4494	Hullinger, Beulah L.	1970/71
17232	Hullinger, C. E.	1999
1918	Humphrey, Adell T.	1976
15124	Hunnicutt, Carolyn D.	1995
708	Hunnicutt, Charles William	1930
14828	Hunnicutt, James A.	1995
14826	Hunnicutt, Virginia A.	1995
7455	Hunt, Bonnie Bess	1980
7813	Hunt, Charles E.	1981
5921	Hunt, Harriet C.	1976
12098	Hunt, Harriet G.	1990
17374	Hunt, Harry L.	1999
17636	Hunt, John W.	2000
7791	Hunt, Lloyd M.	1981
1520	Hunt, Mabel Clara	1951
9610	Hunt, Margardel	1985
9766	Hunt, Mary Louise	1985
2655	Hunt, Robert Allen	1961

File	Deceased	Year
6903	Hunt, William E.	1979
5069	Hunter, Dr. A. C.	1973
9438	Hunter, Bernard A.	1985
855	Hunter, Margaret Beck	1935
10854	Hunter, Margaret Eldora	1987
9202	Huntington, Edwin Ernst	1984
642	Huntington, Fannie R.	1928
1057	Huntington, Sarah	1940
1418	Huntington, Spencer H.	1949
14574	Huntley, H. H.	1994
18304	Huntley, Jeanne A.	2001
3741	Huntley, Marie Eleanor Woefel	1967
16334	Hurley, Paul F.	1997
17346	Hurley, Mina Gobble	1999
4138	Hurst, Alton S.	1969
1519	Hurt, Beatrice Vinning	1951
17412	Hurt, Lewis C. Jr.	1999
6141	Hurtley, Forrest	1976
7557	Husman, Pauline H.	1980
11912	Huss, Alan Jacob	1989
11914	Huss, Margaret S.	1989
18326	Hutches, Clarence Frederick II	2001
4283	Hutchings, Alfred W.	1969
19400	Hutchings, Mildred	2002
1470	Hutchings, Richard L.	1950
17624	Hutchins, Betty A.	1999
4841	Hutchins, Don L.	1972
8667	Hutchins, Eva A.	1983
10738	Hutchinson, Paul	1987
14194	Hutton, Lois Mabel	1993
13468	Huvelle, Verne Garrett	1992
4208	Hyde, Arthur	1969
1828	Hyde, Carrie	1954

File	Deceased	Year
667	Hyde, Guy	1929
1267	Hyde, H. P.	1946
3183	Hyde, Mrs. H. P.	1964
11156	Hyde, Helma Tidwell	1988
7305	Hyde, Ida Bell	1980
5494	Hyde, Josephine	1972/74
782	Hyde, Mrs. L. C.	1933
8917	Hyde, Lillian M.	1984
15136	Hyde, Pauline K.	1995
1040	Hyde, Mrs. S. E.	1940
1824	Hyde, T. M.	1954
2645	Hyde, Walter	1961

I

File	Deceased	Year
18714	Ingenhuett, Carol Ann	2001
8123	Ingenhuett, Warren Peter	1982
16154	Ingram, Robert Lee	1997
SE14	Ireland, Evelyn	1975
17032	Ireland, Leon	1998
12210	Ireland, Winfield S.	1990
8413	Irving, Amy O.	1983
16054	Irving, Lawanda E.	1997
327	Irving, R. J. Sr.	1910
11918	Irving, Willie Mae	1987
1155	Irwin, Alfred	----
15458	Irwin, Warren Lee	1996
16246	Isaac, Charles Lee Sr.	1997
12136	Isbill, Charles Mosley	1990
16718	Isbill II, Jack Donavan	1998
8082	Isenberg, Kelsy C.	1982
15852	Isenberg, Kelcy Coy	1996
12218	Isenberg, Leona	1990
7696	Isenhour, Ethel L. D.	1981

File	Deceased	Year
12696	Ishmael, Gregory Lee	1991
3646	Isinsee, John	----
3140	Isinsee, Lester	----
1094	Ivey, Lillie	----
4012	Ivey, Loice A.	1968
15274	Ivy, Charles I.	1995
18234	Ivy, Cleva Charlen	2001

J

File	Deceased	Year
17556	Jack, Clarence E. Jr.	1999
288	Jack, Mrs. V. H. (Verna)	1908
14186	Jackman, Willis L.	1993
18892	Jacks, Doris Nell	2002
1380	Jackson, Ada	1948
17724	Jackson, Addie Lorne	2000
2838	Jackson, Arthur Le Grand	1962
883	Jackson, Barbara	1926
3767	Jackson, Ben D.	1967
11044	Jackson, Beulah N.	1988
2393	Jackson, Ella	1959
16616	Jackson, Evadean Hardee	1998
8695	Jackson, Forest S.	1983
9260	Jackson, Frances R.	1984
7316	Jackson, Guy R. Jr.	1980
19110	Jackson, Gewndolyn Sue	2002
16320	Jackson, Hazel Irene	1997
8226	Jackson, Herbert L.	1982
2281	Jackson, Irene Baines	1958
1421	Jackson, J. A.	----
16372	Jackson, John (Closed)	1997
395	Jackson, John David	1916
1259	Jackson, John Dee	1946

File	Deceased	Year
18154	Jackson, Josephine B.	2000
18558	Jackson, Mamie Wolforth	2001
17568	Jackson, Osmond D.	1999
13810	Jackson, Sylvia Elaine	1993
10830	Jackson, Vela Miles	1987
7768	Jackson, William M. Jr.	1981
SE64	Jacoby, Harry Peter	1982
9690	Jacobs, Anthony Henry	1985
7965	Jacobs, Edward L.	1981
15654	Jacobs, John Maurice	1996
6711	Jacobson, John A. C.	1978
6146	Jacobson, Virginia A.	1977
4027	Jaeger, Albert	1968
4036	Jaeger, Ethel	1968
11192	Jaeger, Wilma Edward	1988
18146	Jakovich, Ann Stephen	2000
10082	James, Alton	1986
13376	James, Ann Goecke	1992
7442	James, Arlie	1980
15504	James, Bennett W.	1996
CV960083	James, Bennett W.	1996
564	James, Byrd	1924
SE2	James, Frank Sr.	1966
9272	James, Guy L.	1984
1963	James, Helen V.	1955
5704	James, Katherine H.	1975
4859	James, Louis D.	1972
340	James, Malta	1913
44	James, Mary E.	1882
1004	James, Nancy	1938
19374	James, Omega L.	2002
5884	James, Pearl	1975
926	James, Pleas B.	1937
9011	James, Robert Hayes	1984
16914	James, Robert Randolph	1998

File	Deceased	Year
4249	James, W. N. (Bill)	1969
4020	Jameson, A. D.	1968
18142	Jamisoon, Gilbert Leroy	2000
18080	Jamme, Walter J.	2000
17092	Janda, Irene B.	1999
10992	Janda, Robert E.	1988
6114	Janda, Vera A.	1976
15100	Janey, William Price	1995
17050	Janson, Gotthard Jr.	1999
16020	January, Odell D. Jr.	1997
2650	Jarmon, Ella	1961
80	Jarmon, R. B.	1886
1564	Jarmon, Walter	1951
10904	Jarrell, Chester Newton	1987
10910	Jarrell, Letha Marian	1987
15746	Jarrell, L. R.	1996
761	Jarrell, Richard T	1932
16362	Jarvis, Joanne	1997
675	Jauke, W. F.	----
8208	Jay, James W. Sr.	1982
16506	Jefferson, Jean Duerner	1998
17900	Jefferson, Samuel C.	2000
3978	Jemison, W. H.	1968
3693	Jenings, Alice Daisy	1967
12698	Jenkins, John O.	1991
12704	Jenkins, M. Donetta	1991
10068	Jenkins, Roy W.	1986
2295	Jennings, C. G.	1958
17628	Jennings, Fred C.	2000
9462	Jennings, H. Lee	1985
SE11238	Jennings, Isla Mae	1988
16406	Jennings, James F.	1997
12572	Jennings, William Ray	1991
17802	Jenschke, Laura	2000
16536	Jenschke, Leo C.	1998

File	Deceased	Year
5584	Jenschke, Walter M.	1974
6086	Jensen, Emily B.	1976
986	Jensen, Lina	1938
10392	Jensen, Neils J.	1986
2819	Jensen, Thomas Christian	1962
2711	Jerrigan, Eva	1961
4771	Jeter, Alice L.	1972
19262	Jeter, Gladys Lorene	2002
13978	Jeter, Sidney Stell	1993
18866	Jetton, Charles Gaston	2002
SE98-1	Jetton, Heath Aaron	1998
18768	Jewett, Durwood Kent	2001
2044	Jewett, Iva M.	1956
11744	Jitkoff, Andrew N.	1989
7008	Jobes, Bertha C.	1979
4947	Jobes, Noble	1972
8328	Jobes, Roquey G.	1982
14038	Johannessen, Leta	1994
6145	Johns, Elizabeth L.	1976
11204	Johnsen, Elizabeth Mae	1988
7615	Johnsen, Harmon E.	1981
6178	Johnson, A. W.	1976/7
8185	Johnson, Albert Alexander	1982
3120	Johnson, Alice Bradstreet	1964
7338	Johnson, Ann S.	1980
581	Johnson, Asa J.	1926
12146	Johnson, Ben Hearne	1990
10268	Johnson, Bernice	1986
5945	Johnson, Byrdie N.	1976
14654	Johnson, Dan H.	1994
16670	Johnson, Darrell L.	1998
9838	Johnson, Doris	1985

File	Deceased	Year
1406	Johnson, Earl	1949
16840	Johnson, Earl Reed aka	
	Earline R. Johnson	1998
18088	Johnson, Eugene I.	2000
5822	Johnson, Frederich E.	1975
6790	Johnson, George W.	1978
5704	Johnson, Glenn V.	1975
8213	Johnson, James F.	1982
1659	Johnson, Harold	1952
1669	Johnson, Henrietta	1952
13530	Johnson, Herby Leroy	1992
7874	Johnson, Inez A.	1981
3487	Johnson, J. F.	1966
11594	Johnson, J. F. (Billie)	1989
130	Johnson, J. M.	1893
3985	Johnson, James Maurice	1968
11766	Johnson, John Peyton	1989
14158	Johnson, John William	1993
15566	Johnson, Josephine F.	1996
6921	Johnson, L. A.	1979
18086	Johnson, Lois K.	2000
6859	Johnson, Lola L.	1979
17088	Johnson, Marion Pickens	999
7250	Johnson, Marjorie	
	Bender	1980
4317	Johnson, Marvell M.	1970
3958	Johnson, Mary	1968
SE93-1	Johnson, Maurice Wayne	1993
17718	Johnson, Melville L.	2000
17262	Johnson, Mildred	
	Wheeler	1999
4637	Johnson, Morgan W.	1971
16224	Johnson, Nancy Ellis	1997
16422	Johnson, Nathaniel M.	1997
17106	Johnson, Norma Scott	1999

File	Deceased	Year
7212	Johnson, Oren Edward	1980
3079	Johnson, Price King	1964
5475	Johnson, R. J.	1974?
SE47	Johnson, Raymond A.	1978
SE47	Johnson, Raymond A.	1981
5112	Johnson, Richard M.	----
5239	Johnson, Richard M.	----
13592	Johnson, Sarah Naomi	1992
10564	Johnson, Stella Maria	1987
8305	Johnson, Stephania Haberson	1982
10010	Johnson, Virginia Mildred	1986
15002	Johnson, Welford Merlin	1995
2620	Johnston, Annie M.	1961
16748	Johnston, Bobbie L.	1998
644	Johnston, C. H. Jr.	1930
18856	Johnston, Charles H.	2002
1033	Johnston, Elizabeth	1940
15946	Johnston, Ernest R.	1997
10038	Johnston, George H.	1986
8198	Johnston, Henry O.	1982
13058	Johnston, Jean Emch	1992
5160	Johnston, Johnnie B.	----
16808	Johnston, Joseph Ferry	1998
12332	Johnston, Lucille W.	1990
11688	Johnston, Mary Elizabeth	1989
13936	Johnston, Michael H.	1993
12300	Johnston, Newell Crane	1990
18880	Johnston, Pauline	2002
6680	Johnston, Susan Mitchell	1977/8
2810	Johnston, T. W.	1962
16590	Joines, Maggie R.	1998

File	Deceased	Year
14036	Joines, Virgil B.	1993
4813	Jolly, Lula Mae	1972
16952	Jome, Florence J.	1998
2864	Jonas, Robert L.	1962
511	Jonbert, J. Kenry	----
15056	Jones, Alice Mabel	1995
934	Jones, Allen G.	1933
16308	Jones, Anna Amos	1997
13086	Jones, Beatrice R.	1992
12432	Jones, Bertiola	1990
15048	Jones, Bruce Dale	1995
12178	Jones, Carroll L.	1990
10788	Jones, Cecil Orliff	1987
15716	Jones, Charles C. Jr.	1996
11482	Jones, Clarence	1989
9117	Jones, David W.	1984
13428	Jones, De Forest	1992
18565	Jones, Dora Jordan	2001
11908	Jones, Dorothy H.	1989
9698	Jones, Edith I.	1985
8415	Jones, Eleanor Ann	1983
12178	Jones, Ernest	1990
17496	Jones, Florence Edith	1999
10376	Jones, Foster L.	1986
17552	Jones, Gilbert David Sr.	1999
13696	Jones, Glen Keith	1993
15390	Jones, Herman E.	1996
18854	Jones, Hershul T.	2002
4767	Jones, J. D.	1971
7612	Jones, J. E.	1981
2850	Jones, J. Gordon	1962
3733	Jones, Jesse Lee	1967
8995	Jones, Jessie Mayhue	1984
11084	Jones, Juanita Hanna	1988
13156	Jones, Leone	1992

File	Deceased	Year
5121	Jones, Lillian S.	1973
956	Jones, Lillie	----
13776	Jones, Lindsey R.	1993
11600	Jones, Lois	1989
7247	Jones, Marie R.	1980
12000	Jones, Marion E.	1990
19124	Jones, Helen Lenore Christensen	2002
565	Jones, Narcissa C.	1924
6800	Jones, O. P.	1978
17464	Jones, Oakley/Okley	1999
9526	Jones, Obera M.	1985
7757	Jones, Oleander Harrell	1981
1578	Jones, Oscar W.	1951
7556	Jones, Paris	1980
7165	Jones, Prentice William	1979
3534	Jones, R. D.	1966
2827	Jones, R. W.	1962
8325	Jones, Ray B.	1982
11320	Jones, Ray Lamar	1988
8828	Jones, Royce M.	1984
4175	Jones, Rufus M.	1969
10298	Jones, Ruth Jordan	1986
13430	Jones, Ruth Lorraine	1992
6718	Jones, Sue	1978
17802	Jones, Suel	2001
3220	Jones, Susie E.	1964
181	Jones, Tom	----
SE75/76	Jones, Virgil K.	1982
1766	Jones, Walter R.	1954
4584	Jones, William H.	1971
3427	Jones, Willie V. (Mrs.)	1965
9496	Jonon, Ruth Simpson	1985
9206	Jons, Henry Paris Jr.	1984
7518	Jordan, Edwin Riggs	1980

File	Deceased	Year
15758	Jordan, Esther K.	1996
13832	Jordan, John C.	1993
3327	Jordan, William W. Sr.	1965
8894	Jorns, Albert C.	1984
2985	Jorns, Lena Leola	1963
34	Joss, Emil	----
17468	Jost, Evelyn Gaye	1999
5560	Journeay, Percy	1974
19024	Journeay, Wilmer C.	2002
15138	Joy, Donald Gene	1995
15304	Joy, George Carroll	1995
12910	Joy, James A.	1991
16452	Joy, Leonard R.	1998
5820	Joy, Melba	1975
7647	Joy, Oatsie	1981
633	Joy, R.	1927
14074	Juarez, Benita C.	1993
15808	Juarez, Rachel	1996
6347	Judd, Herschel N.	1977
14210	Juenke, Frieda R.	1993
11282	Juenke, Harry W.	1988
17472	Jule, Maxine Richards	1999
2505	Jung, Hulda W.	1960
4046	Junkin, Frederich H.	1968
8563	Junkin, Martha Mc Dowewll	1983
8756	Jurgenson, Dorance R.	1984

K

17518	Kaczmarek, Carl R.	1999
14140	Kain, Douglas	1993
9966	Kain, Grace	1986
4209	Kaiser, Berthold H.	1969

File	Deceased	Year
10822	Kaiser, Emilie H.	1987
9714	Kaiser, Herbert A.	1985
350	Kaiser, Mary	1914
423	Kaiser, W. C.	1917
18870	Kallem, May	2002
15508	Kallem, William	1996
4324	Kalmbach, Brooks	1970
16686	Kalver, Henry T.	1998
11954	Kaminsky, Louis Joseph	1990
16666	Kammer, Fern I.	1998
8360	Kanady, Fred	1982
13740	Kanady, Velma	1993
5891	Kane, G. E.	1976
17608	Kaough, Lois Hill	1999
15490	Karaus, Lewis John	1996
14272	Karcher, Arthur Stalsby	1994
6290	Karcher, Isedor August	1977
2891	Karger, Alex	1962
10400	Karger, Anna L.	1987
1219	Karger, F. A.	1944
16566	Karger, Fritz Albert II	1998
2257	Karger, Harry	1958
-----	Karger, Johann	----
15498	Karnes, Clint Howard	1996
3280	Karger, Lillie	1965
3731	Karper, Mrs. William	1967
SE110	Karwoske, Mary A./E.	1986
2680	Kasey, E. H.	1961
17314	Kash, Karl	1999
8556	Kashanig, Hossein K.	1983
3508	Kasper, Josephine Moore	1966
14088	Kass, Frank A.	1993
116	Kastner, John	----
117	Kastner, John	----
15016	Kastrup, Arnold P.	1995

File	Deceased	Year
4409	Kattner, Lydia L. R.	1970
5101	Kattner, Otto T.	1973
18724	Kaufman, Ralph S.	2001
727	Kaufman, Sam H.	----
5349	Kauss, Carl & Ethel	1974
19052	Kaw, Choo Lian	2002
14518	Kaw, Taik Kee	1994
510	Kaw, Vias Kuce	----
13062	Kay, Elizabeth Butterfield	1992
7804	Kaye, Fred Manuel	1981
14170	Kearney, Michael D.	1993
13240	Kearns, Edward	1992
9594	Kearns, Juanita Dwyer	1985
3998	Keefer, George W.	1968
17564	Keefer, Tollie Mae	1999
14822	Keeling, Georgia K.	1995
17850	Keen, Juanita Puckett	2000
4675	Keen, William H.	1971
18286	Keenon, Mary L.	2001
17972	Keese, Eugene R.	2000
SE16	Keese, Jewel Lorene Chisum	1975
6101	Keese, Jewel L. Chisum	1976
15130	Keese, Vivian	1995
7021	Keester, Earl Leonard	1979
15530	Kehner, Karen Sue	1996
4172	Keidel, Robert P.	1969
5740	Keile, John F. Sr.	1975
13252	Keile, Lillian V.	1992
14646	Keile, Lillian V.	1994
7384	Keiser, Lorence Albert	1979
18844	Keith, Alva C.	2002
17758	Keith, Doris Holden	2000
18044	Keith, Frances Fullwood	2000

File Number	Deceased	Lawyer	Year
16546	Milton, Robert W.	Dolce	1998
15858	Miman, Otis F.	Wallen	1996
7373	Mince, Oscar T.	Lochte	1980
17744	Mincy, Dollie Ruth	LeMeilleur	2000
10626	Minnick, Homer H.	Nagle	1987
1150	Minsch, Walter A.	-----	1943
10166	Mireider, Joszef	Savage	1986
6146	Mitchell, Berger P.	Ervine	1976
5327	Mitchell, Oma	-----	1973/74
4625	Mitchell, Grace I.	-----	1971
12388	Mitchell, Ronald Dean	Kersey	1990
15966	Mittanckm Herbert Guss	King	1997
10934	Mittanck, Ollie S.	Terrell	1988
11672	Mixon, Oleda E.	Prohl	1989
3007	Mize, Austin	Haley	1963
4804	Mock, Oliver L.	-----	1972
13352	Modesitt, Robert Fellows	Schneider	1992
5939	Moeller, Ambrose J.	Goforth	1976
12602	Moeller, Mary Virginia Jett	Wallace	1991
17596	Moeller, William Richard	Wallace	1999
12884	Moffett, Alice Catherine	LeMeilleur	1991
7755	Moffett, Eleanor B.	Wallace	1981
12838	Moffett, Elzo	LeMeilleur	1991
13826	Moffett, Helen H.	Wallace	1993
11382	Moffett, Thomas A.	Wallace	1988
471	Mogford, E. A.	Garrett	1920
3516	Mogford, E. A.	Oehler	1983
11414	Mogg, Herschel Lee	Peters	1988
416	Mohrhoff, George	Garrett	
13850	Molder, L. W.	Jons	1993
7268	Molene, Robert E.	Monroe	1980
5902	Molrgan, May Lines	Harris	1975/76
3042	Molina, Mary D.	Harris	1982
8847	Molter, Charles H.	Pollard	1984
0500	Molter, Ellie B.	Ables	1987
1306	Molter, Jimmie Ray	Wallac	1988
3414	Monkhouse, Charles H.	Leslie	1992
3698	Monkhouse, Eunice	Leslie	1993
2112	Monroe, Dorothy Anita	Oehler	1990
0374	Monroe, George R.	Lochte	1986
030	Monroe, Myrick	Leonard	1963
562	Monrow, S. W.	Barton	1966
9218	Monroy, Salvador	Bailey	2002
32	Montalengo, E.	-----	

File	Deceased	Year
1506	Kelly, Mary Margaret	1950
4371	Kelly, Paul J.	1970
1998	Kelton, Samuel M.	1956
9090	Kemmerer, Carl Edward	1984
8909	Kemmerer, Elizabeth Irene	1984
15848	Kemp, Camilla A.	1996
10558	Kemp, James D.	1987
4005	Kemp, Katherine Daniels	1968
3925	Kemp, Roy	1968
3115	Kemper, Henry Michael	1957
7895	Kendall, Claude	1980
14254	Kendall, Thomas A.	1994
14768	Kendrick, Jack Woods	1994
3507	Kenley, Wilson	1966
SE98-2	Kennedy, Aetna	1998
5033	Kennedy, Albert Jr.	1973
12358	Kennedy, Alice	1990
17196	Kennedy, Alla Mae	1999
4436	Kennedy, Ann Mae	1970
14396	Kennedy, Carrie E.	1994
5010	Kennedy, Edith	1973
5044	Kennedy, Edna G. G.	1973
SE98-2	Kennedy, Esther	1998
3231	Kennedy, Eve D.	1964
SE54	Kennedy, J. Leo	----
2152	Kennedy, Janet F.	1957
14662	Kennedy, John A.	1994
1239	Kennedy, Kate	1945
4435	Kennedy, Levi L.	1970
12444	Kennedy, Louis Dwain	1990
13928	Kennedy, Maggie H.	1993
3326	Kennedy, May L.	1965
16068	Kennedy, Nezzie B.	1997
4343	Kennedy, Oscar E.	1970

File	Deceased	Year
679	Kennedy, S. J.	1924
6376	Kennedy, Theodore A.	1977
5034	Kennedy, Thomas E.	1973
13226	Kenney, V. Clayton	1992
13332	Kenney, Juliana A.	1992
17306	Kensing, Billie R.	1999
14090	Kensing, Kenneth L.	1993
15104	Kensing, Monroe	1995
8805	Kent, Donald F.	1984
5828	Kent, Gordon D.	1975
319	Kent, J. H.	----
17150	Keppler, Philip R.	1999
48	Kernodle, John	----
172	Kerley, James	----
9516	Kerlin, Walter Edward	1985
10742	Kerr, Philip D.	1987
12204	Kerrins, Charles T.	1990
16090	Kessler, Alice Lewis	1984
3642	Key, Ellie	1966
2679	Key, Gussie	1961
17142	Key, Mary Ellen	1999
13846	Key, Roscoe J.	1993
17976	Key, William Oren	2000
18894	Keyes, Glenn A.	2002
16450	Keyes, Mary E.	1998
3527	Keys, James W.	1966
2441	Kichlberg, Alice Dorothy	1959
3918	Kiefer, Albert H.	1968
780	Kiefer, William	1932
18690	Kieffer, George F.	2001
15052	Kieffer, Ruth K.	1995
10532	Kies, Cecilia Yvonne	1987
6213	Kies, Minnie L.	1977

File	Deceased	Year
3161	Kieschnick, G. E.	1964
18162	Kiewitt, Preston G.	2000
3394	Kihlbert, Fred E.	1965
13276	Kilgore, Demetria Kelley	1992
12634	Kilgore, Elmer Herbert	1991
3745	Kilgore, Henry E.	1967
7210	Kilgore, Naida	1979/80
5324	Killer, Edward	1973
19302	Killer, John Edward	2002
635	Killough, B. T.	1927
11218	Killough, Martha A.	1988
771	Killough, R. Lilly	1932
8347	Kimbrow, Bruce Allison	1982
1849	Kime, Imogene R.	1954
2008	Kime, Leonard L.	1954
1223	Kincaid, J. B.	1945
13338	Kincaid, Jact T.	1992
1193	Kincaid, Mollie John	1944
11264	Kincannon, G. E.	1988
5380	Kincy, Kenneth B.	1974
4754	Kindorg, George	1971/72
8446	Kindred, Wilbur A.	1983
555	King, Alma J.	----
8251	King, Annie L.	1982
2310	King, B. H.	1958
5558	King, C. J.	1974
6781	King, Carroll L.	1978
4528	King, Charles M.	1970
13904	King, Charles Robert Sr.	1993
7598	King, Dorothy	1980
13906	King, Dorothy E.	1993
5120	King, Earl Korn	1973
4486	King, Edgar	1970
10960	King, Elizabeth F.	1988

File	Deceased	Year
9354	King, Emma L.	1985
17252	King, Ethel Naomi	1999
5363	King, F. Snyder	1974
6935	King, Griffin Wilson	1979
9916	King, Helen Ruth	1986
9942	King, Horace M.	1986
3674	King, Iva	1967
16956	King, James J. Sr.	1998
3793	King, James P Jr.	1967
5308	King, Jennie W.	1973
19072	King, John Ernest	2002
2104	King, M. M.	1957
7797	King, Marie E.	1981
6906	King, Reuben Cecil	1979
8993	King, Ruth Jane	1984
5648	King, Susan Moody	1975
12622	King, Viola Vertrue	1991
11988	King, Virginia Mae	1990
7033	King, W. L.	1979
5345	King, Walter E.	1974
878	King, William H.	1936
9560	King, Willis J.	1985
11424	Kingsbury, Jerome J.	1988
SE88	Kingston, William Orville	1982
17786	Kinler, Dalton Paul	2000
11946	Kinney, Anna Laura	1990
8032	Kinney, Guy N.	1982
2219	Kinsch, Albert Ralph	1958
11746	Kinsel, J. T.	1989
16522	Kinsel, Jane Townsend	1998
5829	Kinter, Garth M.	1975
7230	Kinton, Ruth Compton	1980
8359	Kipp, Ford Elliott	1982
16492	Kipp, Lillian H.	1998

File	Deceased	Year
6264	Kirby, Arthur B.	1977
6176	Kirby, Ethel W.	1976
9001	Kirby, Ted Taft	1985
4899	Kirchhoff, Leroy	1972
10574	Kirchhoff, Norma B.	1987
450	Kirk, Mrs. C. E.	----
6278	Kirk, Harry L.	1977
SE4	Kirk, Lawrence	1967
13694	Kirk, Rqaymond H.	1993
5143	Kirk, Richard C.	1973
11078	Kirkpatrick, Charles C.	1988
14240	Kirkpatrick, Lalla B.	1994
9722	Kirkpatrick, Mary Snyder	1985
5086	Kirkland, Grace	1973
3207	Kirsapp, Doris E.	1964
14486	Kirscher, Galen P.	1994
11532	Kirscher, Lois E. Ramstack	1989
18424	Kirsh, Lena Virginia	2001
11290	Kisida, Louis	1988
15790	Kiss, Bertha May	1996
10694	Kitch, Kenneth Haun	1987
1422	Kittel, Carl Otto	1949
19248	Kittel, Florence S.	2002
11164	Kittel, Irving	1988
8738	Kittinger, Gillner	1983
14992	Kitto, Elva Pearl	1995
18672	Kitts, Edward Jr.	2001
3663	Kleck, Albert	1966
6168	Kleck, Lizzie	1976
2836	Kleekamp, Bertha	1962
5605	Klein, Ada E.	1974
13214	Klein, Alonzo Christian	1992
10942	Klein, Felix F.	1988

File	Deceased	Year
5075	Klein, Fredda	1973
349	Klein, Frederich	1911?
2495	Klein, Henry	1960
8035	Klein, Hilmer	1982
8367	Klein, Justin Bowen	1982
17888	Klein, Kathryn Louise aka Louise Kathryn	2000
18054	Klein, Lucille	2000
7084	Klein, Mary	1979/80
6239	Klein, Minnie L.	1977
17418	Klein, Neva M.	1999
17594	Klein, Ronald Charles	1999
18422	Klein, Susie Agnes	2001
6647	Klein, W. Conrad	1978
12876	Klein, William Conrad Jr.	1991
14880	Kleinlaus, Fabiola Agnes	1995
1796	Klemstein, Augusta	1954
3288	Klerner, Donald R.	1965
18816	Klewer, Larry T.	2001
15248	Kleypas, Joann	1995
226	Klick, Frauz (??Franz)	----
1852	Klinefelter, Mary E.	1954
11872	Klingemann, James C.	1989
14294	Klingemann, Virginia Goss	1994
3457	Klitsch, Frank	1966
15876	Klombies, Isabella	1996
5660	Klsche, Fred E.	1975
11742	Kluckhohn, Ross E.	1989
5333	Kluever, Hugo	1974
3429	Klugman, Margaret	1965
15780	Knaack, Clarence E.	1996

File	Deceased	Year
17308	Knaack, Esther May Lundell	1999
11279	Knapp, Charles Edward	1988
5930	Knapp, D. R.	1976
14026	Knapp, Charles Howard III	1993
2894	Knapp, Mary Louise	1962
3322	Kneese, Harry E.	1965
10138	Kneese, Thomas M.	1986
12982	Knight, Vivian Havens	1991
12760	Knippers, Howard E.	1991
7938	Knocke, Henry John	1981
SE11714	Knott, Ida May	1989
4519	Known, Eva Ann	1970
16944	Knox, Betty Wilkerson	1998
2876	Knox, John Coffey	1962
14984	Knox, John H.	1995
5935	Knox, Leonard R.	1976
10006	Knox, Velma May	1986
9840	Knoy, Robbie Mae Little	1985
9284	Koch, Henry Lewis	1984
19236	Koch, William T.	2002
1764	Koehler, Catherine L.	1954
14468	Koehler, Elizabeth S.	1994
2115	Koehler, George L. H.	1957
6856	Koehn, Marguerite Johanna	1979
5953	Koenig, John	1976
4420	Koennecke, Bertha E.	1970
12080	Koennecke, Lonnie	1990
15646	Koennecke, Percy	1996
1304	Kohler, John	1946
17604	Koehler, L. F. Earlan	1999
17646	Koehler, Walter C.	2000
5636	Kohlmann, Bernard N.	1975

File	Deceased	Year
19308	Kolb, Donnie Muriel	2002
6021	Konde, Elmer T.	1976
9254	Konde, Hazel June	1984
1202	Konnegay, C.	1944
6496	Koon, C. E.	1977
8744	Koon, Dixie Lee	1983
1594	Koon, J. E.	1951
4832	Koontz, Emery R.	1972
912	Koontz, Julian B.	1936/37
11980	Koopmann, Felton Otto	1990
15636	Koosen, Joseph F.	1996
12666	Koranek, Eddie L.	1991
873	Kordzik, Otto P.	1933
14362	Kornig, Icie Hardy	1994
3639	Kosicki, Jerome L.	1966
19388	Kossuth, Adele Frost	2002
13644	Kotata, Tracey Lee	1992
4240	Kothman, Elma J.	1969/60
17944	Kothman, Lena	2000
4623	Kothmann, R. W.	1971
1415	Kott, Alfred	1949
2081	Kott, Ida	1959
3406	Koval, Johnie & Pauline	1965
1720	Kowalski, Helen	1953
18464	Kraay, Janie C.	2001
8420	Kraay, Oswald Art	1983
1971	Kramer, Albert	1954
18910	Kramer, Catherine G.	2002
14650	Kramer, Charles G.	1994
15422	Kramer, Magdalena Marie	1996
18578	Kramer, Walter C.	2001
18900	Krause, Thomas Fred	2002
567	Kreiss, Fred	----
6097	Kremer, Norman	1976
5035	Krenzel, Margaret E. D.	1973

File	Deceased	Year
4409	Kattner, Lydia L. R.	1970
5101	Kattner, Otto T.	1973
18724	Kaufman, Ralph S.	2001
727	Kaufman, Sam H.	----
5349	Kauss, Carl & Ethel	1974
19052	Kaw, Choo Lian	2002
14518	Kaw, Taik Kee	1994
510	Kaw, Vias Kuce	----
13062	Kay, Elizabeth Butterfield	1992
7804	Kaye, Fred Manuel	1981
14170	Kearney, Michael D.	1993
13240	Kearns, Edward	1992
9594	Kearns, Juanita Dwyer	1985
3998	Keefer, George W.	1968
17564	Keefer, Tollie Mae	1999
14822	Keeling, Georgia K.	1995
17850	Keen, Juanita Puckett	2000
4675	Keen, William H.	1971
18286	Keenon, Mary L.	2001
17972	Keese, Eugene R.	2000
SE16	Keese, Jewel Lorene Chisum	1975
6101	Keese, Jewel L. Chisum	1976
15130	Keese, Vivian	1995
7021	Keester, Earl Leonard	1979
15530	Kehner, Karen Sue	1996
4172	Keidel, Robert P.	1969
5740	Keile, John F. Sr.	1975
13252	Keile, Lillian V.	1992
14646	Keile, Lillian V.	1994
7384	Keiser, Lorence Albert	1979
18844	Keith, Alva C.	2002
17758	Keith, Doris Holden	2000
18044	Keith, Frances Fullwood	2000

File	Deceased	Year

L

File	Deceased	Year
15416	Laas, Perry James Jr.	1996
6550	La Bounty, Eileen S.	1978
18810	La Bounty, Reube May	2001
2940	Lacey, Grace Evelyn	1963
5750	Lackey, B. F. Jr.	1975
SE17	Lackey, Estelle	1975
14796	Lackey, Ethel Barrett	1995
16830	Lackey, Ford F.	1998
665	Lackey, Green	1929
14174	Lackey, Howard B.	1993
9602	Lackey, Iona B.	1985
2544	Lackey, James Robert	1960
19384	Lackey, John Oscar	2002
9330	Lackey, Jonie	1985
14028	Lackey, Josephine	1993
619	Lackey, Mrs. L. J.	----
11590	Lackey, Peggy E.	1989
994	Lackey, Sallie	1938
11658	Lacye, Jack	1989
SE77	La Fleur, Vernon J.	1982
16024	Lain, Ora Mae	1997
11102	Laine, Lucien E.	1988
13064	Laine, Thelma	1992
6462	Laird, Helen Syfan	1977
15842	Laird, Margaret L. Ray	1996
11708	Laird, Reba A.	1989
10286	Laird, Ray Albert	1986
16084	Laird, Wilson M.	1997
15036	Lake, Betty Louise	1995
15038	Lake, Donald Onar	1995
5657	Lamb, Fema C.	1974/75
3175	Lamb, George A.	1964
17042	Lamb, Violet L. Moore	1998

File	Deceased	Year
19184	Lambert, Edward J.	2002
1677	Lamereaux, Lisle W.	1953
12216	Lancaster, Loula Katherine	1990
13870	Land, Eileen V.	1993
14454	Land, Helen R.	1993
11644	Land, Raymond W.	1989
13144	Landay, Charlotte S.	1992
6401	Landay, Hans L.	1977
!3676	Landers, Blanche B.	1993
17098	Landers, Franklin A.	1999
SE76	Landers, John W.	1982
14752	Landgrebe, Daniel Henry	1994
7180	Landreth, Hallye Taylor	1980
4307	Landreth, Victor M.	1969
17138	Landrum, C. R.	1999
17140	Landrum, Hazel G.	1999
1502	Landrum, L. R.	1950
1500	Landrum, Lemuel R.	1950
735	Landry, Atheaory (?sp)	1931
15920	Landry, Clayton F.	1997
15922	Landry, Rovilla May	1997
18956	Lane, Ann Mildred	2002
19364	Lane, Connie E.	2002
1932	Lane, Coy J.	1955
17774	Lane, Girdon W.	----
8460	Lane, Marion Eugene	1983
-----	Lanesen, Sam	----
752	Lanford, W. C.	----
11520	Lang, Francis William	1989
1045	Lang, Garland H.	1940
2534	Lang, Jennie Gribble	1960
1351	Lange, Alvin T.	1947
7650	Lange, Edward William	1981
13630	Lange, Elmer John	1992

File	Deceased	Year
6	Lange, Henry	1865
17146	Lange, Irene	1999
4035	Lange, Lucile W.	1968
1316	Lange, Mrs. M. E.	1947
6542	Lange, Marie	1977
15984	Lange, Mary	1997
942	Lange, R. J.	1937
7304	Lange, R. J.	1980
1512	Lange, W. G.	1951
18668	Lange, William F.	2001
5123	Lange, Wilson G.	1973
6281	Langridge, George F.	1977
8071	Langford, Davis Clinton	1982
14944	Langford, Earl C.	1995
15820	Langford, O'Dessa	1996
15694	Langley, Carl Nelson	1995
11670	Langston, Claude F.	1989
9812	Lanning, Dennis	1985
14168	Lanning, Gertrude W.	1993
8957	Lapham, John	1984
SE10976	Lara, Alberto	1988
12306	Laracy, Elizabeth Coleman	1990
14028	Laracy, Jacqueline Cathryn	1993
16742	Laracy, Stanley Romayne	1998
1187 ½	Larendon, George W.	1944
2080	Larendon, Jennie	1957
9013	Larimer, Laurence M.	1984
11942	Larkins, George C.	1989
1859	Larnard, Ray	1954
8979	Larsen, Minnie Audrey	1984
5300	Larson, Charles C.	1973
1598	La Rue, Florence	1951
15074	La Salle, Mary C.	1995

151

File	Deceased	Year
8586	La Salle, Wilbur M.	1983
8580	Lasley, Linnie Etta	1983
6847	Lasley, William Ray	1979
10066	Lassen, Eula Mae	1986
9204	Lastarjette, Edgar Lee	1984
342	Lathrop, Kenyon C.	1913
14862	Latta, Ruth Sanford	1995
6312	Lauderdale, Evelyn H.	1977
17242	Laue, Helen Louise	1999
74/75	Lauge, Ludwig (?Lange)	1886
11176	Laun, Lillian E.	1988
8324	Laurence, Ruth L.	1982
8202	Lawhon, Robert C.	1982
15894	Lawhorn, Norma Lavinda	1997
15398	Lawless, Melba W.	1996
15804	Lawless, Roy L.	1996
6803	Lawrence, Elva A.	1978
5705	Lawrence, Ernest E.	1975
40	Lawrence, Frances J.	----
12830	Lawrence, Sue Ray Carlen	1991
7983	Lawrence, Walter R. Jr.	1981
4866	Lawrence, William J.	1972
SE00-2	Laws, Daniel Rees	2000
1612	Lawson, M. J.	1952
392	Lawthrop, Mrs, K. C.	1913
430	Layne, L. A.	----
3373	Layton, F. P.	1965
15638	Leach, Edward Curtis	1996
14596	Leach, Jim Phares	1994
18840	Leal, Fernando C.	2002
8452	Leal, Marguerite S.	1983
18164	Leal, Refugio G.	2000
9572	Leary, Anne	1985

File	Deceased	Year
14508	Leatherman, Opal Maxwell	1984
1339	Leazar, William G.	1947
15384	Le Brock, Marth W.	1996
7680	Le Cour, Lillian R.	1981
2356	Ledbetter, Cool B.	1959
11506	Ledbetter, Wilma F.	1989
11432	Lee, Alice R.	1989
19168	Lee, Allen N.	2002
2983	Lee, Bruner S.	1963
11710	Lee, Burnett	1989
14016	Lee, Charlie	1993
8313	Lee, Ethmer E.	1982
15320	Lee, Floyd E.	1995
17846	Lee, Gordon E.	2000
2921	Lee, Grace Evelyn	1963
11614	Lee, Hazel Jean	1989
16270	Lee, Jack William	1997
240	Lee, Laura	----
1640	Lee, Leo A.	1998
12750	Lee, Louis Eldon	1991
12026	Lee, Mary H.	1990
18308	Lee, Mattie Lena	2001
14874	Lee, Rachael Gresham	1995
11466	Lee, Robert E.	1989
18638	Lee, Robert Hayes	2001
7185	Lee, R. T. Sr.	1980
13286	Lee, Tressie H.	1992
5367	Lee, Verna R.	1974
18310	Lee, William Daniel	2001
5397	Leeder, Albert F. W.	1974
1059	Leeder, Gus Sr.	1940
9418	Leeder, Gustav	1985
11818	Le France, Thomas Emory	1989
11956	Legg, Ira Agnes	1990

File	Deceased	Year
2224	Lehman, Guss	1958
13930	Lehmann, Bessie Mae	1993
18076	Lehmann, Frances H.	2000
18534	Lehmann, Marijo	2001
14302	Lehne, Varinna	1994
17702	Leibold, Alice Marie Hoffman	2000
17258	Leibold, Milton Henry	1999
198	Leigh, George L.	1902
4747	Leigh, Lucy E.	1971
8220	Leigh, Virginia M.	1982
219	Leigh, W. B. et al	----
1387	Leigh, William Brewster	1948
18648	Leighton, Martha Elizabeth Horton Briggs	2001
10014	Leinweber, Bessie R.	1986
917	Leinweber, Charles	1936
2185	Leinweber, Corillo	1958
821	Leinweber, Emil	1934
6331	Leinweber, Imogene D.	1977
11476	Leinweber, Jean R.	1989
CV920027	Leinweber, Jean R.	1989
18	Leinweber, John	1870
30	Leinweber, John	1870
2960	Leinweber, John August	1963
13526	Leinweber, John T. aka John Thurston Leinweber	1992
738	Leinweber, L. A.	----
7692	Leinweber, Mildred	1981
8510	Leinweber, Ralph	1983
8614	Leinweber, Ralph E. Jr.	1983
5142	Leinweber, Treva	1973
6546	Leischel, Ruth	1978
7221	Leischel, William	1980

File	Deceased	Year
11772	Le Meilleur, Charles Raymond Sr.	1989
9069	Le Meilleur, Elsie Mae	1984
3864	Le Meilleur, Scott Jr.	1967
13144	Lemmon, Katherine D.	1992
15046	Lemmons, Bessie	----
15028	Lemmons, Marion	1995
13198	Le Moine, Thelma V.	1992
6523	Lemoine, Veal	1978
5692	Lemons, Ernst E.	1975
4079	Lemons, L. J.	1969
10714	Lemons, Marjorie Deleuw	1987
18356	Lemos, Frances Medrano	2001
6244	Lemos, Josephine	1976
6617	Lemos, Romas	1978
12108	Lenard, John H.	1990
17844	Lenhart, Coy S.	2000
6287	Le Noir, James F.	1977
14282	Le Noir, Stellamarie Mannering	1984
3463	Lenord, Ray A.	1965
1325	Lenox, Emma	1947
18574	Leonard, Carolyn	2001
16038	Leonard, Dorothy D.	1997
SE58	Leonard, Hugh R.	1981
9242	Leonard, Joseph F. Jr.	1984
2053	Leonard, Lesa	1956
18800	Lesak, Mary Gay	2001
19128	Lesikar, Albert	2002
2169	Lesley, David Franklin	1957
16396	Leslie, Fern A.	1997
6942	Leslie, Laura Belle	1979
8942	Leslie, Leland Lloyd	1984
16752	Leslie, Oscar Press aka Oscar Press Anderson	1998

File	Deceased	Year
16096	Lesser, George Franklin Jr.	1997
17576	Lesser, Helen	1999
8935	Lessiack, Robert	1984
17322	Lester, Grace Wilburn	1999
18808	Letscher, Carl E.	2001
18760	Letz, Derek	2001
8859	Letz, Hedwig I.	1984
10552	Letz, Udo	1987
12578	Levasseur, Archie James	1991
12598	Levasseur, Sibyl Penelope	1991
10276	Levensailor, Lillie Lee	1986
16720	Leverett, Homer Woodfin	1998
10390	Leverett, Topsy R.	1986
6634	Levering, Marg. Snyder	1978
8391	Levering, Willian H.	1982
1356	Levingston, Ida Alma	1948
12226	Levinton, Cecelia V.	1997
18940	Levinton, Russell S.	2002
8837	Lewis, Barbara Halstead	1984
17286	Lewis, Bill	1999
6360	Lewis, Cynthia	1977
647	Lewis, Danforth R.	1928
11962	Lewis, Edward Lee Jr.	1990
12640	Lewis, Edward Oliver	1991
3943	Lewis, Elizabeth D.	1968
11440	Lewis, Henry	1989
14314	Lewis, Iva Haught	1994
5326	Lewis, James K. Jr.	1974
5355	Lewis, James K. Jr.	1974
15340	Lewis, Jasper Dale	1995
957	Lewis, Lucinda	1937
18016	Lewis, Mabelle Louise	2000
11360	Lewis, Mary Stella	1988

File	Deceased	Year
17912	Lewis, Kelda C.	2000
14244	Lewis, Richard M.	1993
4724	Lewis, Theresa K.	1971
12450	Lewis, Virginia	1990
2561	Lewis, W. T.	1960
5623	Lewis, Wilber M.	1974
8764	Lewis, William Daniel	1983
12596	Lewis, Wilmer M.	1991
17672	Leyden, Robert F.	2000
620	Leyendecker, Alma	----
1167	Leyendecker, Emma R.	1943/44
8624	Leys, Isa	1983
11892	Leys, Victor	1989
18032	Lianza, Mary Jane Dubose	2000
9734	Liao, King Chun Edward	1985
15012	Liberti, Anthony Laurence	1995
94	Lich, Baltoser/Baltasar	1888
1882	Lich, Ernst	1955
16410	Lich, Glen Ernst	1997
16410	Lich, Thelma O.	1997
6584	Lich, Tony	1978
12996	Lich, Victor J.	1991
905	Lich, Wilhelm	1936
16516	Liddle, Ethel Roberta Shelgren	1998
6179	Liddle, Robert M. Jr.	1976
15378	Liebler, Lillian	1996
16442	Liedel, Gayle	1997
8992	Liesmann, A. O.	1984
18914	Light, Asa Calvin	2002
10222	Light, Richard Harry	1986
13874	Light, Rebecca S.	1993
18802	Lightfoot, John E. Jr.	2001

File	Deceased	Year
14470	Lightner, Helen C.	1994
13224	Lightner, Lee M.	1992
4368	Ligon, A. W.	1966
9304	Liljedahl, Edgar Lee	1984
3259	Limberger, Charles F.	1964
483	Limberger, Katrina	1921
3053	Limbert, Lewis Edward	1963
15806	Lime, Freda E.	1996
7625	Liming, Mayme H.	1981
2004	Liming, Meek H.	1956
19282	Lind, Lorean M.	2002
10368	Lindemann, Helen	1986
11228	Lindemann, Vernell	1988
14560	Lindenmeier, Mildred	1994
6909	Lindenmeier, Lee C.	1979
4559	Lindhart, Rosa K.	1971
3380	Lindhart, Walter	1965
14808	Lindhorn, Paul H.	1995
6641	Lindner, Robert M.	1978
16800	Lindsey, James C.	1998
17894	Lindsey, Roy	2000
16050	Linn, Rankin H.	1997
17692	Linn, Winnie H.	2000
6716	Linney, Eleanora B.	1978
10572	Littell, Amy Paterson Howard	1987
12990	Little, Alyeene B.	1991
10036	Little, Mary Finley	1986
2791	Little, Robert O.	1982
19394	Littlefield, Kathryn H.	2002
1000	Littlefield, P. T.	1938
14906	Littlefield, Roy	1995
17390	Littlepage, Randy Bill	1999
19178	Lively, Charles Edmond	2002
7260	Livergood, Kenneth G.	1980

File	Deceased	Year
13838	Livingood, Gerald Still	1993
11436	Livingston, Charles S.	1989
12642	Livingston, Christopher J.	1991
4459	Livingston, Edward N.	1970
18398	Livingston, H. Raymond	2001
6271	Livingston, Leona K.	1977
18806	Livingston, Luise	2001
14978	Livingston, Mildred L.	1995
18959	Livingston, Lucile T. Oglesby	2002
15942	Llines, John C.	1997
3048	Lloyd, A. J.	1963
15992	Lloyd, Leonard	1997
3932	Lloyd, Myrta	1968
6747	Loan, Dorothy B.	1978
726	Lochele, Henry L.	1930
6196	Lochte, Arthur J.	1978
17730	Lochte, Darrell G.	2000
3775	Lochte, Frederick C.	1967
5470	Lochte, Ida	1974
17868	Lochte, James W.	2000
6867	Lochte, Marguerite	1979
3267	Lochte, Pauline E.	1965
1104	Lochte, W.A.	1942
224	Lock, John	1904
228	Lock, Levi	----
6636	Lockamy, Wallace Early	1978
16484	Locke, Arthur James	1998
18952	Locke, Gladys Lorean	2002
2368	Locke, Ransom Lee	1959
282	Lockett, C. C.	1909
4441	Lockett, Joseph L.	----
8558	Lockley, Mary Grace Litsey	1983

File	Deceased	Year
111056	Lockwood, Louise F.	1988
16654	Loden, Ivy Bee	1998
12762	Loden, William Monroe	1991
4263	Lodge, Edmond	1969
14566	Loeffler, Ben E.	1994
10966	Loeffler, Bernice	1988
16510	Loesberg, Jimmie Mae	1998
6997	Loesberg, William	1979
3742	Loftus, Kathryn	1967
5284	Logan, De Alva A.	1973
8588	Lombeh, Mrs. Oskar Morrow	1983
640	Lohman, Gustave	1928
4768	Lohmann, Bernard	1972
16524	Loiselle, Raymond C.	1998
11116	Lomakan, Alexander	1988
10728	Lomax, Lola Bentley	1986
13312	London, Bobbie Lee	1992
6886	London, Evelyn R.	1979
5779	London, William F.	1975/76
10382	Long, Herbert S. Jr.	1986
18618	Long, June H.	2001
7577	Long, Noel Leon	1981
2180	Long, Ophelia F.	1957
18620	Long, Robert A.	2001
7870	Long, Winnie F.	1981
16380	Longworthy, Dorine Mary	1997
14062	Looger, Lloyd L.	1993
12950	Looger, Lillian	1991
17168	Looker, J. Lucille	1999
8351	Looker, James K.	1982
16824	Loosey, Judith K.	1998
15540	Lopez, Adolfo Ramos	1996
3006	Lopez, Camilo	1963
7157	Lopez, Gilbert G.	1979

File	Deceased	Year
17398	Lopez, Raul Jr.	1999
17290	Lopez, Raul G.	1999
9890	Lopez, Victoria Hernandez	1986
2694	Lorenz, Anna	1961
17112	Lorenz, Clara	1999
7550	Lorenz, Walter	1980
-----	Losee, Henry D.	----
10796	Lossen, Warren A.	1987
13586	Lotspeich, Thelma G.	1992
3699	Lott, Arthur	1967
4573	Lott, Emilie E.	1971
8793	Lott, Gilbert Hilmer	1983
3812	Lott, L. C.	1967
15854	Lott, Lewis J.	1996
2016	Lott, Margaret & Clark	1956
2793	Lott, William A.	1962
13072	Loubet, Gertrude W.	1992
11240	Loubet, Mac	1988
1599	Louy, F. A.	1952
9066	Love, Bessye C.	1984
5503	Love, E. B.	1974
13654	Love, Elvira	1992
18158	Love, Gewndolyn	2000
17012	Love, Robert Ernest Sr.	1998
4112	Love, W. E.	1969
2656	Loveland, Howard C.	1961
18138	Loveless, B. G.	2000
14192	Lovett, Gordon H.	1993
5279	Lovett, Sam C.	1973
356	Lowrance, Amanda	1914
1079	Lowrance, B. B.	1941
347	Lowrance, J. S.	1913
685	Lowrance, Leah Ann	1930
3965	Lowrance, Maggie	1963

File	Deceased	Year
612	Lowrance, P. O.	1926
194	Lowrance, William	1902
10026	Lowry, Donald R.	1986
4992	Lowry, Dorothy K.	1973
491	Lowry, J. M.	----
12904	Lozano, Felipe Solis	1991
12230	Luby, Donald V.	1990
12898	Luby, Mary D.	1991
15742	Luby, Mary Jeanette Carr	1996
9806	Luby, Robert Edwin	1985
11148	Lucas, Corynne, Hill	1988
2043	Lucas, Joseph B.	1956
7572	Lucas, Mattie	1981
4610	Lucas, Nell I.	1971
12546	Luckemeyer, Lawrence William	1991
14420	Ludwig, Richard Lester	1994
9904	Luglan, O. L.	1986
SE02-5	Lukasiewiez, Anna	2002
15624	Lumpkin, Isabel C.	1996
1160	Lumpkin, Oney W.	1943
5060	Luna, Lloyd	1973
15762	Luna, Rachael S.	1996
10426	Lundeen, Betty B.	1987
6836	Lundh, John	1978
1879	Lunquest, Polk	1955
18462	Lunsford, Elbert Wm.	2001
5165	Luther, George Dexter	1973
11814	Luther, Horace Norman Jr.	1989
6186	Luther, James	1976
14184	Luther, Leland	1993
5518	Luther, M. K.	1974
8924	Luther, Marjorie Eliz.	1984

162

File	Deceased	Year
8517	Luther, Nellie J.	1983
6519	Lutz, Emerson A.	1978
13054	Lux, Walter H.	1992
9163	Lyle, Minna H.	1984
6012	Lyle, Robert R.	1976
16482	Lyle, William E. Jr.	1998
3448	Lyman, Milton Thayer	1965
8113	Lynch, A. E.	1982
18222	Lynch, Jane T.	2001
12376	Lynch, John A.	1990
8790	Lynch, Marie E.	1983
9324	Lynch, Robert L.	1985
3951	Lyons, Earl G.	1968

M

File	Deceased	Year
570	Maas, Etta	1925
9326	Maatsch, Elmo O.	1985
17414	Mabry, Willie W.	1999
14386	Mac Donald, Donald A.	1994
18010	Mac Donald, Clark H.	2000
16878	Mac Donald, Josephine Bennett	1998
2962	Mac Donald, Paul C.	1963
9804	Mac Dougall, Michael	1985
4674	Macdowell, Athol (Arthur) K.	1971
13538	Macher, Henry	1992
15658	Maciver, Ewlizabeth Ann	1996
5561	Mac Kearly, Florence	1974
2479	Mac Kearly, John S.	1960
18848	Mackey, Marjorie Dorrelle	----
4453	Macklin, Wilbur C.	1970

163

File	Deceased	Year
14	Madison, James	----
15726	Madole, William H.	1996
16684	Madson, Alva Charles	1998
12682	Maebiius, Gertrude F.	1991
12566	Magarian, Martin Kriker	1991
3150	Magee, Bertha A. Wheeler	1964
18960	Magee, Ola Belle	2002
6516	Magee, Phil R.	1977/78
15370	Magee, Sam D.	1996
1228	Maginn, Hugh	1945
6507	Magoon, Fred L.	1977
10100	Mahaffey, Billy Floyd	1986
8349	Mahaffey, John Drayton	1982
5305	Mahan, Earl O.	1973/74
4281	Mahan, Pearl M.	1969
4366	Mahder, Samuel	1970
3245	Mahon, Edward Lamar Sr.	1964
8344	Maize, R. N.	1982
13778	Malcochleb, Edward Alexander	1993
5856	Mall, Tomas Albert	1975
3227	Mallett, Agnes O.	1964
5906	Mallett, Bebe	1975/76
4149	Mallett, Charles J.	1969
10826	Malone, Billy Eugene	1987
9025	Malone, Brian	1984
15622	Maloney, Earle F. Jr.	1996
18396	Maltby, Betty C.	2001
11304	Manes, O. B.	1988
12006	Mangum, Clyde Vickery	1990
18318	Mangum, Jewel M.	2001
11936	Mangum, Laura E.	1989
11154	Mangum, Shelton E.	1988
7614	Mangum, Thelma E.	1981

File	Deceased	Year
14902	Manifold, Kenneth M.	1995
5366	Manley, John D.	1973/74
11108	Manly, H. J.	1988
5091	Mann, A. A.	1973
10180	Mann, Edward C.	1986
11760	Mann, H. Dewey	1989
14882	Mann, mary Lee	1995
5573	Mann, Myrtle L.	1974
10614	Mangham, Parker G.	1987
1982	Manney, Al F.	1956
7544	Manning, Jesse Edward	1980
7182	Manning, Kenneth	1980
13098	Manning, Nannie Brooks Stafford	1992
13328	Manning, William Kenneth	1992
3472	Manny, Eugenia Myers	1966
436	Mansfield, Georgie Ann	----
13426	Mansfield, Gertrude G.	1992
325	Mansfield, J. E.	1912
12326	Mansfield, Richard Bouvier	1990
12524	Manuel, Anna Katherine	1991
12120	Manville Donald T.	1990
16370	March, Lonnie Mae	1997
5157	Marchall, Helen H.	1973
18644	Marchant, Delma Erle	2001
18642	Marchant, Gordon Maitland	2001
7638	Marcum, Raymond Earl	1981
17642	Marek, Walter E.	2000
8124	Margarian, Doris Hilyard	1982
7251	Margequy, Gladys L.	1980
16624	Maris, Gloria Darlene	1998

File	Deceased	Year
17668	Maris, Marjorie B.	2000
13914	Markam, Thomas L.	1993
18590	Markgraf, Edward O.	2001
5875	Markley, T. G.	1975/76
11888	Marks, Emory M.	1989
11126	Marks, Louise Aston	1988
SE105	Marmor, Mark William	1985
10344	Marshall, Adriean Jean	1986
16814	Marshall, Annaliese Christa	1998
12594	Marshall, Betty L.	1990
6515	Marshall, David Boyd	1978
12436	Marshall, Everett E.	1990
13130	Marshall, Everett E.	1992
7817	Marshall, James H.	1981
17474	Marshall, Joseph Earl	1999
15434	Marshall, Marie Frances	1996
8616	Marshall, Richard Leo	1983
15662	Marston, Athur Albert	1996
4224	Marten, Emelia	1969
13256	Marten, Ruth Mary	1992
19158	Martin, Ann	2002
16324	Martin, Byron Everett	1997
6283	Martin, Cleveland	1976/77
11376	Martin, Ednale	1988
6864	Martin, Emmie B.	1979
10266	Martin, Elizabeth A.	1986
8691	Martin, Etta B.	1983
13944	Martin, Faye Cameron	1993
10256	Martin, Frank D.	1986
413	Martin, Garrett	----
418	Martin, Garrett	----
419	Martin, Garrett	----
16970	Martin, Gary Howard	1998
15366	Martin, Harry C.	1996

File	Deceased	Year
12974	Martin, James Harrison	1991
4491	Martin, James L.	1970
9384	Martin, James Madison	1985
7561	Martin, John H.	1980
18018	Martin, John J.	2000
4055	Martin, Josh	1968
10264	Martin, Josh W.	1986
6405	Martin, Leila Mae	1977
19224	Martin, Lucille C.	2002
5227	Martin, Maria S.	1973
8105	Martin, Mary E.	1982
15630	Martin, Mildred L.	1996
11140	Martin, Richard Sargeant	1988
SE96-1	Martin, Robert E.	1996
14498	Martin, Robert R.	1994
4840	Martin, William G.	1972
2597	Martinez, Pablo	1960
9111	Martinko, Mike	1984
10632	Martyn, Glenn E.	1987
16002	Mason, Albert F.	1997
16216	Mason, Charles Wayne	1997
10410	Mason, E. L.	1987
6503	Mason, May Louise	1976/77
14772	Mason, Steward R.	1994
2892	Massey, Ben	1962
15632	Massey, Clyde T.	1996
14636	Massey, Fred N.	1994
17528	Massey, Fred W.	1999
10204	Massey, Harold Lee	1986
611	Massey, John	1926
14340	Massey, Katy G.	1994
6995	Massey, Louise	1979
4357	Massey, Norma	1970
11986	Massey, William Houston	1990

File	Deceased	Year
12702	Massey, Woodrow W.	1991
7578	Massie, Doc	1981
7160	Massie, Nita	1979
17488	Masters, John E.	1999
13954	Masters, Lorraine T.	1993
17020	Masterson, Ransom Eugene	1998
7267	Mate, Alexander John	1980
7624	Matejka, Franklin K.	1981
7953	Matheny, Beatrice Eva	1981
5008	Matheson, John N.	1972
9908	Mathews, Anne Bratton	1908
13898	Mathews, Bobby Lavelle	1993
5268	Mathews, Laurence Oldham Jr.	1973
18294	Mathiason, Bertha Jean	2001
1145	Mathis, A. N.	1943
1225	Mathis, Henry C.	1945
14834	Mathisen, Jack E.	1995
7401	Mathison, Carney O.	1980
5519	Mattei, Julia	1974
8788	Matter, Elmaer Clifford	1983
14844	Matter, Jesse Jordan	1995
16884	Matter, Raymond L.	1998
6877	Matteson, David Douglas	1979
11972	Matteson, Lillian Hall	1990
13912	Matthews, Charles Wilburn Sr.	1993
10952	Matthews, Choice B.	1988
6913	Matthews, Henry Andrew	1979
15690	Matthews, James H.	1996
12556	Matthews, Jane Elizabeth	1991
7372	Matthews, Katherine S.	1980
16542	Matthews, Katie S.	1998

File	Deceased	Year
3867	Matthews, Mary M.	1967
12768	Matthews, William Paul	1991
3447	Matthews, William R.	1965
4392	Matthews, Zell I.	1970
2267	Matthiesen, August	1958
16628	Mattiason, Omer S.	1998
1522	Mattingly, Benjamin J.	1951
6622	Mattingly, Mary Mason	1978
16818	Matula, Henry A.	1998
13494	Matula, Myra R.	1992
4743	Maulcahay, Eleanor F.	1971
257	Mauldin, Mrs. F. J.	----
5944	Mauldin, S. C.	1976
9672	Maurer, Alice	1985
18588	Maurer, Clemens Willie	2001
297	Maurer, Mary E.	----
14216	Mavor, Hyacinth Russell	1993
8939	Mavor, James E.	1984
14750	Maxson, Beverly Bixby	1994
15260	Maxson, Leo Jr.	1995
3202	Maxwell, Grace Martha	1964
1410	Maxwell, Jesse J.	1949
16426	Maxwell, Jimmie Ruth	1998
8286	Maxwell, Margaret	1982
18980	Maxwell, Marta Emma	2002
18378	Maxwell, Raymond Paul	2001
14492	Maxwell, Thomas James	1994
13768	May, Twillarea L.	1993
933	May, Vivian B.	1937
13176	Mays, Margaret Feser	1992
13446	Mayer, Arlene Elizabeth	1992
7263	Mayer, Clare Ellen	1980
16284	Mayer, Robert Ray	1997
15850	Mayfield, Alice Lee	1996
12488	Mayfield, Boyd Hart	1990

File	Deceased	Year
12542	Mayfield, Graydon S.	1991
5563	Mayfield, Julia	1974
6217	Mayfield, Mamie Ray	1976
6740	Mayfield, Mamie Ray	1978
19164	Mayfield, Norma Carol E.	2002
1335	Mayhugh, Emma E.	1947
1364	Mayhugh, John C.	1948
2331	Mayners, Herman	1959
14734	Mc Afee, Grace C.	1994
3799	Mc Angus, Gertrude	1967
2653	Mc Angus, Hugh	1961
19360	Mc Anally, Henrietta V.	2002
14138	Mc Anally, Raymond L.	1993
SE13	Mc Annalley, Inez	1975
14202	Mc Ashan, Elizabeth S.	1993
15584	Mc Askill, Mary L.	1996
9450	Mc Askill, W. N.	1985
14778	Mc Atter, Shirley Yeager	1994
SE80	Mc Aulay, Garland O.	1982
10708	Mc Bride, Arthur R.	1987
15454	Mc Bride, Laura Mays	1996
13502	Mc Bryde, Cleo Nowlin	1992
3889	Mc Bryde, Douglas G.	1968
1688	Mc Bryde, Ida	1953
SE44	Mc Bryde, Lorita Gibbens	1977
9502	Mc Bryde Marvin B.	1965
13148	Mc Bryde, Rankin Carol	1992
703	Mc Bryde, T. A.	1930
3520	Mc Caffety, William Howard	1966
1173	Mc Cain, Helen M.	1943
14708	Mc Cain, Wescott William Jr.	1994

File	Deceased	Year
14864	Mc Caleb, Catherine	1995
15952	Mc Caleb, Novella	1997
5752	Mc Call, Charles D.	1975
17452	Mc Call, Charles Hartman	1999
13908	Mc Call, Nina	1993
9820	Mc Candless, Theodore W.	1985
18122	Mc Cardell, Darwin E.	2000
13535	Mc Carron, Donald F. Sr.	1992
14766	Mc Carron, Reba P.	1994
18046	Mc Carty, Jacquelyn Jo Shannon	2000
10254	Mc Carty, Ollie L.	1986
4194	Mc Carty, Robert Talley	1969
666	Mc Cauley, Emmett B.	1929
15970	Mc Causland, Alfred G.	1997
2682	Mc Chesney, Ira D.	1961
15192	Mc Cillan, Leondas S.	1995
18056	Mc Clain, Anciel Lee	2000
15436	Mc Clelon, Alton Franklin Jr.	1996
19392	Mc Clellan, Mildred O.	2002
17086	Mc Clendon, Raymond T.	1999
6873	Mc Clung, C. C.	1979
8600	Mc Clure, Dorothy Wolf	1983
6380	Mc Clure, Jack Francis	1977
1110	Mc Clury, Mrs. J. S.	1942
5461	MC Comas, Thomas R.	1974
8093	Mc Connel, William H.	1982
19160	Mc Connell, Dixie	2002
13146	Mc Connell, Lloyd S.	1992
SE49	Mc Cord, L. W.	1980
16828	Mc Corkle, Manley L.	1998
2511	Mc Cormick, Alice C. R.	1960
1249	Mc Cormick, H. C.	1945

File	Deceased	Year
13580	Mc Cormick, Kenneth S.	1992
5412	Mc Coun, Lloyd C.	1974
3192	Mc Cown, Jim B.	1964
10372	Mc Coy, Edward C.	1986
9960	Mc Coy, Ethel Ellis	1986
10718	Mc Coy, Eva Mae	1987
2066	Mc Coy, George Carroll	1956
1099	Mc Coy, L. W.	1942
3597	Mc Coy, Roger	1966
15210	Mc Cray, Mildred Smith	1995
7917	Mc Crea, Ethel	1981
3185	Mc Creight, Loraine B.	1964
11740	Mc Creless, John F. Jr.	1989
11716	Mc Crorey, Jean	1989
16940	Mc Crum, Juanita Rhea	1998
14060	Mc Crum, Ruth S.	1993
2366	Mc Cullock, Frances Emily	1958
5645	Mc Cullock, Lelia B.	1974
18728	Mc Cullough, Katherine B.	2001
SE35	Mc Cullough, William Alexander	----
2618	Mc Culley, Emmett F.	1961
8207	Mc Dade, Lemuel A.	1982
9310	Mc Dade, M. W.	1984
10566	Mc Daniel, Alva	1987
13306	Mc Daniel, Cecil A.	1992
5987	Mc Daniel, Charles L.	1976
12378	Mc Daniel, Curtis Lee Sr.	1990
7204	Mc Daniel, Fred	1980
SE95-3	Mc Daniel, Hattie Mary	1995
19386	Mc Daniel, Helen M.	2002
9188	Mc Daniel, Jane Estell	1984

File	Deceased	Year
15360	Mc Daniel, Jo An Rutledge	1996
17132	Mc Daniel, Leonard	1999
14076	Mc Daniel, Sharon Sarah Elizabeth	1993
6970	Mc Daniel, William Thomas	1979
14236	Mc David, Maggie	1994
14440	Mc David, Nora A.	1994
2481	Mc Donald, B. O.	1960
16488	Mc Donald, Bernette P.	1998
13030	Mc Donald, Charlie Richard	1991
12266	Mc Donald, Clovis Dalton	1990
12354	Mc Donald, Clovis W.	1990
2829	Mc Donald, Elbert M.	1962
1655	Mc Donald, I. G.	1952
1038	Mc Donald, J. E.	1940
16994	Mc Donald, Jimmie Lee	1998
17298	Mc Donald, Johnnie Ola	1999
13070	Mc Donald, Lester Willard	1992
8911	Mc Donald, Mabel Inez	1984
6214	Mc Donald, Richard T.	1974
9650	Mc Donlad, Samuel Robert	1985
271	Mc Donald, W. A.	1908?
2270	Mc Donald, W. E.	1958
7220	Mc Dougal, Bertha M.	1980
4204	Mc Dougall, Myrtle	1969
18270	Mc Dougall, Nina Faye	2001
11288	Mc Dougall, Stanford A.	1988
13542	Mc Duff, Martha Agnes	1992
4058	Mc Eachern, Don J.	1968

File	Deceased	Year
2874	Mc Elrath, George D.	1962
2450	Mc Elroy, George	1958
6548	Mc Elroy, Grace	1978
680	Mc Elroy, Joseph L.	1929/30
200	Mc Elroy, Kate & J. L.	1901
991	Mc Elroy, S. G.	1938
17038	Mc Ewen, Pearl	1998
55	Mc Fadin, Alfred	----
366	Mc Farland, Louise	1912
5963	Mc Garry, Henry S.	1976
91	Mc Gaughey, G. W.	----
14086	Mc Gehee, Charles D.	1993
15296	Mc Gehee, Frank Owen Sr.	1995
14456	Mc Gehee, James Everett	1994
5916	Mc Ghee, Evelyn Thomas	1975
17990	Mc Gill, Edward Everett	2000
19338	Mc Gill, Jeanne Marie	2002
18836	Mc Ginnis, Anna Marie	2002
11266	Mc Ginnis, Atha Fellmy	1988
7939	Mc Ginnis, Charles Edward	1981
6635	Mc Govern, Mildred	1978
4739	Mc Greevy, Charles H.	1971
SE12262	Mc Greevy, Marjorie Anna	1990
16780	Mc Grew, Albert D.	1998
11734	Mc Grew, Martha Ann	1989
SE01-6	Mc Guff, William Arthur Jr.	2001
15332	Mc Guffin, Jack L.	1995
15318	Mc Guffin, Katherine O.	1995
3875	Mc Henry, W. H.	1967
13208	Mc Hugh, Artie Mae	1992
5594	Mc Hugh, J. E.	1974
2847	Mc Ilmoyl, Edith M.	1962

File	Deceased	Year
4853	Mc Ilmoyl, Harry W.	1972
5019	Mc Ilmoyl, Lillian Loyd	1973
17486	Mc Ilveen, Thomas Albert Jr.	1998
2399	Mc Jimsey, A.	1955
5204	Mc Jimsey, Laura W.	1973
7110	Mc Kay, Ira	1979
5410	Mc Kay, J. R.	1974
5463	Mc Kean, Pearl E	1974
16042	Mc Kee, Charlie F.	1997
6232	Mc Kee, Charlton W.	1977
14116	Mc Kee, Fannie Jean	1993
9508	Mc Kee, Hartwell F.	1985
17038	Mc Kee, Vera K.	1998
7009	Mc Kellip, A. W.	1930
37	Mc Kie, W. M.	----
9974	Mc Killop, James M.	1986
590	Mc Killys, Kate	----
3387	Mc Kim, Clar Smith	1965
8519	Mc Kinney, F. L.	1983
11462	Mc Kinney, Margaret Louise	1989
18358	Mc Kinnis, Fayne Albert	2001
10736	Mc Kinnon, Alieda	1987
16690	Mc Knight, Daniel	1998
16692	Mc Knight, Eleanor N.	1998
12672	Mc Knight, Eloise Roe	1997
11094	Mc Knight, James Oliver	1988
6325	Mc Knight, Margaret M.	1976
7807	Mc Kune, William James	1981
3997	Mc Lane, Sam Brooks	1968
18052	Mc Laughlin, Annie L.	2000
12470	Mc Lean, Ada C.	1990
8675	Mc Lellan, Laura Muir	1983
16646	Mc Lemore, Ernest J. M.	1998

175

File	Deceased	Year
1142	Mc Leod, Dwight	1943
1697	Mc Leod, Louise	1953
12872	Mc Loughlin, Dorothea Elaine	1991
2474	Mc Loughlin, George W.	1960
7828	Mc Loughlin, Myrtle	1981
17862	Mc Loughlin, Thomas R.	2000
6846	Mc Mahon, Ernest Graham	1979
868	Mc Mahon, Jim	1935
760	Mc Mahon, John Edward	1932
12610	Mc Mahon, Maureen Shockley	1991
14264	Mc Mahon, William D.	1994
1324	Mc Manes, Estella Maude	1944
4475	Mc Manimie, Margery Willard	1969
2631	Mc Manimie, Vera	1961
1542	Mc Manus, Alma E.	1951
15062	Mc Michael, Jack Brame	1995
6628	Mc Millan, Ernest Lewis	1978
12270	Mc Millan, Irene M.	1990
6898	Mc Millan, Jack A. Sr.	1979
4278	Mc Millan, Jewel	1969
6910	Mc Millan, Neil G.	1979
6897	Mc Millan, Odell Salomon	1979
7859	Mc Millan, Velma	1981
42	Mc Minn, Sarah	1882
8	Mc Minn, Robert	1869
2802	Mc Mullen, James G.	1962
10916	Mc Murray, Crawford Andes	1987
16664	Mc Murray, Edna Mae/May Thomas	1998
8212	Mc Murray, Lillie M.	1982

File	Deceased	Year
4630	Mc Murry, George J.	1971
6922	Mc Murtrey, Asa Evans	1979
10710	Mc Nabb, J. W.	1987
17924	Mc Nally, Robert E.	2000
12062	Mc Nay, Drexell Caraway	1990
18518	Mc Nay, Edna H.	2001
11616	Mc Nay, William H.	1989
572	Mc Neal, Cordelia	----
925	Mc Nealy, Jessie O.	1937
1698	Mc Nealy, Jesse Orville	1953
1209	Mc Nealy, Mary E.	1944
6980	Mc Neely, John F.	1979
585	Mc Nees, David Franklin	1925
1205	Mc Nees, Sarah F.	1941
1208	Mc Nees, Sarah F.	1941
4365	Mc Neil, Jobe	----
11706	Mc Nutt, William F.	1989
16678	Mc Phail, Joe L.	1998
7789	Mc Pherson, Estelle Wilkes	1981
4102	Mc Pherson, Floyd	1969
3090	Mc Pherson, H. A.	1964
14166	Mc Pherson, Harold	1993
10002	Mc Pherson, Omega M.	1986
15982	Mc Phillips, John James Sr.	1997
18814	Mc Quinn, Helen Ruane	2001
357	Mc Rae, Minnie	1914
3565	Mc Reynolds, Leila E.	1967
5385	Mc Shan, Berta Lee	1974
7059	Mc Shan, C. Hunter	1979
8353	Mc Shane, John V.	1982
15698	Mc Wha, Robert Edward Sr.	1996
525	Mc Williams, Florence	1923

File	Deceased	Year
18794	Meacham, Lucille	2001
15358	Mead, Charle J.	1996
17130	Meadors, Dorothy F.	1989
4381	Meadow, Essie Horn	1970
15114	Meadow, Keith S.	1995
2252	Meadow, William W.	1958
10080	Meadow, Wilma Maxine	1986
18820	Meadows, Glenn Olin Jr.	2002
18284	Meadows, Martha Brown	2001
11960	Meares, Fern Marvin	1990
15814	Mears, Paula B.	1996
9074	Mecom, Lois Chamber	1984
13284	Mecom, William H.	1992
14094	Medearis, Jewell R.	1993
8959	Medina, Ruben	1984
16104	Medlin, James Hall	1997
8420	Medlin, Myretta	1983
14082	Mefford, Milton O.	1993
6983	Meehan, Dorothy (Dora)	1979
3494	Meehan, Hiram A.	1966
71	Meehan, John	----
18998	Meehan, Mildred S.	2002
17526	Meek, Carl D.	1999
12084	Meek, Cleo A.	1990
15240	Meek, Clyde Hortense	1995
9990	Meeker, Burton C.	1986
2376	Meeker, Ernest Wade	1958
14492	Meeker, Franklin Wade	1994
4671	Meeker, Hallie Frances	1971
4424	Meier, Freda C.	1970
7836	Meighen, Jay M.	1981
10856	Meighen, Melva Pauline	1987
1396	Meikel, Della Rucks	1948
3289	Meikle, Edward	1965
13066	Meinecke, Ida Jewel	1992

File	Deceased	Year
3877	Meitzen, Anita B.	1967
3064	Meitzen, R. W.	1963
15502	Melberg, Robert Lee	1996
10946	Melberg, Sally Larson	1988
4270	Melear, Francis Emmett	1969
9762	Mellott, Grace E.	1985
741	Melton, C.B. & Alice	----
17674	Melton, Mary Jane Turner	1999
18874	Menchaca, Lily Chacon	2002
662	Menendez, Joe	----
17076	Mengel, John H.	1999
16094	Menke, Clifford C.	1997
12850	Menn, Hugo F.	1991
16390	Merchant, Mary Cleo	1997
4406	Meredith, Clara B.	1970
5407	Meredith, J. A.	1974
5493	Meredith, Katie G.	1974
2605	Meredith, Roderick Allan	1961
16222	Merrel, Harold Alton	1997
13622	Merrell, Velna Spence	1992
6916	Merrell, Vergil	1979
15898	Merrill, Charmaine Mary	1997
388	Merritt, A. D.	----
1775	Merritt, B. Foster	1954
6352	Merritt, Eva	1977
10636	Merritt, King	1987
344	Merritt, Kirzzire	----
1250	Merritt, Lizzie	1945
12748	Merritt, Nell Moore	1991
1445	Merritt, Robert R.	1949
1217	Merritt, Viola K.	1944
16210	Merritt, William H.	1997
6256	Mertz, Edwin	1977

179

File	Deceased	Year
19162	Mertz, Floyd Elsworth	2002
919	Mertz, Minea	1937
908	Mertz, Theodore	1936
12172	Messer, Perle R.	1990
12530	Messerili, Mayme Letha	1991
SE10340	Messerli, Louis R.	----
1161	Metcalf, Edna	1943
SE62	Metcalf, Orena	1982
7953	Metheny, Beatrice Eva	1981
9958	Methvin, Percy C.	1986
13114	Metzger, Russell E.	1992
3525	Meyer, Anna Marie	1966
5418	Meyer, Arnold	1974
2640	Meyer, Arthur E.	1961
4650	Meyer, Fred Anthony	1971
3587	Meyer, Julius C.	1966
4507	Meyer, Pauline	1970
4223	Meyer, Robert Werner	1969
1742	Meyer, Walter	1953
9192	Meyers, Boyd L.	1984
10458	Meyers, Cornelius Robertson	1987
18226	Meyers, Gladyne J.	2001
13296	Meyers, Jacqueline A.	1992
10522	Meyers, Robert Earl	1987
14966	Meyners, Wilma Janice Tiemann	1995
10970	Michalak, Charlotte	1988
10386	Michelson, Elliot Leonard	1986
17082	Michon, August Domingues	1999
92	Michon, A. Francoise	1886
11162	Michon, Ella Marie	1988
777	Michon, F. J.	1932

File	Deceased	Year
259	Michon, John	----
53	Michon, L.	----
6481	Michon, Lucy Smith	1976/77
3371	Michon, Regina Heimann	1965
5824	Mickel, Roland	1974/75
14324	Mickelsen, Hazel Leticia Carpenter	1994
6860	Mickelsen, William Frands	1979
8651	Mickle, Raymond M.	1983
17720	Mickle, Rosalyn P.	2000
14462	Mickna, Eva A.	1994
5038	Mickna, Leo P.	1972
SE94	Middlebrook, John	1982
15904	Middleton, Betty Joe	1997
1632	Middleton, George M.	1952
11480	Middleton, Helen Eliz.	1989
2088	Middleton, Isabel P.	1957
6955	Middleton, William Robert Sr.	1979
8184	Midkiff, Hattie Mae	1982
15230	Midkiff, Margaret Jo	1995
9456	Midkiff, T. O. Jr.	1985
13876	Miears, Edna J.	1993
14038	Miears, Jerry Jean	1993
15612	Miears, William Thomas (W. T.)	1996
1272	Miers, C. Hale	1946
1789	Miers, George H.	1954
17852	Miers, Mary	2000
13588	Miers, William T.	1992
3773	Mika, John J.	1967
18072	Mikeska, Jeannine	2000
4359	Milars, L. T.	1970

File	Deceased	Year
16086	Miles, Elizabeth Payseur Tait	1997
4076	Miles, Frank Harry	1969
2388	Miles, Margaret	1959
8435	Milholland, Jay Guy	1983
6885	Milhous, Ivan C.	1979
10480	Millard, James Nolan	1987
18522	Millard, Ronald G.	2001
3224	Miller, A. B. Sr.	1964
14040	Miller, Alvin Berthold Jr.	1993
13372	Miller, Anette Belinda	1992
18042	Miller, Ann	2000
8977	Miller, Anna G.	1984
10962	Miller, Annie Lee	1988
14312	Miller, Antoinette	1994
4262	Miller, Arthur B.	1969
2873	Miller, Barbara	1962
15750	Miller, Benjamin Peter	1996
19398	Miller, Beverly Jean Pickens	2002
11690	Miller, Dorothy F.	1989
1359	Miller, Edgar M.	1948
14684	Miller, Edmund W.	1994
13004	Miller, Elizabeth Karger	1991
SE97-6	Miller, Eric Paul	1997
18416	Miller, Evelyn F.	2001
5384	Miller, Evelyn K.	1974
5408	Miller, Forrest B.	1974
15514	Miller, Fred	1996
16264	Miller, Fred L.	1997
1884	Miller, Frona Ellen	1955
4213	Miller, George B.	1969
16834	Miller, George M. Jr.	1998

File	Deceased	Year
16992	Miller, George Martin	1998
18028	Miller, Harry	2000
603	Miller, Henry	1925
14976	Miller, Howell L.	1995
18458	Miller, James Harold	2001
19032	Miller, Joe Davis	2002
10208	Miller, John Robert	1986
6013	Miller, Julia S.	1976
14892	Miller, Leon O. Jr.	1995
7758	Miller, Leroy Robert	1981
16582	Miller, Marie V.	1998
14268	Miller, Marilyn Adele	1993
18140	Miller, Mary Kent	2000
15582	Miller, Mary Lee	1996
4762	Miller, Mary Mann	1971
6249	Miller, Mollie G.	1977
2254	Miller, Nelson Arthur	1958
16080	Miller, Oliver E.	1997
14222	Miller, Ollene S.	1993
3147	Miller, Otto	1964
2301	Miller, Otto D.	1958
15096	Miller, Paul H.	1995
10778	Miller, Pearle H.	1987
2135	Miller, R.	1957
13500	Miller, Retah Harl	1992
1606	Miller, Robert S.	1952
7001	Miller, Ruby H.	1979
18468	Miller, Ruth Marilyn	2001
9848	Miller, Ruth Murphy	1986
17386	Miller, Sudi G. aka Susannah G.	1999
3738	Miller, Susie Elizabeth	1967
10922	Miller, Thaddeus	1987
1569	Miller, W. W.	1951
3860	Miller, W. W. Jr.	1967

File	Deceased	Year
9136	Miller, Wallace V.	1984
9136	Miller, Wallace V.	1984
2790	Miller, William J.	1993
13942	Milligan, Clark C.	1993
17592	Mills, A. Lynn	1999
13124	Mills, Christine	1992
9900	Mills, Doris	1986
10642	Mills, Edward J.	1987
2721	Mills, Eula Slaughter	1961
2507	Mills, James Henry	1961
15368	Mills, Ora	1996
6206	Mills, Thomas Estyl	1976
10996	Milner, Luella Egg	1988
5340	Milner, Milo Allan	1974
3439	Milthaler, Royce	1998
26546	Milton, Robert W.	1998
15858	Miman, Otis F.	1996
7373	Mince, Oscar T.	1980
17744	Mincy, Dollie Ruth	2000
10626	Minnick, Homer H.	1987
1150	Minsch, Walter A.	1943
10166	Mireider, Joszef	1986
6146	Mitchell, Berger P.	1976
5327	Mitchell, Oma	1973/74
4625	Mitchell, Grace I.	1971
12388	Mitchell, Ronald Dean	1990
15966	Mittanckm Herbert Guss	1997
10934	Mittanck, Ollie S.	1988
11672	Mixon, Oleda E.	1989
3007	Mize, Austin	1963
4804	Mock, Oliver L.	1972
13352	Modesitt, Robert Fellows	1992
5939	Moeller, Ambrose J.	1976

File	Deceased	Year
12602	Moeller, Mary Virginia Jett	1991
17596	Moeller, William Richard	1999
12884	Moffett, Alice Catherine	1991
7755	Moffett, Eleanor B.	1981
12838	Moffett, Elzo	1991
13826	Moffett, Helen H.	1993
11382	Moffett, Thomas A.	1988
471	Mogford, E. A.	1920
8516	Mogford, E. A.	1983
11414	Mogg, Herschel Lee	1988
416	Mohrhoff, George	----
13850	Molder, L. W.	1993
7268	Molene, Robert E.	1980
5902	Molrgan, May Lines	1975/76
8042	Molina, Mary D.	1982
8847	Molter, Charles H.	1984
10500	Molter, Ellie B.	1987
11306	Molter, Jimmie Ray	1988
13414	Monkhouse, Charles H.	1992
13698	Monkhouse, Eunice	1993
12112	Monroe, Dorothy Anita	1990
10374	Monroe, George R.	1986
3030	Monroe, Myrick	1963
3562	Monrow, S. W.	1966
19218	Monroy, Salvador	2002
132	Montalengo, E.	----
4314	Montel, Alice	1970
4118	Montel, R. M.	1969
9490	Montgomery, David P.	1985
10050	Montgomery, Elynor Hatheway	1986
787	Montgomery, Etta B.	1933

File	Deceased	Year
7705	Montgomery, Garnet L.	1981
SE89	Montgomery, James Wesley	1982
6771	Montgomery, L. Wilma	1978
4493	Montgomery, Lee W.	1970
19192	Montgomery, M. H.	2002
10594	Montgomery, Mabel Wade	1987
16294	Montgomery, Ned A.	1997
6881	Montgomery, Paul B.	1979
13128	Montgomery, Thomas Ed	1992
909	Montgomery, Vernon W.	1936
14300	Montgomery, Violet Ardell	1994
11090	Moody, Clifford Burnett	1988
13180	Moody, Dorothy M.	1992
18184	Moody, Dov Alfred	2000
5031	Moody, Leslie W.	1972
17352	Moon, Edward Dean	1999
17350	Moon, Mary Alice	1999
10098	Mooney, Albert W.	1986
7586	Mooney, Arthur B.	1981
715	Mooney, Minnie Jones	----
16310	Moore, A. C.	1997
427	Moore, A. S.	----
1474	Moore, Andrew Franklin	1950
5452	Moore, Anna A. M. B.	1974
12644	Moore, Arch Douglas	1991
4318	Moore, Augusta	1970
14996	Moore, Beatrice Hilburn	1995
4294	Moore, Boyd	1969
19120	Moore, Carole	2002
6768	Moore, Clare A.	1978
296	Moore, D.	----
SE25	Moore, Davis S.	----
12168	Moore, Dewey L.	1990

File	Deceased	Year
7178	Moore, Dora Atwood	
	Latham	1980
15058	Moore, Ellen	1995
12788	Moore, Elizabeth M.	1991
2309	Moore, Elsie G.	1958
3621	Moore, Eugenia I.	1966
280	Moore, F. M.	----
5452	Moore, Frank	1974
2756	Moore, George E. (Ed)	1962
18832	Moore, George Henry	2002
8052	Moore, Gladys E.	1982
9614	Moore, Harry Leonard	1985
-----	Moore, Henry	1860
273	Moore, J. F.	----
12660	Moore, J. I.	1991
18276	Moore, Jack Wilmot	2001
3917	Moore, James F.	1968
3255	Moore, Jennie	1964
9145	Moore, Jennie Ann	1984
2805	Moore, Jennings Tolbert	1962
5055	Moore, John Alder	1973
13784	Moore, Kenneth R.	1993
6349	Moore, Leone A.	1977
2055	Moore, Lillie Mae	1956
89	Moore, M. F.	1886
5146	Moore, Margaret R. E.	1973
1114	Moore, Mary	1942
6200	Moore, Mary R.	1976
18992	Moore, Maryon Starkey	2002
481	Moore, Mittie	----
927	Moore, Mrs. M. A.	1937
7294	Moore, Nell Ross	1980
1090	Moore, O. Mc Leod	1940/41
1820	Moore, Samuel F.	1954
16726	Moore, T. Jasper	1998

File	Deceased	Year
14110	Moore, Thomas E.	1993
4040	Moore, Tom J.	1968
7749	Moore, Violet L.	1981
9230	Moore, Virginia Chaney	1984
14888	Moore, Waldon E.	1995
11880	Moore, Walter C.	1989
13264	Moore, Walter H.	1982
33	Moore, Wesley	----
12976	Moore, William C.	1991
377	Moore, William J.	----
1029	Mooring, Cora L.	1939
18110	Moorman, Taylor Worley	2000
93	Moose, A. J.	----
10310	Moose, Minnie Mae	1986
7935	Moran, Joseph John	1981
865	Morales, Guillermo	1935
9762	Morales, Ronald C.	1985
11024	Moran, Alton	1988
11950	Moreau, David	1990
9970	Moreau, Ed	1986
10224	Morehead, Dorothy S.	1986
9022	Moreland, Robert Clell	1984
17212	Moreno, Francisca F.	1999
10436	Moreno, Francisco E.	1987
12814	Moreno, Guadalupe F.	1991
792	Moreno, Maria G.	1933
2146	Morgan, Agnes	1957
14784	Morgan, Agnes	1994
2343	Morgan, Bessie L.	1959
12280	Morgan, Carolyn E.	1990
4272	Morgan, Corrine O.	1969
757	Morgan, D.	1932
9530	Morgan, Edward O.	1985
4335	Morgan, Elmer A.	1970
17470	Morgan, Elvie Louise	1999

File	Deceased	Year
10758	Morgan, Gladys Daniel	1987
4057	Morgan, Howard Pinker	1968
9352	Morgan, Lester R.	1985
2725	Morgan, Mack	1961
12096	Morgan, Mark C.	1990
13142	Morgan, Morris G.	1992
13042	Morgan, William Edward	1991
14758	Morgart, Lela M.	1994
17284	Moriarty, Francis	1999
12124	Moritz, Lawrence J.	1990
17226	Morlett, Opal W.	1999
19306	Morris, Annie L. C.	2002
11975	Morris, Bobby Neal	1990
1869	Morris, C. E.	1954
797	Morris, C. M.	1933
11990	Morris, Christine Thomas	1990
13894	Morris, Clifford V.	1993
13642	Morris, Dorothy Eileen	1992
16298	Morris, Earl Elroy	1997
SE13968	Morris, Edward	1993
4522	Morris, Ethel M.	1970
5074	Morris, Everett E.	1973
18764	Morris, Floyd Marshall	2001
582	Morris, George	1925
6385	Morris, James Emmett	1977
6632	Morris, Jewett T.	1978
9256	Morris, Joseph Magee	1984
18778	Morris, Lois Jean Fine	2001
425	Morris, Mary Ann	----
653	Morris, Robert L.	----
15754	Morris, Roy E.	1996
10782	Morris, Russell Winters	1987
6402	Morris, Ruby Curry	1977
4693	Morris, Sam J.	1971

189

File	Deceased	Year
9548	Morris, William Elbert	1985
10684	Morrison, Beatrice	1987
11194	Morrison, Elmo W.	1988
7457	Morrison, Imogene Merritt	1980
SE37	Morrison, John Ray	1980
15354	Morriss, Edward L.	1996
5499	Morriss, Ferrol R.	1974
3226	Morriss, Hada	1964
8915	Morriss, Loma Snodgrass	1984
2882	Morriss, Robert H. A. Jr.	1962
4961	Morrow, George Ike	1972
3206	Morrow, George L.	1964
9750	Morrow, George W.	1985
16186	Morrow, Gerald Lamar	1997
12882	Morrow, James Albert	1991
3514	Morrow, Joe H.	1966
2452	Morrow, L. A.	1959
9512	Morrow, Mildred L.	1985
15478	Morse, Anne C.	1996
11686	Morse, Robert Allen	1989
18426	Morton, Lawrence Delbert	2001
16552	Morua-Pina, Jose Reyes	1998
12956	Mosby, Willie D.	1991
12744	Mosby, Willie M.	1991
6219	Mosel, Alvin Henry	1977
7058	Mosel, Edna E.	1979
7533	Mosel, Emma Louise	1980
3012	Mosel, H. Ben	1963
8257	Mosel, H. Ben	1982
1534	Mosel, Herman	1951
14316	Mosel, Hertha Elfreda Carpenter	1994

File	Deceased	Year
11404	Mosel, Johnnie L.	1988
5221	Mosel, Lois	1973
2467	Moseley, B. E.	1960
4472	Moseley, Effie Myrtle	1970
SE01-5	Moseley, Marvin Laurence	2001
11568	Moses, Andrea S.	1989
12954	Moses, Marlowe G.	1991
15298	Moses, Ruby	1995
3996	Mosley, Jesse L.	1968
1134	Mosou, Lee	1943
14694	Moss, Anita M.	1994
9822	Mossbarger, Christine Chaney	1985
3449	Moston, Harry L.	1965
17812	Mosty, Agnes Cecilia Straluch	2000
14550	Mosty, Charles H.	1994
1307	Mosty, Elizabeth	1946
18150	Mosty, Esther D.	2000
12268	Mosty, Evlyn	1990
2280	Mosty, Harvey	1958
3143	Mosty, Julia I.	1964
14444	Mosty, Julia W.	1994
3257	Mosty, Karl	1964
3109	Mosty, Lee	1964
1308	Mosty, Lee A.	1946
2434	Mosty, Margaret Lee	1959
12756	Mosty, Mark	1991
14246	Mosty, Raymond F.	1994
18984	Mosty, Robert Lee	2002
SE42	Moten, Mary	----
18570	Motheral, Vera E.	2001
11632	Motherspaw, Jack Martin Sr.	1989

File	Deceased	Year
7148	Motley, Crystal Pearl	1979
16858	Motley, Delmer Harvey	1998
11562	Motley, Lenore	1989
13606	Motteram, Helen M.	1992
16012	Moulton, Willetta Stringfellow	1997
9037	Mounger, Mary M.	1984
15112	Mouton, Albert J.	1995
17376	Moyer, Mary Margaret	1999
9091	Moyers, Delbert O. Sr.	1984
17555	Much, Elsie K.	2000
13920	Muck, George J.	1993
7763	Muck, Mary	1981
10156	Mueller, Dorothy L.	1986
13952	Mueller, Ernest W.	1993
18026	Muenker, Annie Gertrude	2000
7108	Mugge, ohn Wofford	1979
4742	Mulcahay, John McMurray	1971
6272	Mulett, Minnie	1977
396	Mull, Christina	1916
3657	Mull, Wyle	1966
88914	Muller, Ernest D.	1984
6052	Mullin, Maud M.	1976
1920	Mullin, Peter J.	1955
1660	Mullinax, P. H.	1952
3660	Mullins, M. H.	1966
9015	Mullins, Marion Mayrine	1984
3707	Munhall, Alfred N.	1967
6330	Munhall, Mabel McKneely	1977
448	Muniz, Felipe	----
11412	Munk, Rex E.	1988
12980	Munzel, Elrane V.	1991
13636	Murcott, Arthur M.	1992
16916	Murcott, Elizabeth Marie	1999

File	Deceased	Year
1639	Murdock, A. E.	1952
16958	Murdock, Patricia Jane	1998
6741	Murff, Carroll E. III	1978
-----	Murff, Daniel (Murphy)	1856
14450	Murphy, Elizabeth Ann Murray	1994
5048	Murphy, Ella A.	1973
12798	Murphy, George Byrne Jr.	1991
3939	Murphy, Guy H.	1968
16060	Murphy, John L.	1997
19012	Murphy, Mindy W.	2002
1754	Murphy, William Sr.	1953
10406	Murphy, William T. A. Jr.	1987
13254	Murnane, William Joseph	1992
8083	Murray, Florence V.	1982
2642	Murray, John M.	1961
6430	Murray, John Roberts	1977
12740	Murray, Katie Lou	1991
12730	Murray, Margaret Lou	1991
765	Murray, Patrick J.	1932
9244	Murray, Thomas H.	1984
6084	Murray, Winkie	1976
18048	Muse, Louise	2000
SE3	Muse, Richard Howard	1965
18988	Muse, Violet	2002
8967	Musso, Frederick G.	1984
3721	Mustain, Tommie Denson	1967
6045	Mutzig, Lorenz P.	1976
SE95-5	Myatt, John Michael	1995
15302	Myatt, John Michael	1995
CV960062	Myatt, John Michael	1995
5864	Myer, Willard J.	1975
16066	Myers, Carl R.	1997
18882	Myers, Richard Randy	2002

File	Deceased	Year
17248	Myers, Wanda L.	1999
15940	Myers, Warren W.	1997
6735	Myran, Leslie D.	1978

N

6715	Nabers, Nell Whitewood	1978
1509	Nabours, Cranfiel LeRoy	1947
2523	Nagle, Albert J.	1960
967	Nagel, Elizabeth	1938
19354	Nagle, Frances Y.	2002
19548	Nagle, Frank	2002
19040	Nall, Walter Forrest	2002
10740	Nance, Archer Lebus	1987
14358	Nance, Bennett A.	1994
544	Nance, Gypsie	1926
3711	Nance, Lucy Ann	1967
11778	Napoleon, David Wayne	1989
14442	Naredo, Mary Woolverton	1994
16794	Narramore, Eulali Roundten	1995
5575	Nash, A. L.	1974
960	Nation, Homer	1937/38
10772	Naul, Merle Jane	1987
13666	Nauman, Hazel Mae	1992
!5268	Naumann, Carol Alice	1995
15266	Naumann, John William	1995
15270	Naumann, Tiffany Marie	1995
13032	Nawrocki, Emmy Oelze	1992
7768	Nawrocki, John J.	1981
5549	Naylor, Howard M.	1974
19348	Neal, Arvella Viola	2002
2531	Neal, Frances	1960
11408	Neal, Frank Earl	1988

File	Deceased	Year
8560	Neal, John E.	1983
109	Neal, J. J.	----
17730	Neal, Marvin R.	1999
14270	Neal, Merrill Francis	1994
4383	Neal, Robert Lee	1970
4764	Neal, Thomas Albert	1972
440	Neale, Emma	----
9162	Needham, Doris Romiae	1984
11624	Needham, Harold L.	1989
12056	Needham, Henrietta A.	1990
12266	Neeley, Elsie M.	1990
18826	Neeley, Madeline F.	2002
9694	Neely, Jean H.	1985
10918	Neely, Otis K.	1987
2860	Nees, Ruth Johnson	1962
10244	Neff, Annette Lummis	1986
9936	Nehs, Elizabeth Jane Monger	1986
2698	Neill, Alexander Leonard	1961
15346	Neill, James C. Jr.	1995
1717	Neill, Marjorie Virginia	1952
SE68	Nelezen, Arnold Martin	1982
18528	Nelms, Avie Marye Elkins	2001
8798	Nelms, Elizabeth W.	1983
14538	Nelms, Lucian W.	1994
16412	Nelms, Thomas Paisley Sr.	1997
16046	Nelson, Ada	1997
401	Nelson, Allen	1915?
4360	Nelson, Ben	1970
SE22	Nelson, Chester B.	----
511	Nelson, Christine	1973

File	Deceased	Year
12016	Nelson, Dorothy G.	1990
7905	Nelson, Earl W.	1981
1645	Nelson, Frank C.	1952
18872	Nelson, Glenn Roy	2002
4417	Nelson, Grace K.	1970
504	Nelson, H. L.	1922
1540	Nelson, Hanny B.	----
5	Nelson, Hiram	1862
15882	Nelson, Irene A.	1996
17070	Nelson, Joyce Eileen	1999
15404	Nelson, Kenneth Howard	1996
12224	Nelson, Lawrence Mc Kee	1990
11542	Nelson, Leona	1989
8098	Nelson, Lloyd R.	1982
16434	Nelson, Margaret L.	1998
6377	Nelson, Nels Christian	1977
12294	Nelson, Ray Alton	1990
12480	Nelson, Robert Frederick	1990
2634	Nelson, Willis W.	1961
3682	Nesbitt, Frank W. III	1967
	Nestler, Lillie Littia	1976
6182	Neslter, Mabelle McElvain Miller	1983
2363	Nettles, Gussie M.	1959
14686	Neuman, Otis Glen	1994
7747	Neumann, Mamie E.	1981
8308	Neunhoffer, Albert	1982
14942	Neunhoffer, Geneva K.	1995
1203	Neunhoffer, Hilda	1944
13310	Neunhoffer, Julius R.	1992
6185	Neunhoffer, Oscar	1976
211	Neunhoffer, William	1904
2476	Neuschafer, Clara	1960
2279	Neuschafer, George	1958

File	Deceased	Year
15232	New, Walter	1995
6779	Newbury, Olive Clinton	1978
7440	Newcomer, J. M.	1980
11200	Newcomer, Winnie M.	1988
13302	Newell, Horace Mead	1992
13028	Newell, Olive Longstreet	1991
11316	Newlon, Dorothy Grace Berry	1988
10820	Newlon, Lawrene Dale	1987
12340	Newman, Karen Clark Cole	1990
18362	Newsom, William Taylor	2001
1097	Newton, Mary	1941
5649	Newton, Mary A.	1975
9196	Newton, Oliver H. III	1984
11334	Nibert, Benjamin Everett	1988
11666	Nibert, Geneva Urban	1989
4952	Nickel, Allison M.	1972
10562	Nicholaisen, Andreas	1987
SE102	Nicholas, Elbert Arvin	1985
6381	Nicholl, Edwin Robert	1977
9682	Nichols, Alford L.	1985
1778	Nichols, Amie W.	1954
18100	Nichols, Billie G.	2000
4688	Nichols, Clara B.	1971
4315	Nichols, E. H.	1970
9498	Nichols, Elizabeth V.	1985
712	Nichols, Eva	1930
9236	Nichols, Howard O.	1984
13572	Nichols, Irene S.	1992
8653	Nichols, Johnnie Lynn	1983
7105	Nichols, Leota Peters	1979
4694	Nichols, Mary Elizabeth	1971

File	Deceased	Year
11508	Nichols, Paul R.	1989
1976	Nichols, R. V.	1955
13592	Nichols, Ralph A.	1992
3352	Nichols, Robert Roy	1965
1	Nichols, Roland (William Roland)	1859
6011	Nichols, Wesley Frederick	1976
7333	Nichols, William Losson	1980
4998	Nicholson, Larry E.	1973
5000	Nicholson, Evander M.	1973?
8039	Niederhiser, Floyd E.	1982
10670	Niederhiser, Lizetta	1987
16966	Niedermann, Rosemary L.	1998
2498	Niedles, Albert J.	1960
3470	Niehaus, Henry J.	1966
11052	Nielsen, Estella Ingeborg	1988
4904	Nielsen, Thorvald Veldermar Sr.	1975
5772	Nielsen, Thorvald Valdermer Jr.	1975
3217	Nielson, Estella E.	1964
11112	Nielson, Jamie Ruth	1988
14586	Nier, Marie C.	1994
9592	Niklas, Ernst	1985
605	Nimitz, Anna	1926
4846	Nimitz, Louise H.	1972
2477	Nimitz, Otto	1960
1137	Nimitz, William	1943
3219	Nimms, Victor R.	1964
7023	Nims, Myrtle R.	1979
539	Nink, John Julius	----

File	Deceased	Year
11546	Nippert, Mabel Irene Hensley Douglass/Paul aka Mabel I. Paul	1989
14832	Nixon, James Franklin	1995
19114	Nixon, June La Nell	2002
12408	Noble, Chesley	1990
14390	Noble, Gordon Otis	1994
7216	Noblett, Irwin A.	1980
5851	Noel, Dora M.	1975
15460	Noder, Osker Wilhelm	1996
14130	Nogues, James Carter	1993
6431	Noland, Joseph	1977
6332	Nolen, Katherine A.	1977
17958	Noll, Elizabeth Kelly	2000
1581	Noll, George Henry	1951
592	Noll, Dr. Julius	1925
4226	Noll, Stella Hodges	1969
482	Noll, W. W.	----
7610	Nolte, Minnie Beatrice	1981
17756	Nordquist, Armand D.	2000
15308	Nordquist, Margaret Z.	1995
9276	Norman, Andrew Edward Sr.	1984
3701	Norman, Frank F.	1967
1897	Norman, James Lee	1955
13230	Norman, Josephine Maude	1992
10704	Nomer, Howell F.	1987
11464	Norris, Elizabeth	1989
9920	Norris, Elwood Bernard	1986
9622	Norris, Floyd	1985
8354	Norris, Ira N.	1982
9194	Norris, Rosa Mae	1984
19340	Norris, Sammie Nell	2002
9626	North, Elsie Agnes	1985
52	North, Elizabeth	1883

File	Deceased	Year
16690	North, W. J.	1998
3114	Northrup, Elizabeth H.	1964
14970	Northrup, Mary Elizbeth Herpin	1995
7069	Norton, Irene B.	1979
19212	Norton, Lennos C.	2002
11626	Norton, Norman Eugene	1989
7068	Norton, Oral A.	1979
5253	Norwood, Charles C. (Mickey)	1973
13322	Norwood, Joe Waites (Joe W.)	1992
16456	Noser, Edward C.	1998
13602	Novak, Lumir F.	1992
19330	Nowak, Eugene L.	2002
7498	Nowak, Helen E.	1980
19018	Nowak, Nadyne G.	2002
5763	Nowlin, Annie L.	1975
14612	Nowlin, Hazel	1994
1363	Nowlin, Henry M.	1948
184	Nowlin, J.	1898
18478	Nowlin, John Elson	2001
2469	Nowlin, Lilla Mae	1960
1889	Nowlin, Oscar	1955
11992	Nowlin Richard B.	1989
2468	Nowlin, Roy	1960
595	Nowlin, Susan Arabella	1925
6918	Noyes, Alice Hitchcock	1979
15896	Noyes, Anna Louise Baker	1997
10404	Noyes, Richard Field	1987
3713	Nuernberger, Carla	1967
15430	Nuernberger, Ernst	1996
621	Nuernberger, Ida	1927
11882	Nuernberger, Linda	1989

File	Deceased	Year
2352	Nuernberger, Rudolf	1959
11002	Nuernberger, Walter	1988
9158	Nugent, Ada Beth Teresa	1984
9159	Nugent, Edward William	1984
SE72	Nunemaker, David B.	1982
6657	Nunley, Stella Doria	1978
14912	Nunneley, Samuel K.	1995
11630	Null, Wallace R.	1989
6938	Nutter, C. N.	1979
9086	Nutter, Josephine Reid	1984
2023	Nutter, Julia G.	1956
1400	Nyc, Frederick Francis	1948

O

File	Deceased	Year
3459	Oates, Dell R.	1966
11346	Oatman, J. E.	1987
15252	Oberg, Ernest R.	1995
6359	Obergfell, Audrey	1978
7395	Obergfell, Jennie E.	1980
17644	Oberlander, Robert G.	2000
16354	O'Brien, Beatrice Marguerite	1997
13122	O'Bryant, Claris B.	1992
15580	O'Bryant, Dorothy K.	1996
4093	O'Bryant, Laurence M.	1969
18438	O'Connor, Helen M.	2001
18678	O'Connor, Jack W.	2001
18368	O'Connor, Oscar L.	2001
5416	Odem, Agnes B.	1974
1465	Oden, William Thomas	1949
11838	Odena, Charles Frederick	1989
16454	Odena, Mary Soper	1998

File	Deceased	Year
817	Oehler, Adolph E.	1930
10794	Oehler, Carl A.	1987
5637	Oehler, Ella L.	1969
9388	Oehler, Golda Walls	1985
1895	Oehler, Henry	1954
8812	Oehler, Herbert E.	1984
6558	Oehler, Hervie	1978
7094	Oehler, Johnnie Karl	1980
1179	Oehler, Paul	1943
1924	Oehler, Maude T.	1955
7595	Oehler, Max D.	1981
3456	Oehler, Theodore	1966
6829	Oehler, Theodore John	1978
16304	Oeland, Raymond Wieson Jr.	1997
18968	O'Hara, Mary P.	2002
14740	Ohern, James Bryce	1994
15018	Ohl, Calvin H.	1995
6956	Ohls, John A.	1976
17360	Ohls, Lucille B.	1999
18390	O'Kelley, Esther M.	2001
18388	O'Kelley, Frank	2001
1148	Oldham, Alice	1942
3136	Oldham, Anna M.	1984
6769	Oldroyd, Jeanette B.	1978
15306	Oldroyd, John B.	1995
6805	Olds, Emory Bracken	1978
11920	O'Leary, Charles Frederick	1989
14700	Olen, Alice Mc Kaughan	1994
CV950091	Olivares, Ida Juarez aka Aguida J. Juarez & Aguda J.	1995
6520	Olive, Eulalia	1978
13706	Oliver, Anna B.	1992

File	Deceased	Year
6786	Oliver, J. B.	1978
3700	Oliver, Symmes F.	1967
9648	Oliver, Winona Neuman	1985
18860	Olney, James H.	2002
15596	Olreach, John Jr.	1996
5502	Olsen, Charles O.	1974
5530	Olsen, Charles Benedict	1974
5510	Olsen, Florence M.	1974
9234	Olson, Frank Walworth	1984
15818	Olson, Norman L.	1996
14089	Olson, Orvin A.	1993
7794	Olson, Ruby L.	1981
18039	Olson, Thomas H.	2000
5685	Olvey, Joseph R. Sr.	----
15926	Oman, Frank B.	1997
188	O'Neill, Henry	----
15294	Oney, John A.	1995
17364	Onion, James Collins	1999
11722	Onion, Margaret Eliz.	1989
16556	Orasco, Asencion A.	1998
5190	Orchard, Charles Dan	1973
1968	Orchard, Elma	1955
988	Orcutt, S. A.	1938
8014	Orgain, John Clifford	1982
15714	Orgain, Marvel Weeks	1996
14366	Orman, Emma B.	1994
8875	Orman, Sybil Bernice	1984
10334	Orr, Clara R.	1986
14600	Orr, Corrine Palmer	1994
8755	Orr, Floyd F.	1983
18168	Orr, Helen Dietert	2000
3389	Orr, James Al.	1965
1187	Orr, J. W.	1944
4670	Orr, Raymond	1971
10536	Orr, Robert Payne	1987

File	Deceased	Year
5534	Orr, Wilburn D.	1974
14672	Orton, Oris	1994
6047	Osborne, Charles P.	1976
17960	Osborne, Hattie May	1999
3760	Osborne, Herbert C. Jr.	1967
18546	Osborne, Lula Rae	2001
393	Osborne, Mason S.	1921
16770	Osborne, Orin Alex	1995
19028	Osborne, Wilma Jones	2002
1981	Oster, Kenneth E.	1956
7908	Ostreich, Hattie M.	1981
8372	Oswalt, Etta Dietert	1982
8312	Oswalt, J. D.	1982
8411	Ottinger, Leo E.	1983
10538	Ottinger, Leslie L.	1987
5353	Ottinger, Lula M.	1973
6485	Ottinger, Mildred K.	1977
12784	Ottmers, Roy R.	1991
13864	Outhouse, Donald Wayne	1993
16402	Overmyer, Lucretia M.	1997
16786	Overstreet, Faye B.	1998
7954	Overstreet, Lester M.	1981
15076	Owen, Jesse Lee	1995
2087	Owens, B. H.	1957
16890	Owens, Della	1998
19320	Owens, Jean Agnes Kersting	2002
12236	Owens, Paul L.	1990
16242	Ozuna, Elena	1997
4777	Ozuna, Urbano C.	1972

P

3020	Paak, Herman	1963

File	Deceased	Year
6149	Pace, John	1977
12626	Pace, Vara Oletta	1991
8389	Pacheck, Joe W.	1982
1934	Pacheck, Marguerite	1955
13792	Pack, Emagean V.	1993
8758	Packard, Duan E.	1983
14006	Packard, Eleanor S.	1993
7067	Padden, Dorothy B.	1979
4757	Padden, Rosie M.	1972
1653	Padgett, Mary	1952
1692	Paduk, Charlotte	1953
4023	Pafford, Cynthia Ann	1968
1989	Pafford, Etta	1956
16854	Page, Frances Lorene	1998
9480	Page, George A.	1985
5435	Page, Hattie	1974
18754	Page, Helen Eva	2001
1967	Page, J. E.	1955
389	Page, John T.	1913
4328	Page, Odis	1970
4139	Page, Seth E.	1969
694	Page, W. H.	1929
15452	Paine, Louise Tips	1996
4348	Pakkila, Helga M.	1970
1749	Palacio, J. H. & Pablo	1953
911	Palmer, Ada A.	1936
16296	Palmer, Arthur Leroy	1997
18788	Palmer, Cheryl Anne	2001
6677	Palmer, Emma Mae	1978
910	Palmer, Ernest E.	1936
316	Palmer, George	1912/13
10900	Palmer, George W.	1987
17182	Palmer, Hilda Rather	2000
5807	Palmer, John Wallace	1975
17878	Palmer, Keith Franklin	2000

File	Deceased	Year
5186	Palmer, Nannie	1973
17342	Palmer, Velva D.	1999
15656	Palmer, Virginia E.	1996
772	Pampell, Annie	1932
2311	Pampell, J. L.	1958
19762	Pampell, Lucile P.	1987
5460	Pampell, Milton L.	1974
15708	Pancake, Belva J.	1996
7825	Pancake, Jack M.	1981
8499	Pankey, Guy H.	1983
SE29	Pankratz, Albert	----
1956	Pankratz, Bodo	1955
8839	Pankratz, Dora Wiedenfeld	1984
526	Pankratz, Otto Sr.	----
5230	Pankratz, Otto	1972
11842	Pankratz, Pansy	1989
659	Pankratz, Theodore	1928
4925	Pankratz, Walter	1972
16838	Papa, Omer L. Del Jr.	1998
18776	Pape, Clarence Alvin	2001
12492	Pape, Dorothy M.	1990
12284	Pape, Paul E.	1990
1401	Paradowski, Edward	1948
2553	Parfait, Edward	1960
18502	Parham, Beverly Dodson	2001
18410	Paris, Andrew B.	2001
18412	Paris, Lorena S.	2001
2796	Park, C. R.	1962
13392	Park, Kenneth Puzz	1992
5521	Park, Menla E.	1974
CV940081	Park, Russell Barfield	1994
3218	Parker, Barton N.	1964
SE95	Parker, Edward E.	1982

File	Deceased	Year
8887	Parker, Emily H.	1984
13814	Parker, Everette M.	1993
17934	Parker, Frank Peyton aka Francis Peyton Parker Sr.	2000
10572	Parker, Gladys L.	1987
1567	Parker, John Lewis	1951
12810	Parker, L. L. Fox Jr.	1991
11418	Parker, Raymond	1988
11958	Parker, Raymond L.	1990
8573	Parker, Vivian L.	1983
3441	Parker, W. R.	1965
8376	Parks, Amy Menges	1982
14244	Parks, Blanche P.	1994
11836	Parks, Hal B.	1989
7036	Parks, Margaret Fraser	1979
16774	Parks, Renee	1998
6452	Parks, Robert Lee	1977
7863	Parks, Thoedore	1981
18550	Parr, Audrey A.	2001
SE96-2	Parr, Emma Charlene	1996
11016	Parr, Lloyd T.	1988
SE96-4	Parramore, Charles Ray	1996
6152	Parrott, Maude E.	1976
17740	Parsley, Helen Margaret Emig	2000
1760	Parson, Augusta	1954
1739	Parson, Bert	1953
682	Parson, Mary A.	1929
11964	Parsons, Ethel	1990
136	Parsons, R.	----
8287	Partain, Ira G.	1982
13268	Partain, Ruth Mae	1992
18062	Partridge, Ellen Ruth Whitaker	2000

File	Deceased	Year
8342	Partridge, John M.	1982
6262	Partridge, Katherine H.	1977
14616	Parvin, Alene C.	1994
11384	Pashai, Abbas	1988
6653	Passmore, Pauline T.	1978
5396	Passmore, Stephen A.	1974
15505	Pasternacki, Billie J. Stubbins	1996
13278	Pate, Earl Edward	1992
6453	Pate, Earl R.	1977
6117	Pate, Henry J.	1976
16614	Patrick, Elsie Ruth Henry	1998
18530	Patrick, Wallace L.	2001
1479	Pattee, Callie E.	1950
13734	Patten, Charles G.	1993
17544	Patterson, Alice Stevenson	1999
16978	Patterson, Camilla E.	1998
9972	Patterson, Edith May	1986
11198	Patterson, Frank Milton	1988
13078	Patterson, George A.	1992
10698	Patterson, Joseph Minton	1987
SE112734	Patterson, Marion Reed	1991
7496	Patterson, Norma J.	1979
18954	Patterson, Ruth H.	2002
18696	Patterson, T. A.	2001
13140	Pattison, James W.	1992
10434	Patton, Benjamin J.	1987
5043	Patton, E. H.	1973
6041	Patton, Elizabeth C.	1976
6454	Patton, Hattie V.	1977
15324	Patton, Joan Gaines	1995

File	Deceased	Year
9938	Patton, Joseph Desha	1986
16016	Patton, Norma T.	1997
10886	Patton, Zula Mae	1987
18372	Patty, Alton Boyd	2001
1288	Paul, H. L.	1946
7858	Paul, H. T.	1981
17224	Paul, Jack Cousins	1999
11546	Paul, Mabel I.aka Mabel Irene Henchy Paul Nippert	1989
15924	Paul, Mary B.	1997
7756	Paul, Meta Henke	1981
11548	Paul, Ruth P.	1989
5422	Paulson, James R.	1974
16802	Pauly, Arthur James	1998
14582	Paxson, Charles W.	1994
19250	Paxson, Glenda R.	2002
6329	Payne, Alexander Otto	1977
775	Payne, Kirk C.	1932
15624	Payne, Mary E.	1996
11474	Payne, R. C.	1989
10812	Payne, Robert A. Jr.	1987
779	Payne, Winnie D.	1932
19196	Pazdral, Lucie Mae	2002
7839	Pazdral, Tod	1981
14438	Peace, Nadine R.	1994
11618	Pearce, Florence S.	1989
12154	Pearce, Henry F. Jr.	1990
12256	Pearce, Pauline	1990
8499	Pearce, Robert W.	1983
9376	Peare, Dorothy B.	1985
5096	Peare, Reve S.	1973
12410	Pearson, Calvin	1990
5125	Pearson, James E.	1973
3986	Pearson, Laura E.	1968

File	Deceased	Year
828	Pearson, Rayburn	1933
8552	Pearson, Thelma Brosch	1983
17288	Peays, Thomas A.	1999
15278	Peck, Charles W.	1995
4918	Peck, Ida	1972
10888	Peckham, Janet Young	1987
1845	Pederson, Andrew C.	1954
1846	Pederson, Ellen C.	1954
15122	Pederson, Rhoda Marie	1995
9880	Peebles, Ramona	1986
17558	Pebworth, William S. Jr.	1999
9171	Peel, Katherine M.	1984
15796	Peel, Margaret K.	1996
10102	Peese, Julia Helmers	1986
17892	Peirce, Clara Andreas	2000
16160	Peirce, Michael	1997
SE13364	Pelton, "Jack" Elvie Edith/Ruth	1992
15146	Pelton, Nellie	1995
14226	Pemberton, Carolyn E.	1993
16232	Pemberton, Carolyn Elizabeth	1997
16866	Pendleton, Paula W.	1998
18346	Pendley, Roy I.	2001
18068	Pendola, Lucile G.	2000
15722	Penn, Aldan B.	1996
SE97-5	Penney, Gertrude M.	1997
SE97-4	Penney, Luther Terry	1997
14436	Pennick, Beulah	1994
1135	Perez, F. E.	1943
2643	Perez, Marcos G.	1961
1678	Peril, J. A.	1953
7445	Perkin, Mary E.	1980
2236	Perkins, Edith	1958
11680	Perkins, George	1989

File	Deceased	Year
4026	Perkins, Gladys M.	1968
10576	Perkins, Jack T.	1987
7257	Perkins, May Preston	1980
11682	Perkins, Susie O'Bryant	1989
10438	Perkins, Walter Robert	1987
13368	Perlowaki, Sigmund A.	1992
18346	Perry, J. H.	2001
17776	Perry, John H. Jr.	2000
14336	Perry, Mary Frances	1993
4910	Personnett, C. D.	1972
651	Peschel, Filomenn	----
6549	Peters, Albert	1978
9640	Peters, Beatrice	1985
9978	Peters, Beatrice V.	1986
9644	Peters, Beatrice	1985
5058	Peters, C. J.	1973
13556	Peters, Conrad A. Jr.	1992
10468	Peters, Donald B.	1987
16798	Peters, Donald Lee	1998
4616	Peters, E. M.	1971
14328	Peters, Eleanor Henke	1994
3099	Peters, Georgia Elleff	1964
11890	Peters, Ida Gray	1989
4573	Peters, Reine	----
478	Peters, S. Ross	1921
7113	Peters, Stanford D.	1979
913	Peters, Winnie S.	1936
1574	Petersione, D. F.	1951
4714	Petersione, Edna May	1971
857	Peterson, Ayleen	1935
7947	Peterson, Beulah C. Nichols	1981
1757	Peterson, Charles V.	1953
11062	Peterson, Elizabeth Dryden	1988

File	Deceased	Year
12764	Peterson, Esther A.	1991
15874	Peterson, Francis K. D.	1996
6254	Peterson, George G.	1977
2785	Peterson, Hal	1962
7966	Peterson, J. Arvid	1981
2194	Peterson, Joe Sid	1958
1582	Peterson, Myrtle	1951
1830	Peterson, Norris J.	1954
4785	Peterson, Ruby	1972
1025	Peterson, Sid	1938/39
17026	Petrson, Sue Hallmark	1998
895	Peterson, W. G.	1936
673	Peterson, W. S.	1929
3529	Peterson, Walter Carl	1966
11888	Petrie, Joseph Nicholas	1989
14814	Petron, George John	1995
15284	Petron, Lillian F.	1995
3656	Petsch, Glenn	1966
1124	Petsch, Walter	1942
14616	Pettit, Emma Ruth	1994
10986	Pettit, John W.	1988
16754	Pettitt, Linda E.	1998
5701	Pettit, Maynard H.	1975
4770	Pettitt, F. J.	1971
14746	Petty, Arvis Oran	1994
4483	Petty, James E.	1973
10752	Petty, James Kenneth	1987
10936	Petty, John Allan	1988
14384	Petty, Marie H.	1994
17302	Pfaff, Albert G. III	1999
15140	Pfaff, Anna V.	1995
3568	Pfannstiel, F. E.	1966
18508	Pfeiffer, Arnold Charles	2001
17764	Pfeiffer, Carolina	2000

File	Deceased	Year
13012	Pfeiffer, Herman	1991
7992	Pfeiffer, Louis	1981
7387	Pfenfer, Carl T.	
	(?Pfeufer)	1980
14620	Pfeuffer, Howard E.	1994
1912	Pfeuffer, Louie	1955
3063	Pfeuffer, Nettie	
	Ruth W.	1963
1319	Pfeuffer, Rosa	1947
6417	Phalen, Alfred E.	1977
6348	Phalen, Dorothy E.	1977
14590	Phares, Gladys Esther	1994
11582	Phelps, Ella	1989
18202	Phelps, Hazel B.	2000
14160	Phillips, C. C.	1993
7713	Phillips, Gerald Bert	1981
14640	Phillips, Grace E.	1994
2378	Phillips, Henry	1959
12958	Phillips, James Henry	1991
1210	Phillips, John E.	1944
1725	Phillips, Lorreta	1953
1917	Phillips, Marvin	
	Bradley	2002
16948	Phillips, Olive Frances	1998
1745	Phillips, Russell A.	1953
2144	Phillips, Stanley	1957
4993	Phillips, Stella	1973
1207	Phillips, Walter	1944
14634	Philp, Sarah	1994
1604	Pickard, Matthew W.	1952
17194	Pickens, Elva V.	1999
10824	Pickens, Eugenia	1987
1831	Pickens, Tom	1954
5416	Pickett, Guy	1974

File	Deceased	Year
6751	Pickett, Hildred C.	1978
10424	Pickett, John S.	1987
6752	Pickett, Johnnie C.	----
4244	Pickett, Willis J.	----
4508	Pieper, Alma	1970
13852	Peiper, Edward August	1993
15024	Pieper, Eula Griffin	1995
18240	Pieper, Frederich G.	2001
4711	Pieper, Henry	1971
15834	Pieper, Henry Jr.	1996
17444	Piepgrass, Bernice E.	1999
9664	Piepgrass, Ben P.	1985
18440	Pierce, Dorothy	2001
8656	Pierce, James L. Jr.	1983
18874	Pierce, Nelson Ross	2002
13386	Pierce, Robert L.	1992
15958	Pierson, Becky	1997
18422	Pierson, Ruth E.	2001
10579	Pierz, Richard C.	1987
12034	Pike, Beulah Anderson	1991
7536	Pike, Bruce	1980
15108	Pike, Jean Springer	1995
15724	Pike, Richard Thomas Sr.	1996
16296	Pilkerton, Betsy N.	1997
CV990198	Pilkerton, Betsy N.	1999
8548	Pimlott, Berta R.	1983
16552	Pina, Jose Reyes Morua	1998
16076	Pinder, Donald	1997
5273	Pineo, Archibald Lee	1973
4386	Pines, Maude D.	----
4726	Piper, Christopher Michael	1972
6767	Pipkin, Charles C.	1978
3948	Pitchers, Mary E.	1968
12234	Pitkin, William	1990

File	Deceased	Year
3560	Pitman, Hallis M.	1966
13736	Pittman, Jonathon William	1993
16668	Pittman, Mikel Joe	1998
13418	Pittman, Ouida C.	1992
6267	Pitts, Richard K.	1977
8305	Pitts, Rose Ellen	1982
13772	Pitts, William B.	1993
4239	Plach, Kenneth B.	1969
15532	Plangman, Solange Boutin	1996
13118	Plahm, Arthur O.	1992
11700	Plahm, Hazel	1989
6369	Plant, Lou Visa	1977
17536	Plant, Wesley	1999
13540	Planzer, Pearlie Jean	1992
11448	Ploetz, William F.	1989
7541	Plumlee, Betty J.	1980
12316	Plumlee, Irene Schulz	1990
SE95-1	Plumly, Glen P.	1995
7164	Plummer, Olivia Flato	1979
12812	Plummer, William Alexander Sr.	1991
7951	Plautz, Sanford C.	1981
14348	Podgorny, Barbara Allen	1994
12790	Poe, G. A.	1991
9950	Poe, Ruby Mae	1986
12158	Poehler, Kenneth Cole	1990
4939	Poehnert, Alice Nelson	1972
13188	Poehnert, Harry	1992
3984	Poehnert, Otto Frank	1968
5102	Polish, Virginia Marie	1973
12484	Polk, Carlo B.	1990
3957	Pollard, Henrietta	1968
7848	Pollard, L. W.	1981

File	Deceased	Year
7637	Pollard, Margery H.	1981
12250	Ponton, Gene Edward	1990
12302	Ponton, James Edward	1990
12066	Poole, Elizabeth C. aka Mrs. J. C. Poole & Eliz. Carpenter Poole	1990
2927	Poole, J. C.	1963
11246	Poole, M. James	1988
3104	Poore, Homer H.	1964
18506	Poore, Thomas J.	2001
4189	Poorman, Sam	1969
12500	Poot, William J.	1990
3538	Pope, Annie E.	1966
1296	Pope, Mattie	1946
5082	Pope, R. B.	1973
11512	Popkin, Fritz E.	1989
15134	Poplin, Margaret Matilda	1995
13382	Poppe, Erich Willi Walter	1992
9200	Porche, Clement Edward	1984
638	Porras, Marcelo	1928
4419	Porter, B. F.	1970
6443	Porter, Donald R.	1977
1340	Porter, E. H.	1947
10172	Porter, Kitty J.	1986
18244	Porter, Louise L.	2001
668	Porter, Malta	1928
7471	Porter, Paul A.	1980
17930	Porter, Wayne	2000
10354	Posey, Robert	1986
6974	Poshepny, Lucy	1979
11202	Post, Marvin H.	1988
16572	Poth, Hilda	1998
16052	Poth, Jay L.	1997

File	Deceased	Year
6058	Potschernick, Emilie	1976
7960	Potts, Arthur G.	1981
9702	Powell, Amcil	1985
3276	Powell, Annie V. (Jennie)	1965
6241	Powell, B. D.	1977
16544	Powell, Carl L.	1998
13120	Powell, Doyce L.	1992
13628	Powell, Doyce L. Jr.	1992
560	Powell, James	----
561	Powell, James	1925
830	Powell, James	1933
11770	Powell, James Wallace	1989
16368	Powell, Lorene	1997
4558	Powell, Milann	1970/71
17952	Powell, Willis M. Jr.	2000
14916	Powers, Donald D.	1995
9520	Powers, Mary Grace	1985
7636	Powers, Muriel Mc Cann	1981
3947	Powers, W. Earl	1968
10242	Prater, Jeff	1986
9141	Pratt, Alice Mc Anally	1984
7531	Pratt, Jack Sr.	1980
1318	Pray, Harry	1947
14618	Preddy, Jane Ann	1994
7425	Preddy, Linna Herma	1980
15544	Preer, Helen Brinson	1996
17348	Prell, Noel	1999
9500	Prentess, Viola	1985
15782	Prentice, Fred T.	1996
10940	Preslar, Elizabeth Margaret	1988
12858	Presley, Beatrice	1991
6297	Presley, Edwin C.	1977
5164	Pressler, Charles	1973

217

File	Deceased	Year
16428	Preston, Barbara	1998
5264	Preston, Mrs. Cleo	1973
923	Prestridge, Dicey J.	1937
928	Prestridge, Dicey J.	1937
6568	Prestridge, Joyce Eliza.	1978
15586	Prestwood, Cleo Edwards	1996
11578	Prestwood, Frank B.	1989
9120	Price, Anna Belle	1984
18496	Price, Bobby Jess	2001
441	Price, David	----
17492	Price, Floyd Virgel	1999
5804	Price, Forrest Marion	1975
19122	Price, Irvie	2002
7973	Price, J. Lillard	1981
17190	Price, Lonnie J.	1999
5231	Price, Susie Hardin	1973
11656	Priddy, Arthur P.	1989
4719	Priddy, William C.	1971
11786	Pridemore, Cleave Henry	1989
17008	Prilwitz, Sophia	1998
17216	Prince, Carolyn W.	1999
9332	Prince, Edna Wolff	1985
17368	Prince, Jack Edward	1999
17410	Prince, Jack Edward	1999
5876	Prince, Kerman	1976
19358	Prindle, Barclay Lewis	2002
6974	Pringle, Ira Lee	1979
6968	Pringle, Tera Louollie	1979
10586	Prinzing, Henry W.	1987
5880	Prinzing, Pearl	1975
1081	Priour, A. B.	1940/41
1491	Priour, Henry	1950
6807	Priour, J. W.	1978
5816	Priour, James W.	1975
3523	Priour, Thomas Franklin	1966

File	Deceased	Year
14208	Priour, Velma	1993
15666	Priour, Winona	1996
18540	Pritz, Donald D.	2001
17100	Probst, Kurt Martin	1999
17052	Procopio, Barbara A.	1999
12776	Prothro, Fred A.	1991
9656	Prout, Timothy John	1985
8147	Pruett, Helen I.	1982
19002	Pruitt, Gail Terry	2002
11558	Prumeda, Tetra H.	1989
SE46	Puccini, Pearl F.	----
17680	Puckett, Leon L. Sr.	2000
16262	Puckett, Ruby	1997
15022	Pulkrabek, Franklin Delano	1995
5382	Pulliam, Helen L.	1974
2430	Pullin, George W. Sr.	1959
18994	Pullin, Marjorie M.	2002
2355	Pullin, Mary Pearl	1959
6554	Pump, Raymond Edward	1978
10096	Pumphrey, Jack E.	1986
7605	Pumphrey, Lucian T.	1981
18812	Pumphrey, Kitty West	2001
17480	Punzel, Robert L.	1999
9176	Purdy, Bernice V.	1984
9652	Purdy, Winona	1985
9262	Purvis, Frances	1984
13922	Purvis, L. H.	1993
3126	Purvis, Minnie	1964
9302	Puryear, E. C.	1984
11554	Putman, Alam Grace	1989
18556	Putman, Jack G.	2001
17820	Putnam, Ilah Fay	2000
3892	Pylander, W. E.	1968

File	Deceased	Year
10192	Pyle, Coy	1986
12430	Pyle, Gilbert Eward	1990

Q

File	Deceased	Year
12502	Qualtrough, Cleo Bryson	1990
5580	Qualtrough, Lucille B.	----
12314	Qualtrough, Pearl E.	1990
12624	Qualtrough, Raymond Hayden	1994
14506	Qualtrough, Walter F.	1994
2681	Queen, Johnson	----
13690	Quinn, B. E. Jr. aka Benjamin Edmund Jr.	1993
15488	Quinn, Charles F.	1996
6344	Quinn, Helen S.	----
10988	Quinn, Lettie Viola	1988
16098	Quinn, Margaret M.	1997

R

File	Deceased	Year
3879	Raaz, Frieda	1967
6286	Raatz, W. A.	1977
13490	Rabalais, Dovie	1992
6328	Raborn, Willie Reed	1977
17466	Raburn, M. Merle	1999
418	Radez, Ursula (Redey)	1917
15072	Radleff, Ernest F.	1995
14666	Radeleff, Eugenia H.	1994
1701	Radeleff, Fritz	1953
5309	Radeleff, Minnie D.	1973
17784	Radenz, Shirley O.	2000
2406	Ragland, Corles Simpson	1959

File	Deceased	Year
5126	Ragland, Eddie Lucile	1972
541	Ragland, F. S.	1923
18450	Ragland, Ruby L.	2001
1039	Ragland, Susan M.	1940
233	Raiborn, Edwina	----
10418	Raiford, A. H.	1987
18676	Raiford, Ada F.	2001
6776	Raiford, Beulah Pearl	1978
6783	Raiford, Beulah Pearl	1978
3691	Raiford, Grace Jewel	1967
11166	Raiford, Ira L.	1988
5913	Raiford, J. G.	1975/76
9894	Raiford, Lloyd	1986
14782	Raine, Joseph V.	1994
9906	Raine, Thomas W.	1986
14852	Rains, Ada Dee	1995
14398	Rains, Richard Kerr	1994
4327	Ralston, A. J.	1969
10720	Ramelli, Roland	1987
10252	Ramirez, Blas	1986
9408	Ramirez, Felix Castillo	1985
15162	Ramirez, Gabriel Valdez	1995
13394	Ramsden, Violet Phoebe Frances	1992
3697	Ramsey, Alma	1967
6648	Ramsey, Harold L.	1978
1983	Ramsey, Jeanette	1956
1868	Ramsey, Jeanette E.	1954
1845	Ramsey, Jeanette E.	1955
3571	Ramsey, Loyd E.	1966
1875	Ramsey, O. P.	1955
9430	Randel, Floyd L.	1985
12914	Randel, John Lee	1991
15000	Randell, Ola Lee	1995
15912	Randell, Rosella Mae	1997

File	Deceased	Year
4543	Randell, Willie G.	1970
16312	Randle, Jacqueline W.	1997
7235	Raney, Cecil E. Sr.	1980
6161	Raney, Walter	1976
6927	Ranft, Everette O.	1979
7016	Ranft, Mamie S.	1979
12188	Ranger, Gladys Jacob	1990
5313	Rankin, Vera	1973
15766	Ranne, Willard D.	1996
10728	Ransleben, Mabel Burney	1987
10982	Rappolee, Bess Aileen	1988
9356	Rappolee, Jean Lucian	1985
13150	Rasmus, James Wendell Sr.	1992
17580	Ratcliffe, Goldie B.	1999
17366	Ratcliffe, Sara Eastwood	1999
18522	Rath, Albert Earnest	2001
571	Rathmann, Carl A. L.	1923
12592	Ratliff, Arch Sr.	1991
15412	Raubfogel, Grace F.	1996
15822	Raubfogel, Manuel Forster	1996
1042	Rauch, Adolph	1940
10656	Rauch, Beatrice H.	1987
2128	Rauch, Chester	1957
3696	Rauch, Oscar R.	1967
2357	Rauch, Wayne C.	1949
902	Raute, Otto	1936
7009	Ravenna, Melanie E.	1979
1751	Rawls, Martha	1953
798	Rawls, Robert R.	1933
953	Rawson, Florence	1937
955	Rawson, Florence	1937
859	Rawson, Herbert	1935

File	Deceased	Year
861	Rawson, Herbert	1935
17796	Rawson, Melinda Louise Southerd Smith	2000
723	Rawson, W. H.	1931
11046	Ray, Charles Sr.	1988
13228	Ray, Charles Melvin	1992
14034	Ray, Dewey G.	1993
SE01-7	Ray, Edward Franklin	2001
7206	Ray, E. P.	1980
4429	Ray, F. A.	1967
5365	Ray, James Harry	1974
6650	Ray, James Henry	1978
18594	Ray, Kathleen Olive	2001
16200	Ray, Ruby Brunson	1997
5755	Rayburn, Avian T.	1975
9830	Rayburn, James Clifford	1985
5913	Rayford, J. G.	1975/76
16760	Raymer, Geoffery M.	1998
17340	Raymer, Harriet F.	1999
10182	Raymond, Alice Jean	1986
2310	Raymond, Orville Leon	1958
2137	Raymond, William Apffel	1957
3081	Reader, Thomas Ernest	1964
8153	Reagan, Dora	1982
1182	Reagan, T. M.	1944
719	Real, Albert	1930
2917	Real, Amanda	1963
2936	Real, Amanda	1963
7585	Real, Amie W.	1981
1095	Real, Casper	1942
1100	Real, Casper	1942
4347	Real, Elmer	1970
4347	Real, Elmer O.	1967
5047	Real, Esther R.	1972
4504	Real, Ettie	1970

File	Deceased	Year
8992	Real, Felix R.	1984
7470	Real, Frankie Flach	1980
1215	Real, Gretchen	1944
14370	Real, Hugo	1994
3645	Real, Johanna	1966
1198	Real, Julius	1944
10380	Real, Loma Moss	1986
7824	Real, Louis A.	1981
300	Real, Marie	1910
935	Real, Robert	1937
4415	Real, Victor	1967
1252	Real, Walter	1945
12856	Reaves, Frances M.	1991
16630	Reaves, Ralph L.	1998
815	Rebitz, Christian	1934
12212	Redden, Dorothy Oels	1990
6259	Redden, Edward N.	1977
5501	Redford, Louise T.	1974
5013	Redland, Arthur J.	1972
SE19	Redman, Francis	1977
16112	Redmon, James Robert Jr.	1997
6929	Reed, Ardice Wanetta	1979
16946	Reed, Clyde F.	1998
9628	Reed, Dorothy M.	1985
11220	Reed, Everette Laverne	1988
11718	Reed, Forrest K.	1989
10034	Reed, Jack M.	1986
8923	Reed, La Fayette F.	1984
1913	Reed, Margaret H.	1955
1342	Reed, Mary Hamburg	1947
11552	Reeder, Albert Gordon	1989
5996	Reeh, Olga P.	1976
2072	Reeh, William & Emilie	1957
1503	Rees, Albert	1950
435	Rees, Anna C.	----

File	Deceased	Year
193	Rees, D. A.	1901
3011	Rees, D. A.	1963
12608	Rees, D. D.	1991
14298	Rees, Dorothy Louise	1993
4544	Rees, Elizabeth L.	1970
1756	Rees, Ellen Ora	1953
245	Rees, Emily	1906
2228	Rees, Herman C.	1958
755	Rees, Ida Stieler	1932
630	Rees, James C.	1923
17810	Rees, Lenore L.	2000
2978	Rees, Louis L.	1963
6816	Rees, Marie Jensen aka Alice Marie Harris	1978
2989	Rees, Nowlin Freeman	1963
4345	Rees, Sidney B.	1967
16568	Reesa, Sylvia Theriet	1998
7454	Reese, Aubra G.	1980
13688	Reese, Earl Littleton	1993
1871	Reese, Edward Eugene	1954
6791	Reese, Howard W.	1978
18212	Reeves, Ann Lee	2000
1805	Reeves, D. C.	1954
17942	Reeves, Ruth Taylor	2000
964	Reffelt, William	1938
18710	Regner, Daniel Thomas	2001
5559	Regnes, Mathilda	1974
2932	Rehberger, Ferdinand	1963
6449	Rehm, Harry	1977
9214	Rehm, Marvel Dell	1984
2490	Reicherd, Charles R. S.	1960
13024	Reid, A. E. Jr.	1991
13342	Reid, Albert Nettleton	1992
1283	Reid, H. P.	1946
6545	Reid, Helen K.	1978

File	Deceased	Year
8808	Reid, Howard C.	1984
13344	Reid, Margaret Musselman	1992
8585	Reifel, Gertrude Mary	1983
8216	Reifel, Ormond Francis	1982
5260	Reiffert, Nancy Patricia	1973
10280	Reiger, Joe B.	1986
11756	Reilly, Annette C.	1989
18720	Reimers, Karl August	2001
15948	Reinbach, Max O.	1997
15358	Reinhard, Bertha Faye	1995
12536	Reinhard, Charles	1991
4237	Reinhard, Clara	1967
793	Reinhard, J. P.	1933
2451	Reinhardt, Lena	1959
652	Reinhardt, P. J.	----
10296	Reinsch, Carl A.	1986
1077	Reiter, Catherine	1941
5480	Reiter, Charles A. Sr.	1974
14720	Reiter, Diane T.	1994
13610	Reiter, Mary	1992
SE12390	Reither, Velna Lee aka Reither, Velma Lee	1990
14472	Reither, Virgil Robert	1994
4004	Remschel, Claribel D.	1968
3132	Remschel, J. B.	1964
6370	Remschel, Laura Frances	1977
6129	Remschel, R. A.	1976
7241	Renfro, A. A.	1980
14534	Renfro, Edith	1994
10556	Renfro, Holly L.	1987
16010	Renfro, Lowell Edvin Jr.	1997
14540	Renfro, Robert Jackson	1994

File	Deceased	Year
15976	Reno, Edward Willian aka Bill E. Childers	1997
10316	Rentz, Jack C.	1986
9023	Ressel, Lorraine A.	1982
15652	Ressler, Ivon R. Jr.	----
8589	Reynolds, Arthur W.	1983
9252	Reynolds, Charles Luther	1984
4364	Reynolds, Charles M.	1967
14206	Reynolds, Conway F.	1993
12232	Reynolds, Dorothy Hall	1990
3853	Reynolds, Edith	1967
4518	Reynolds, Eugene I.	1970
16698	Reynolds, Jodie L. aka Joe L.	1998
8621	Reynolds, John A.	1983
8740	Reynolds, Joyce Marie Owen	1983
7056	Reynolds, Marvin W.	1979
499	Reynolds, Nelson A.	1922
14648	Reynolds, P. T.	1994
14204	Reynolds, Sibyl M.	1993
12562	Reynolds, Velva Sue	1991
13986	Rhea, Leonard Doyle	1993
11444	Rhoads, Daisy Katherine	1989
2415	Rhoden, Emmett W.	1959
6774	Rhoden, James G.	1978
15380	Rhodes, Carl Eugene	1996
5932	Rhodes, George E. F.	1976
18420	Rhodes, Lillie B.	2001
10370	Rhorbeck, Ruby	1986
10620	Rhudy, Jack D.	1987
11442	Rhuddy, Jo H.	1989
17484	Rhyne, Harvey Glenn	1999
6242	Rice, Albert J.	1977

File	Deceased	Year
1449	Rice, Edythe L.	1949
9740	Rice, Ernest Robert	1985
6057	Rice, F. C.	1976
684	Rice, F. A.	1930
11000	Rice, Henry C.	1988
9350	Rice, Jesse Clyde	1985
10896	Rice, Mabel Moore Floyd	1987
9404	Rice, Naomi	1985
1872	Rice, T. Burt	1954
2072	Rice, William B.	1957
7664	Rich, John George	1981
5927	Rich, John R.	1976
1034	Richards, B. C.	1940
11596	Richards, Charlotte F.	1989
13360	Richards, Dorothy B.	1992
16254	Richards, Ida C.	1997
6137	Richards, Nelson A.	1976
4358	Richardson, Bertha O.	1967
514	Richardson, C. E.	1922
10802	Richardson, Curtis Arthur	1987
12794	Richardson, Elsie B.	1991
15470	Richardson, Eugene E.	1996
2767	Richardson, Farrah Dane	1962
7485	Richardson, Mary Mann	1980
10178	Richardson, Nova G.	1986
10654	Richardson, Thorton R.	1987
11570	Richardson, Walter R.	1989
2997	Richardson, William A. Sr.	1963
14112	Richardson, William S.	1993
18736	Richerson, Ilera Pauline	2001
18300	Richerson, Malcolm Murry	2001

228

File	Deceased	Year
4277	Richeson, G. L.	1967
4935	Richeson, Iva Byas	1972
815	Richeson, Jewel	1934
18774	Richmond, Curtis R.	2001
18129	Richmond, Earl H.	2000
17272	Richter, Joseph Dudley	1999
6552	Rickard, C. E.	1978
15172	Rickbeil, Clara E.	1995
16576	Ricker, John Milton	1998
12894	Ricketts, Alma L.	1991
8826	Ricks, Philip A.	1984
7004	Riddle, Evelyn	1979
7137	Riddle, Melville G.	1979
15692	Ridgaway, Robert E.	1996
1586	Ridgaway, Lewis S.	1951
14426	Ridgaway, Ora M.	1994
2313	Ridgaway, Will	1958
7426	Ridgaway, Willie	1980
3780	Ridge, Paul K.	1967
554	Ridgway, Fred	1923
17160	Rieger, Velma Vae	1999
4409	Rieke, Lydia L.	1967
14578	Riesel, Erich	1994
15282	Riesmeyer, John F.	1995
10640	Riexinger, Albert	1987
18260	Rigano, Virginia E.	2001
8179	Rigsby, Herbert Prentice	1982
10832	Riggens, Dale D.	1987
14500	Riggs, McElroy Denson	1994
886	Riggs, Nancy	1936
18934	Rigsby, Doris L.	2002
16064	Riley, John Lemuel	1997
17962	Riley, Marguerite	2000
15334	Riley, Marguerite Eliz.	1995

File	Deceased	Year
14874	Riley, Olga Marie	1995
6655	Riley, T. W.	1978
15	Rine, George J.	----
12130	Riney, Helen L.	1990
6563	Ring, Carlon Earl	1978
12574	Riojas, Concepcion R.	1991
15872	Riopelle, Biddie C. Campbell	1996
10674	Rios, Jose H.	1987
11446	Rios, Socorro S.	1989
14416	Rippek, Edgar Otto	1994
15374	Riquelmy, Clara Mae	1996
13926	Ris, J. Spencer	1993
16034	Rische, James Irwin	1997
1329	Rishworth, W. H.	1947
1085	Rishworth, W. T.	1941
14656	Ritch, Nancy Smith	1994
12126	Ritcheson, Homer Alvin	1990
466	Ritchie, Joseph Harrison	1920
3972	Ritchie, Mrs. L. L.	1963
15472	Ritter, Harold Glen Jr.	1996
14228	Ritter, John William	1993
4889	Rittiman, Eugene W.	1972
4150	Rittimann, Elgin O.	1967
14692	Rittimann, Lucille H.	1994
1180	Ritz, Emil	1943
1251	Ritzenthaler, Henry W.	1945
1618	Ritzenthaler, Nettie E.	1952
18216	Rivera, Jose Garcia	2001
9460	Rives, John	1985
12226	Rives, Odile Sonnier	1990
7584	Riviere, Louise R.	1981
5364	Riviere, William T.	1973
14010	Roach, Philip D.	1993

File	Deceased	Year
17156	Roach, Walter L.	1999
15410	Roaten, Shelley P.	1996
3101	Robb, Edgar A.	1964
451	Robb, George Carmichael	----
10308	Robb, Vera Curtis	1986
8886	Robbins, Abbie Lee	1984
10596	Robbins, Billie Marvin	1987
16876	Robbins, Earnestine M.	1998
7368	Robbins, Harvey W.	1980
7770	Robbins, W. J.	1981
4552	Roberson, Leslie C.	1971
16592	Roberts, Adella Agnes	1998
1379	Roberts, Alfonso A.	1948
15868	Roberts, Arthur M.	1996
16268	Roberts, Bob Brown	1997
19154	Roberts, Charles C.	2002
13796	Roberts, Claude	1993
12426	Roberts, Clifford Jesse	1990
2677	Roberts, Gertrude Mulett	1961
17622	Roberts, Gladys Lundstrum	1999
7575	Roberts, Jay	1981
4545	Roberts, Katherine	1970
2661	Roberts, Madona Martin	1961
3000	Roberts, Mary M.	1963
922	Roberts, W. D. (Bill)	1937
880	Roberts, W. F.	1936
13380	Roberts, William Fowler	1992
17422	Roberts, William Jett	1999
18246	Roberts, Willie Mae	2001
4574	Robertson, Anna Lee	1971
14176	Robertson, Betty Jane	1993
6633	Robertson, Charles F.	1978
13828	Robertson, Dorothy	1993

File	Deceased	Year
6420	Robertson, Iva Jane	1977
8170	Robertson, Josephine	1982
7746	Robertson, John L.	1981
888	Robertson, Lake	1936
16846	Robertson, Lola	1998
5072	Robertson, Lorraine	1972/73
13678	Robertson, Mable M.	1993
4333	Robertson, O. B.	1970
4232	Robertson, Thomas H.	1967
14332	Robertson, Vada C.	1994
16182	Robertson, William A. Sr.	1997
6861	Robertson, William Howard	1979
6736	Robertson, W. R. Sr.	1978
8504	Robertson, Winnie Travis	1983
11050	Robey, Marie T.	1988
14840	Robinson, Addie Ann	1995
237	Robinson, Allen D.	1945
249	Robinson, Cecil D.	1906
13629	Robinson, Effie G.	1992
99	Robinson, Fannie E.	1887
11762	Robinson, Harold R.	1989
247	Robinson, J. D. & Estelle (Estelle Died in 1904)	1904??
1481	Robinson, J. W.	1950
4180	Robinson, Mattie Jean	1967
7819	Robinson, Merice Charles	1981
11022	Robinson, Merice Charles	1988
3557	Robinson, Roy L.	1966
3375	Robinson, Ruby Reid	1865

File	Deceased	Year
2435	Robinson, Sue	1959
8846	Robinson, William Leon	1984
5200	Robinson, Willie Eugene	1973
4969	Rockey, Harry	1972
1466	Rockey, Winnifred	1950
8136	Roddy, Allie Peters	1982
10330	Rode, Mayme	1986
12920	Rodecape, Lucile B.	1991
17816	Rodgers, Arthur G.	2000
2100	Rodgers, Charles A.	1957
11350	Rodgers, Elva Mae	1988
7365	Rodgers, Loyas Ray	1980
14728	Rodgers, Thomas Allen Sr.	1994
9922	Rodriguez, Able V.	1986
16544	Rodriguez, Alice J.	1998
17540	Rodriguez, Blas Sr.	1999
16962	Rodriguez, Elvira M.	1998
5991	Rodriguez, Emmet Vargas	1976
16864	Rodriguez, John D.	1998
SE99-4	Rodriguez, Jose A.	1999
17542	Rodriguez, Juana G.	1999
SE99-5	Rodriguez, Samuel M.	1999
6365	Roe, Hilmer Jack	1977
1818	Roe, William Robert	1954
4890	Roeder, Joe J.	1972
4891	Roeder, Pauline	1972
4870	Roeder, Ruben	1971
12420	Roehl, Rudolph J.	1990
6991	Roesler, Fred A.	1979
13976	Roessing, Hilda N.	1993
15802	Roetzler, Gladys Gertrude	1996
7400	Roetzler, Thomas J.	1980
18622	Roever, Mary June	2001

File	Deceased	Year
10876	Rogan, Virgil K.	1987
15748	Rogers, Earnest A.	1996
17732	Rogers, Ella Louise aka Ella Wolfe Rogers	2000
13440	Rogers, Era W.	1992
12936	Rogers, Francis A.	1991
18616	Rogers, Freda F.	2001
16586	Rogers, Jacob Harley	1998
10502	Rogers, John E.	1987
19070	Rogers, Lola Mae	2002
4038	Rogers, Losson C.	1968
6505	Rogers, Nan Swayze Kellan	1977
5014	Rogers, Norman Will	1972
6273	Rogers, Ralph E.	1976
1111	Rogers, Ray B.	1942
12202	Rogers, Stephanie M.	1990
6375	Rogers, Witt	1977
13444	Rohe, Bernard	1992
14988	Roehl, Mildred A.	1995
15556	Roesler, Elizabeth M.	1996
4609	Rohn, Elizabeth Bochman	1971
9056	Rohrbeck, Alfred	1984
10214	Rohrbeck, Ruby	1986
10370	Rohrbeck, Ruby	1986
13674	Rolander, George R.	1994
16352	Roland, Anna Belle	1997
11400	Rolland, C. A.	1988
15246	Rollen, Edith T.	1995
4150	Roller, Dora L.	1967
9248	Rollo, Charles	1984
9606	Rollo, Ira	1985
17902	Romero, Josephine	2000
13020	Romigh, Orin Lambert	1991

File	Deceased	Year
5177	Romine, A. E.	1973
4539	Romine, Mary Frances	1970
9146	Rommel, Alexander Ross	1984
13600	Ronk, Cleo Eugene	1992
6934	Rosales, Victor Alcorta	1979
806	Rose, J. D.	1933
1255	Rose, John D.	1945
15406	Rose, Paul Roland	1996
8503	Rose, Robert V.	1983
8470	Rosemann, Guenther J. H.	1983
14128	Rosenbaum, Evelyn Louise	1993
1429	Rosenberg, A. F.	1949
11692	Rosenblum, Alex M.	1989
17908	Rosenthal, Adela M.	2000
1293	Rosenthal, Annie	1946
15986	Rosenthal, Robert L.	1997
16662	Roser, Etta Louise	1997
9826	Rosilier, John A.	1985
18842	Rosin, Arline L.	2002
7091	Ross, Daisy R.	1979
5411	Ross, Egbert H.	1974
7677	Ross, George E.	1981
17524	Ross, Leona Rutledge	1999
17742	Ross, Luther W. Jr.	2000
10008	Ross, Ruth E.	1986
1253	Ross, W. K.	1945
4971	Rosson, J. G. (Joe Gray)	1972
SE96-5	Rossiter, Harry A.	1996
SE96-5	Rossiter, John Albert	1996
19058	Rossotto, Meta Eunice	2002
6318	Rotge, Amie August	1977

File	Deceased	Year
826	Rotge, Hypolite	1934
1221	Rotge, Joseph A.	1945
1224	Rotge, Louise	1945
9988	Rotge, Lucy Eckert	1986
887	Rothchild, William	1936
14430	Rothrock, James A.	1994
3977	Roundtree, Michael Cox	1968
11268	Rouse, William Raymond	1988
18922	Rowland, Albert V.	2002
393	Rowland, Hattie B.	1912
8280	Rowland, Nell Wheat	1982
58	Rowlings, Keziah	----
10760	Rowsey, Gentry L.	1987
18404	Rowsey, Merl A.	2001
6601	Roy, Alton L.	1978
7065	Roye, Ruth Roberts	1979
4210	Rubio, Lula	1967
14022	Rubey, Martha Ferguson	1993
6195	Ruby, Arthur Carson Jr.	1976
11340	Rucker, Edith Jean	1988
18230	Rucker, Esther Montel	2001
17068	Rucker, James	1999
6509	Rucker, William P.	1977
7691	Rudasill, Catherine A.	1981
6531	Rudasill, Katherine Ann	1977
7452	Rudasill, Nichols H.	1980
SE11132	Rudd, Carroll Gene	1988
15442	Rudine, Margie E.	1996
14884	Ruff, Alma M.	1995
4253	Ruff, Lena	1967
4534	Rugel, Gus L.	1970
18670	Runberg, Marioin L.	2001
18552	Rupley, Blanche G.	2001
13808	Ruppert, George Omar	1993
10948	Rusch, Leroy	1988

File	Deceased	Year
1960	Ruse, Ada Payne	1955
4960	Rush, Maude	1972
16328	Rushing, Stephen O.	1997
12690	Rusling, Charles James Jr.	1991
8572	Rusling, Thelma	1983
13554	Russ, Elizabeth Koudelka	1992
13552	Russ, Rudolph	1992
6710	Russell, Abner H.	1978
1710	Russell, Ammons B.	1953
11992	Russell, Bess M.	1990
583	Russell, Dan/Don	1923
3166	Russell, Frank Allen	1964
10000	Russell, Harry Fuqua	1986
5381	Russell, Howard Kenneth	1973/74
2957	Russell, J. W.	1963
9684	Russell, Rex G.	1985
15020	Russell, Robert R.	1995
1109	Rut, Leonard J.	1990
11820	Ruth, Esther	1989
9173	Rutherford, Effie L.	1984
1589	Rutherford, William W.	1951
3334	Rutledge, May B.	1965
SE13786	Ruttan, Hilda Mae Doney	1993
7727	Ryan, Lynne	1981
8575	Ryan, Philip J.	1983
12742	Ryan, Richard George	1991
10090	Ryberg, Carl Gunner	1986
7173	Rydberg, Gladys Evelyn	1979
13884	Rye, Doyle S.	1993
1723	Rylander, Eva	1953

File	Deceased	Year
	S	
9161	Sabel, Jack Sidney	1984
13232	Sabins, Edna Brooks	1992
14622	Sabins, Elizabeth Secour	1994
14848	Sabins, Lonnie Dean	1995
9986	Sabins, Mavis	1986
8858	Sabins, R. L. Sr.	1984
12716	Sabins, R. l. Jr.	1991
18580	Sabom, Felicia S.	2001
12948	Sabom, William O.	1991
9368	Saenger, Arthur A.	1985
1907	Saenger, Emil Edmond	1955
12554	Saenger, Marion D.	1991
1588	Saenger, Robert Sr.	1951
2992	Saenger, T. H.	1963
SE10318	Saffell, Nettie Loyce Duncan	1986
7277	Safferstone, Hattie Mae	1980
8067	Safferstone, Irving B.	1982
15914	Sailer, Elly E.	1997
6948	St. Clair, Clarence R.	1978
12428	St, Clair, Dorothy A.	1990
5254	St. Clair, John Allen	1973
3298	St. Germain, Bert J.	1965
3333	St. Germain, Leta B.	1965
2846	St. Germain, Raymond J.	1962
3461	St. John, Herbert L.	1966
2619	St. John, Margaret H.	1961
13744	Sakraida, Frank T.	1993
10122	Sallee, Clinton M.	1986
SE11230	Salinas, Melquides	1988
687	Salter, C. E.	1929

File	Deceased	Year
8463	Salter, Camilla Elizabeth	1983
14544	Salter, Forrest A.	1994
9170	Salter, Jeanne Claire	1984
7815	Salter, Louise Eliza.	1981
687	Salter, Winnifred Alain	1930
14528	Salvaggio, Joe Jr.	1994
17176	Salvaggio, Robert Lee	1999
16106	Salvaggio, Toaslie Clara	1997
375	Sammons, Albert	----
14448	Sample, Beulah S.	1994
7669	Sample, Earline L.	1981
9744	Sample, Ernest E.	1985
8871	Sample, Fred J.	1984
10260	Sams, Farris Vernon	1986
2156	Samuels, Elsie	1957
15102	Sanchez, Antonio	1995
14798	Sanchez, Francisca	1995
16776	Sanchez, Louis L.	1998
18206	Sanchez, Margaret Ellen	2000
1560	Sandefer, Annie	1951
6085	Sandedge, C. M.	1976
3417	Sandedge, G. T. Sr.	1965
SE11856	Sandel, Roland A.	1989
5482	Sandell, Elizabeth Duke	1974
6308	Sander, Helen Anne	1976/77
12342	Sanders, Beulah	1990
9021	Sanders, Clyde Jr.	1984
2616	Sanders, Ernest L.	1961
11318	Sanders, Hubert E.	1988
6334	Sanders, Lewis J.	1976/77
6339	Sanders, Lewis J.	1976/77
2739	Sanders, Melver Mae	1961
15954	Sanders, Nancy Marga.	1997

File	Deceased	Year
SE112944	Sanderson, Christine C.	1991
11294	Sandidge, Annie B.	1988
17822	Sandidge, Jean Baker	2000
16272	Sandidge, John	1997
2027	Sandidge, Minnie	1956
8642	Sandlin, William Thomas	1983
11858	Saner, Dorothy R.	1989
1442	Saner, O. B.	1949
18730	Saner, William Bryant Sr.	2001
3717	Sanford, Allan D. Jr.	1967
9902	Sanford, Blanche Bell	1986
937	Sanford, Edgar B.	1936
SE21	Sanford, Grace	----
12440	Sanford, John D.	1990
10030	Sanford, Rosalee Vetter	1986
13472	Sapp, Betty JO	1992
CV940028	Sapp, Betty Jo	1992
13458	Sapp, John James	1992
10956	Sapp, John P.	1988
170060	Sargent, John Chester	1999
234	Sauballe, Mary	----
341	Saubelle, Nicholas	1913
360	Saucier, Henrietta C.	1913
137	Sauer, A.	----
733	Sauer, Mary A.	----
1704	Saul, J. J.	1953
9051	Sauls, Mary Letha	1984
9510	Saunders, Alan Wiafield Jr.	1985
14914	Saunders, Dorothy Mae	1995
6491	Saunders, Harold C. Jr.	1977
14876	Saunders, Orena G.	1995
740	Saur, Fritz	1931

File	Deceased	Year
368	Saur, Minna	----
11256	Saur, Selina	1988
9019	Savage, George Walter	1984
14818	Savage, Grace R.	1995
6073	Savage, Maggie E.	1976
17422	Savoie, Ulric G.	1999
744	Savoir, Hiram	1931
15862	Saylor, Charles E.	1996
7358	Scales, Fran Mc Neeley	1980
12684	Scantlin, Lester Wayne	1991
SE13378	Scarborough, Annie C.	1992
8916	Scarborough, Eleanor Grace	1984
5506	Scarborough, Frank	1974
3193	Schad, Joseph F.	1964
6866	Schad, Vera Braden	1979
17420	Schaefer, James D.	1999
8027	Schaper, Pearl	1982
795	Scharnberg, Ida	1933
14252	Scharnhorst, Myrtle Geneve	1994
1490	Schatt, Sophie	1950
7522	Schackelford, John Charles	1980
19270	Schaefer, Adis Adean	2002
9312	Scheaffer, Edna S.	1984
SE95-2	Scheer, Larell Powell	1995
10869	Scheirton, George W.	1987
134	Schellhase, Gottfried	1892
14442	Schellhase, Roland	1994
444	Schellhase, Otto	----
10198	Scherdin, Carl William	1986
17768	Scherer, Leon E.	1998
7242	Scherer, Lewis Frederic	1980
13988	Scherer, Margaret Lois	1993

241

File	Deceased	Year
7754	Schiller, Horace F.	1981
4689	Schilling, Louis F.	1971
3694	Schirch, Harry	1967
8863	Schiwetz, E. M.	1984
10216	Schiwetz, Ruby Lee	1986
9334	Schladoer, Eugene	1985
107	Schladoer, Hugo	1891/92
-----	Schladoer, Robert	----
18902	Schlather, James G.	2002
5539	Schlunegger, Ueli	1975
12916	Schlup, Walter Dale	1991
8115	Schmerbeck, Aimee Garrett	1982
19258	Schmerbeck, Edith H.	2002
17590	Schmerbeck, Garrett G.	1999
11026	Schmerbeck, Robert L. Jr.	1988
5495	Schmerber, Leonor	1974
1812	Schmidt, Charles	1954
13882	Schmidt, Chester	1993
13626	Schmidt, Clara Mae	1992
3522	Schmidt, Eddie	1966
381	Schmidt, Edward	----
5336	Schmidt, Edward J.	1974
4937	Schmidt, Eleanor E.	1972
6583	Schmidt, Ella	1978
6126	Schmidt, Jay H.	1976
15450	Schmidt, Marie H.	1996
5219	Schmidt, Oscar F.	1973
16758	Schmidt, Robert William	1998
5823	Schmitz, Francis J.	1975
11510	Schmidtz, Grace	1989
10058	Schmisseur, Edward R.	1986
14704	Schmitt, Robert George	1994

File	Deceased	Year
15300	Schmuck, Myla Frances Padgett	1995
15812	Schmuck, Rudolph H.	1996
16926	Schneider, Mildred Jean	1998
10792	Schneider, Ruth Medlin	1987
16282	Schock, Gwendoline B.	1997
1409	Schoenwolf, A. F.	1949
8603	Schoettler, Erna B.	1983
19228	Schofield, David Patrick	2002
5209	Scholibo, Charles	1973
12854	Scholl, Agnes Mcbeth aka Macbeth Ashworth Scholl aka Macbeth A. Scholl	1991
9608	Schorer, Freeda	1985
1447	Schott, Bruno	1949
4086	Schrampfer, Ernest	1967
875	Schreiner, A. C.	1935
3076	Schreiner, A. C. Jr.	1964
11236	Schreiner, Audrey Phillips	1988
623	Schreiner, Charles	1927
18428	Schreiner, Charles III	2001
781	Schreiner, E. Mae	1933
2811	Schreiner, Gus F.	1962
1164	Schreiner, Huldah	1943
9140	Schreiner, Josephine Carr	1984
18684	Schriener, Louis Albert II	2001
4751	Schreiner, Myrtle B.	1969
2293	Schreiner, Myrtle Scott	1958
1724	Schreiner, Nellie G.	1953
790	Schreiner, W. R.	1933

File	Deceased	Year
4300	Schreiner, W. Scott	1969/70
3975	Schroeder, John	1968
10890	Schroeder, Lillian B.	1987
14008	Schubert, Betty	1993
1843	Schuepbach, Elise Hopf	1954
5153	Schuettig, Alvin E.	1973
2445	Schuett, Harry C.	1959
1274	Schuetze, Fritz	1946
6099	Schuetze, Hubert	1976
19268	Schuh, Margaret Ann	2002
1707	Schuh, Swanette	1953
9892	Schulgen, Walter A.	1986
6646	Schultis, Emanuel H.	1978
9784	Schults, Melissa J.	1985
6932	Schulz, Ottilie	1979
1473	Schulze, Augusta Anna	1950
1266	Schulze, Herman	1946
1513	Schulze, Walter	1951
13262	Schumacher, B. N.	1992
16256	Schumacher, Dorothy J.	1997
98	Schumacher, Elizabeth	1887
9782	Schumacher, Gustine M.	1985
SE56	Schumacher, Houston C.	1981
1245	Schumacher, John R.	1945
15704	Schumacher, Jonny Hascol	1996
7202	Schumacher, Zella Secrest	1980
14690	Schuster, George III	1994
12180	Schwandt, Gerhardt	1990
18224	Schwartz, Albert George	2001
13432	Schwartz, Ruth	1992
SE00-1	Schwartz, Sidney S.	2000
11438	Schwarz, Charles E. Sr.	1989
19104	Schwarz, Marie K.	2002

File	Deceased	Year
10342	Schwarz, Mary L.	1986
12758	Schwarz, O. E.	1991
8703	Schweitzer, Norma	1983
1163	Schwethelm, Bruno	1943
17548	Schwethelm, Harry F.	1999
1608	Schwethelm, Johanna	1952
7737	Schwethelm, O. B.	1981
13154	Schwethelm, Ysabel Faltin	1992
1407	Schwetze, Louise	1949
1901	Schwetzer, Charles L.	1954
4812	Schwiening, Fred	1972
398	Scoble, Annie E.	1916
2123	Scogin, G. N.	1957
15592	Scogiin, Garland C.	1996
SE83	Scotka, A. J.	1982
SE23	Scott, Clyde O.	1977
263	Scott, E. D.	----
2166	Scott, Earl D.	1957
14928	Scott, Ethel	1995
13050	Scott, Fay P.	1991
12514	Scott, Ferne	1991
16130	Scott, Frances T. aka Ima Frances Scott	1997
2649	Scott, Gertrude	1961
4019	Scott, John W.	1968
10530	Scott, Leslie Dale Sr.	1987
6753	Scott, Lillian May	1978
15594	Scott, Lynn Dykes	1996
6872	Scott, Neva Viola	1979
11916	Scott, Margaret G.	1989
15310	Scott, Robert Wilson	1995
96	Scott, W.	1887
2674	Scott, Wilbur G.	1961
10240	Scroggins, Earl Keith	1986

File	Deceased	Year
1289	Scroggs, J. W.	1946
9446	Scruggs, Jackson Columbus	1985
9634	Scruggs, Juanita Bruton	1985
16772	Seagraves, Maydee	1998
10454	Seale, Charles Taze	1987
13980	Seale, Philip	1993
16594	Seamons, Benjamin O.	1998
9678	Searcy, Alfred Lee	1985
9760	Searcy, Fleda Jo	1985
17898	Searcy, Jack	2000
9774	Sears, Charles Lee	1985
2352	Sears, George DuBose	1959
19286	Sears, Jack Vaughn Sr.	2002
3677	Sears, Walter G.	1967
5050	Seaver, Harold Edward	1972/73
19150	Sebesta, Carol S.	2002
5311	Sechrist, F. B.	1973
12836	Sechrist, Norris	1991
15538	Secor, Beulah Adkins	1996
15166	Secor, Creighton	1995
950	Secor, William Lee	1936
4653	Secor, Willie Beatrice	1970
2862	Secrest, F. H.	1962
1556	Secrest, Leacy	1951
5536	Seeback, E. John	1974
14488	Seeger, Roe E.	1994
5100	Seeligson, Jeff Lewis	1973
2565	Segar, Gordon L.	1960
19402	Segerson, Willard	2002
3716	Seide, Carl	1967
15040	Seidel, Joshua	1995
16904	Seidel, Terry Wayne	1998
9514	Seidensticker, Elise Doebbler	1985

File	Deceased	Year
12458	Seidensticker, Elmer Roy	1990
15190	Seidensticker, Joyce E.	1995
14754	Seidensticker, Margaret Sarah	1994
9187	Seitz, Grace	1984
11106	Selbo, Lyle W.	1988
1777	Self, A. E.	1954
12778	Seller, Helen M.	1991
1242	Sellers, Fannie Augusta	1945
1291	Sellers, James	1946
18370	Sellers, Raymond Leo	2001
19190	Semple, Bernice M.	2002
11586	Semple, John	1989
9030	Sencenbough, Leslie E.	1984
3506	Sentesi, Frank J.	1966
7621	Sessums, George E.	1981
8248	Sessums, Marguerite	1982
6571	Seth, Olga Carolyn	1977/78
825	Sevanson, Alfred	1934
14286	Sevey, Fred Warner	1994
14298	Sewell, Lester Avent Sr.	1994
12422	Seyfert, Ethel M.	1990
204	Seyfert, Herman	----
16950	Seyler, Carey Milford	1998
14762	Seymour, Gladys Luciel	1994
13164	Shafer, Cleve Otis	1992
12886	Shafer, George Raymond	1991
8763	Shafer, Shelton S.	1983
14926	Shafer, Virginia D.	1995
7190	Shaffer, David Cross	1980
11738	Shaffer, Elsie I.	1989
632	Shaffield, Maurine	----
6978	Shafter, Wilson M.	1979
5320	Shaheen, Richard F.	1974

File	Deceased	Year
9366	Shamel, Fannie A.	1985
14720	Shanahan, Olive Elaine	
	Mc Duffee	1994
3233	Shanklin, Edith L.	1965
2264	Shanklin, J. L. (Dr.)	1958
5139	Shannon, Charlotte E.	1973
13358	Shannon, Robert	1992
18188	Shannon, Sally B.	2000
1053	Shapiro, I.	1940
17710	Shapiro, Martin B.	2000
19344	Sharpless, Ralph G.	2002
4581	Shares, H. L.	1968
SE85	Shaw, Bernon F.	1982
322	Shaw, Claricy	----
17808	Shaw, Doris Marie	2000
2239	Shaw, Hilda	1958
13562	Shaw, Hubert M.	1992
2049	Shaw, John C.	1956
SE95-6	Shaw, Kenneth A.	1995
16156	Shaw, Mary Margaret	1997
SE85	Shaw, Vernon F	1983
15492	Shay, Connor Patrick	1996
11638	Shay, Mildred H.	1989
2443	Shearn, Laura R.	1959
15500	Sheaves, Harry	1996
7549	Sheckles, Loyd W.	1980
19078	Skeckles, Theo Myrtle	2002
-----	Sheerhotz, Louis	----
2600	Sheffield, Frank D.	1960
18990	Sheffield, Hugh Donald	2002
5233	Sheffield, Setella C.	1973
9554	Sheffield, Theodore	
	Ferdinand	1985
10518	Shelgren, Carl H.	1987
7474	Shelton, Burl L.	1980

File	Deceased	Year
2271	Shelbourne, Lalah G.	1958
16144	Shelburne, Charles Wesley	1997
18516	Shelburne, Wilma Kathleen	2002
1347	Shelhunne, R. A.	1947
9550	Shellman, Elmer William	1985
SE02-4	Shelton, Horace H.	2002
11870	Shelton, J. D.	1989
14296	Shelton, Robert R.	1994
3434	Shepard, Mary V.	1965
14536	Sheppard, Alfred Edgar	1994
6649	Sheppard, Harriet Lucy Rees	1978
16804	Sheppard, John Wayne	1998
8374	Sheppard, Marshall Lott Jr.	1982
1675	Sheppard, Mary	1953
14352	Sheppard, Thomas Odell	1994
17180	Sherlock, Edward J. Jr.	1999
3846	Sherman, Claud	1967
5413	Sherman, Nina Mae	1974
17006	Sherman, Norman Glenn	1998
2582	Shern, Charles P. Jr.	1960
8057	Sherrell, Saidee Day	1982
10838	Sherrick, Josephine O.	1987
9412	Sherwin, Dan Clark	1985
3585	Sherwood, Eugene W.	1966
6269	Sheyock, Herbert M.	1976/77
12036	Shidel, Frederic Charles	1990
15800	Shields, Florine E.	1996
464	Shikell, C. E.	----

File	Deceased	Year
16416	Shilling, Mayfield R.	1997
19240	Shilling, Merle	2002
1561	Shinn, Jesse W.	1951
1550	Shinn, Susie M.	1951
9928	Shipman, Fannie K.	1986
8194	Shirley, Mary Ida	1982
7124	Shock, Jake	1979
10460	Shoemaker, Barbara Ruth	1987
12014	Shoemaker, Benjamin H.	1990
12034	Shoemaker, Benjamin Howe	1990
6592	Short, Cleveland L.	1978
13314	Short, James Clyde	1992
661	Short, Lawrence H.	----
14512	Short, Marvin Clyde	1994
14558	Short, Theda Merle Kiefer	1994
17778	Shotts, Patricia Taylor	1999
12476	Shouts, Alzina E.	1990
16548	Shows, Frances Faye	1998
19204	Shroyer, Dalton P. Jr.	2002
15396	Shroyer, Melvin A.	1996
1839	Shudde, Florence Wood	1954
10384	Shults, Leana R.	1986
12994	Shults, Bill	1991
13616	Shultz, Virginia H.	1992
11012	Shumate, Willaim A.	1988
16704	Sichel, Betty Emily	1998
8591	Sickert, Inda	1983
13242	Siel, Harry A.	1992
13608	Siel, Midge B.	1992
2753	Sifford, Joshua Green	1962
2854	Sifford, Maggie M.	1962
3347	Sigler, Maud L.	1965
3663	Sikes, Charles E.	1966

File	Deceased	Year
518	Sikes, Mrs. Guy Abner	----
8232	Sikes, Jewell Mangum	1982
3163	Sikes, L. C.	1964
5301	Sikes, Mamie M.	1973
17154	Silva, Bessie R.	1999
14660	Silvas, Estefana Enriquez	1994
3606	Silvey, Earl H.	1966
10864	Simler, Frank R.	1987
13726	Simler, Kathryne Hartshorn	1993
8356	Simon, George	1982
17690	Simon, Janice Kay Jacobs	2000
18634	Simon, Wyona	2001
6022	Simmonds, Fred Hartt	1976
1590	Simmonds, J. M.	1951
537	Simmons, Charles M.	----
16682	Simmons, Elizabeth Anne Richards	1998
12952	Simmons, Jimmie Eliz.	1991
1907	Simpson, George	1955
7508	Simpson, Harris Duane	1980
1443	Simpson, Ida B.	1949
1444	Simpson, Ida B.	1949
1987	Simpson, Ida B.	1955
3367	Simpson, Linda	1965
3070	Simpson, R. K.	1962
18824	Simmons, Andrew K.	2002
CV950184	Simmons, Eugene B. Jr.	1995
12384	Simmons, Ernest Wilson	1990
15400	Simmons, Frances Loraine	1996
14878	Simmons, James D.	1995
2147	Simmons, Mary	1957
9488	Sims, Charles H.	1985

File	Deceased	Year
14414	Sims, Frances	1994
3490	Sims, Irene J.	1966
6981	Simms, Nona B.	1979
15602	Simpson, Dorothy Frances Tiberghiem Higgins	1996
14482	Simpson, Tom Bowen	1994
15520	Simpson, Zella M.	1996
12924	Sinclair, Roy L.	1991
2121	Sing, J. C.	1957
11806	Singleton, Bonnie	1989
6391	Singleton, Charles] Morgan	1977
18364	Sinningerm, Charlotte M.	2001
16374	Sinninger, Dwight V.	1997
19140	Sippy, Stewart D.	2002
9934	Sivert, Loyd Carson	1986
12532	Sivert, Velma B.	1991
3615	Skaggs, Charles Luther	1966
4940	Skaggs, Erna Louise	1972
1721	Skaggs, Lee Andrew	1953
3196	Skeen, Matt	1964
5842	Skidmore, Carl Everett	1975
13388	Skinner, William Ross	1992
1641	Skillin, Marjorie F.	1952
6732	Skipworth, Ophus N.	1978
7126	Slader, Eleanor J.	1979
15262	Slape, Estelle Myrtle Wood	1995
3487	Slater, Gertrude	1966
6707	Slater, Sibyl Smiley	1978
18482	Slaughter, Lola Belle	2001
6840	Slater, William Allen	1978
15254	Slatt, James Leroy	1995
8262	Slaytor, James E.	1982

File	Deceased	Year
4884	Slaven, Connie Theodore	1972
326	Sleet, E. A.	----
8164	Sleet, Nayla L.	1982
7048	Sleet, Russell B.	1979
11572	Sliger, Lola Le Mae Long	1989
15178	Slimpin, William B.	1995
17694	Slavich, Jerold B.	2000
2090	Sloan, Florence	1957
18180	Sloane, Harold J.	2000
7118	Slocum, Frances Marie	1980
13216	Slocum, James Robert	1992
8152	Sloss, Mercedes	1982
177	Sly, Emelie	1899
15720	Smalley, Bernadyne Stokes	1996
6310	Smalley, Harriet R.	1977
180	Smallwood, Amelia	----
179	Smallwood, Ed	1899
17080	Smallwood, Lillie Mae	1999
18292	Smart, Dorothy Hughs	2001
9582	Smart, John W.	1985
7375	Smart, Lon R.	1980
2266	Smith, Albert	1958
9930	Smith, Alfred M.	1986
17440	Smith, Amos Lee	1999
12162	Smith, Archie	1990
3303	Smith, Arthur	1965
2214	Smith, Ava M.	1958
2234	Smith, Bertha	1958
6205	Smith, Bertha E.	1976
11224	Smith, Betty J.	1988
966	Smith, Blakely	1938
1353	Smith, C. R.	1947
10476	Smith, Carl G.	1987

File	Deceased	Year
13324	Smith, Cecil R.	1992
18040	Smith, Cecil Ray	2000
19098	Smith, Cecile S.	2002
16924	Smith, Chloe Bessie Hess	1998
5174	Smith, Claude H. Sr.	1973
SE74	Smith, Claude J.	1982
12414	Smith, Clayton Elmo	1990
13758	Smith, Cullen James	1993
408	Smith, Cora	1916
16706	Smith, Dale Outward	1998
17520	Smith, Delilah	1999
11878	Smith, Della	1989
17904	Smith-Hoston, Delores L.	2000
17458	Smith, Delphia B.	1999
6645	Smith, Dora Elizabeth	1978
15418	Smith, Doris Lee	1996
14520	Smith, Dorothy A.	1994
1405	Smith, Ed F.	1948
14792	Smith, Edaline Mildred	1994
2761	Smith, Ella May	1962
3605	Smith, Emma	1966
18380	Smith, Eugene Leo	2001
8662	Smith, Eura M.	1983
10168	Smith, Evelyn Louise Mayes	1986
10056	Smith, Frank Forsythe	1986
9167	Smith, Franklin Gilbey	1983
14604	Smith, Graydon Merle	1994
11518	Smith, Gunhilde A.	1989
14664	Smith, Hal W.	1994
10064	Smith, Harold E.	1986
17688	Smith, Hazel Lee	2000
9948	Smith, Horace E.	1986
17926	Smith, Irvin Lee	2000

File	Deceased	Year
3273	Smith, J. B.	1965
14198	Smith, J. H.	1993
6666	Smith, Jackson K.	1980
7226	Smith, Jackson Kelly	1980
2821	Smith, Jake L.	1962
10250	Smith, James W.	1986
175	Smith, Jane	1899
16214	Smith, Jay Bruce	1997
12928	Smith, Jennie Lee	1991
16116	Smith, Jewel D.	1997
1910	Smith, Jim H.	1955
524	Smith, Joe A.	----
8926	Smith, Joe W.	1983
8562	Smith, John	1983
8912	Smith, John De Lacy	1984
3167	Smith, John Reagan	1964
8514	Smith, Jubell Earl	1983
5964	Smith, Kelly C.	1976
17438	Smith, Klea M.	1999
10528	Smith, Lawrence N.	1987
17670	Smith, Lena Mae Wootton	2000
6255	Smith, Leslie H.	1977
17660	Smith, Lonnie Phillip Jr.	2000
17118	Smith, Lucile	1999
14688	Smith, Lucille E.	1994
2339	Smith, Mae M.	1959
5439	Smith, Martha K.	1974
6386	Smith, Mary Bernhard	1977
18738	Smith, Mary W.	2002
9818	Smith, Matthew	1985
9466	Smith, Maxine Christy	1985
15138	Smith, Mercedes	1995
1112	Smith, N. B.	1942
3558	Smith, Nettie Mae	1966

File	Deceased	Year
503	Smith, Ollie	----
6590	Smith, Ollie Agnes	1978
12908	Smith, Orval L.	1991
18750	Smith, Otis M.	2001
2830	Smith, P. M.	1962
13170	Smith, Paris A.	1993
17454	Smith, Phillippa B.	1999
3974	Smith, Powell Augusta	1968
18374	Smith, Raymond Leo	2001
10462	Smith, Ree G.	1987
14350	Smith, Richard C.	1994
7448	Smith, Roland	1980
10786	Smith, Ruby Rogers	1987
6197	Smith, Rudolph P.	1976
SE10786	Smith, Ruby Rogers	1987
12806	Smith, Sarah Ravndal	1991
18940	Smith, Thelma Elizabeth	2002
16610	Smith, Tyson Christopher	1998
3540	Smith, Verda Kathryne M.	1966
12298	Smith, Vermeille Sears	1990
218	Smith, Mrs. W. E.	----
9868	Smith, W. D.	1986
258	Smith, W. E.	1907
9940	Smith, William Joseph	1986
12048	Smith, Winston W.	1990
11086	Smith, Youel Curtis Sr.	1988
17456	Smith, Zane R. Jr.	1999
11468	Snealy, Gladys	1989
11058	Sneathen, Ivey William	1988
2006	Sneed, Maggie	1956
8379	Sneed, Carlos A.	1982
5071	Sneed, Methiel	1973
1858	Snelgrove, Marjorie	1954

File	Deceased	Year
1232	Snellgrove, George Fleming	1945
8022	Snelling, Gladys D.	1982
11774	Snelling, Harry F.	1989
16652	Snider, Ray	1998
8709	Snitker, Arlan Jack	1983
16168	Snodgrass, Bryce	1997
2051	Snodgrass, Georgie	1956
22	Snodgrass, Otis W.	----
11032	Snow, Carlton W.	1988
13940	Snow, Helen D.	1993
9794	Snow, Virginia Lee	1985
17572	Snyder, Barton Haschke	1999
18386	Snyder, Emma J.	2001
10290	Snyder, Florence Mary	1986
16446	Snyder, Joe A.	1998
8104	Sodich, Josephine	1982
7034	Sodich, Walter Peter	1979
11898	Sokalyk, Wasyl	1989
7558	Solcher, O. J.	1980
8246	Soleday, Josephine W.	1982
5187	Soles, George W.	1973
5488	Soles, Lessie Lake Forehand	1974
5737	Soliz, Mary Lou	1975
1695	Somers, Bertha	1953
6201	Sommer, Elsa Marie	1976
1601	Sommers, Della	1952
1605	Sommers, Della	1952
2188	Sonnen, Birdie Mae	1958
2383	Sonnen, Louis Jr.	1959
12494	Sontag, Merwyn R.	1990
19030	Soos, John P.	2002
14638	Sorell, Charles Frank	1994
3554	SoRelle, Andrew C. Sr.	1966

File	Deceased	Year
13308	Soth, Charles H.	1991
7806	Soth, Henry	1981
8565	Sottosanti, Anthony J.	1982
18610	Soukup, Lena W.	2001
6017	Souter, Mary Mc Kenna	1976
14744	Sowards, Mildred B.	1994
19176	Sowell, Thomas Wynns	2002
6992	Spalding, Henry Moses	1979
17510	Spalding, Sallye M.	1999
14368	Spangler, Tiana C.	1994
3512	Spann, Albert L.	1966
6810	Spann, Ethel Carroll	1978
11120	Sparenberg, George Russell	1988
7690	Sparkman, Bessie	1981
16634	Sparks, Charles W.	1998
15094	Sparks, Newton J.	1995
15092	Sparks, Pearl E.	1995
7948	Sparks, Mary Ruby	1981
6175	Spear, Gwenolyn	1976
11250	Spear, Clara Durrette	1988
1616	Spearman, J. B.	1952
17296	Speakmon, Frank Leroy	1999
411	Spears, Albert	----
12754	Spears, Helen D.	1991
7921	Spears, Russell Alan	1981
9316	Spears, Samuel L.	1985
10958	Speath, Alfred	1988
11216	Speath, Lillie	1988
13752	Speck, J. W.	1993
15644	Speck, Philip Laurence	1996
232	Speed, Julia	1904
1322	Speice, William C.	1947
4643	Spellman, Jessie V.	1969
5252	Spellman, Paul R.	1973

File	Deceased	Year
12244	Spence, Alice M.	1990
6486	Spence, John E.	1977
2202	Spence, Sallie	1958
15856	Spencer, Alexander Burke	1996
10124	Spencer, Robert L.	1986
SE81	Spencer, George Rutland	1982
6247	Spencer, Myrtle W.	1976
3338	Spenrath, Dan	1965
18312	Spenrath, Dan Jr.	2001
8641	Spenrath, Emma N.	1983
168	Spenrath, Frauz (?Franz)	1896
1635	Spenrath, Gertrude	1952
1076	Spenrath, Gustav	1941
1554	Spenrath, Louis	1951
166	Spenrath, Margaret	----
3384	Spenrath, Martin	1965
951	Spenrath, May	1936
9151	Spenrath, Peter	1984
589	Spenrath, William	1925
9238	Sperber, Ruth Marion	1984
3914	Sperry, Mabelle F.	1968
16350	Spice, Rowlin T.	1997
4001	Spicer, J. S. A.	1968
954	Spicer, James	1936
18298	Spicer, Mary	2001
970	Spicer, Robert	1938
836	Spicer, Robert E.	1934
5168	Spicer, Robert L.	1973
835	Spicer, Ruth Nelson	1934
13860	Spies, Olive Eastman	1993
4732	Spies, Warren T.	1971
16106	Spirek, John	1997
18292	Spirek, Ruth C.	2001

File	Deceased	Year
18466	Splaine, Gerard J.	2001
14068	Spooner, Fay Henry	1993
6203	Spooner, Lee Ira	1976
3689	Spooner, Ralph Francis	1967
59	Spotts, S. B.	----
3140	Spragg, Grances I.	1964
2783	Sprague, Chebe Ann	1962
2784	Sprague, Lloyd Annan	1962
11968	Sprang, Barbara I.	1990
736	Sprenace, Anzehan	1931
2093	Spriggs, Florence	1957
2506	Spriggs, Jessie	1960
2637	Spriggs, William B. R.	1961
9864	Springer, Ernst	1986
171	Sprinkles, M. J. (?M. S.)	1894
10784	Sproles, Jay Tracy	1987
2588	Sprott, Felix	1960
3880	Sproul, Annie Kaiser	1968
3454	Sproul, Dora	1966
446	Sproul, Margaret	1917
1974	Sproul, R. A.	1955
4736	Sproul, R. A. (Annie Kaiser)	1969
447	Sproul, W. W.	1918
602	Spruill, John Fred	1925
8151	Squire, Vera M.	1982
12022	Squires, James Hilton	1990
6900	Stacey, Hugh Grieve Jr.	1979
1125	Stacy, William G.	1942
17966	Stafford, Allen E.	2000
18402	Stafford, Jerry D.	2001
11754	Staglik, Louis George	1989
14288	Stahelin, George L.	1994
16738	Stakes, Eloi	1998

File	Deceased	Year
8006	Stalcup, J. Ray	1998
16502	Stalcup, Rebecca	1998
2789	Stalder, Dorothy Guenther	1962
8304	Stalder, Marvin F.	1982
6651	Stalker, Nellie W.	1978
4657	Stallings, Jessie Frances	1971
8776	Stallings, Laura Heathe	1983
18002	Stallsmith, Melissa K.	2000
8718	Standifer, Sarah	1983
7042	Stanfoid, William Simeon	1979
13060	Stanford, Fannie Dobie	1992
5256	Stanford, Helen A.	1973
16604	Stanford, Iva Mae	1998
5194	Stanford, R. W.	1973
5198	Stanford, William S.	1973
3664	Stanish, Chester K.	1966
18536	Stanley, Bobbie J.	2001
16626	Stanley, Jean Wood	1998
10074	Stanley, Jerry	1986
SE36	Stanley, Kent	----
1458	Stanley, William M.	1949
10092	Stansbury, Guy L.	1986
3285	Stapp, Jessie B.	1965
5907	Stark, Claud	1976
2510	Stark, James C.	1960
3941	Stark, Maggie	1968
18690	Stark, Novella Gertrude	2001
1275	Starkey, A. L.	1946
19366	Starkey, Alma Broadway	2002
2716	Starkey, Gordon Rankin	1961
19272	Starkey, J. W.	2002
18958	Starkey, Martha Lillie	2002

File	Deceased	Year
6361	Starkey, Patti Ruth	1977
3452	Startzmann, I. L.	1966
3050	Staudt, A. K.	1963
13646	Stayton, Zachary Scott	1992
871	Steagall, Josephine	1935
314	Steagall, P. M.	----
17228	Stedifer, Effie P.	1999
15202	Stedifor, Martha Irene	1995
12074	Steed, Margaret Elizabeth	1990
16040	Steed, William C.	1997
18360	Steele, Barbara Jean	2001
17922	Steele, Dick Ray	2000
16078	Steffey, Melvin Dewey	1997
14152	Steger, Hazel	1993
18432	Stegmann, Henry B.	1981
7587	Stegmollrt, Emil A.	1981
8210	Stehling, Estelle	1982
16826	Stehling, Loretta M.	1998
16280	Stehling, Martin F.	1997
2558	Stehling, Rudolf	1960
3854	Steiler, Edgar	1967
8527	Steiler, Josie	1983
15608	Stein, John Charles	1996
16712	Stein, Ruth Georgia	1998
7258	Steiner, John A.	1980
7252	Steiner, Michelle Denise	1980
8199	Steitle, Willaim A.	1982
16238	Stell, Georgia Monroe aka Georgianna M.	1997
18566	Stelter, Lydia	2001
8311	Stelzer, Walter E.	1982
16932	Stemmler, Hazel B.	1998
12576	Stephen, Tressie Lee	1991

File	Deceased	Year
9458	Stephens, C. M.	1985
13200	Stephens, Don M.	1992
10230	Stephens, Dorothy	1986
10964	Stephens, Edgar Allen	1988
6110	Stephens, Edward Benjamine	1976
9474	Stephens, George A.	1985
14250	Stephens, George A.	1994
8073	Stephens, Jacelyn Spellman	1982
14150	Stephens, Jewel W.	1993
14030	Stephens, John Allen	1993
8933	Stephens, M. V.	1984
10616	Stephens, Thad	1987
17220	Stephenson, Bess C.	1999
12862	Stephenson, Grace L.	1991
7704	Stephenson, Paul Christy	1981
11428	Stephenson, Paul E.	1989
13756	Sterling, Wilma D.	1993
5306	Stern, Emma R.	1973
12834	Stern, Lydia Juenger	1991
15864	Stern, Raymond L.	1996
3153	Sterne, Blanche K.	1964
6078	Sterne, Blanche K.	1976
8660	Stevens, Floyd V.	1983
8802	Stevens, H. N.	1984
17066	Stevens, Juanita W.	1999
17734	Stevens, Lester D.	2000
17683	Stevens, Loleen Eliz.	2000
18324	Stevens, Juanita	2001
4697	Stevens, Mary Linton	1971
10174	Stevens, Norman F.	1990
4823	Stevens, O'Dell	1972
15978	Stevens, Roy T.	1997

File	Deceased	Year
14188	Stevens, Virginia	
	Mc Gown	1993
3566	Stevenson, Frank R.	1966
4	Steves, G. C.	1862
2205	Stewart, A. H.	1958
3763	Stewart, Albert L.	1967
6067	Stewart, Alice	1967
14732	Stewart, Anabel M.	1994
3945	Stewart, Bettie B.	1968
13824	Stewart, Buell H.	1993
17950	Stewart, Carrie W.	2000
12482	Stewart, E. R.	1990
12072	Stewart, Helen Brehn	1990
2095	Stewart, John Heron	1957
7219	Stewart, Laurel G.	1980
8118	Stewart, Lewin R.	1982
1762	Stewart, Pauline	1954
3080	Stewart, Roscoe E.	1964
12612	Stewart, Rose M.	1991
16306	Stewts, Ralph W.	1997
443	Stiebeck, Auston August	----
15960	Stieber, Wanda L.	1997
7012	Stiefel, Earl E.	1979
11358	Stiefel, Ruth Anderson	1988
7057	Stieler, Adolf	1979
18096	Stieler, Elmer A.	2000
10306	Stieler, Evelyn W.	1986
11170	Stieler, Hilmer	1988
12160	Stiles, Jeanette D.	1990
9748	Stimson, Silas	
	Newton Sr.	1985
12070	Stine, Walter Dougles	1990
13374	Stinson, Clyde A.	1882
8816	Stinson, Meta Raver	1984

File	Deceased	Year
16892	Stobbe, Grace Mary Chandler Malicote	1998
2195	Stockton, B. M.	1958
3513	Stockton, Iolah	1966
863	Stockton, S. E.	1935
10416	Stodghill, Margaret C.	1987
18454	Stockwell, Marshall D. Jr.	2001
1681	Stoetzner, Mary Sabrina	1953
5955	Stoetzner, Walter U.	1976
9670	Stokes, James Edward	1985
2742	Stokes, Koger	1961
13766	Stolte, Opal	1993
18114	Stoltenberg, Wilmer David	2000
17664	Stolz, Eugene William	2000
19278	Stolz, Mercia Ahnnay	2002
14986	Stolz, Simy	1995
5268	Stone, Aaron R.	1973
16408	Stone, Bernice Bumpus aka Bernice Elaine	1997
3623	Stone, Charlie	1966
1024	Stone, Evans	1939
8733	Stone, Edna Bobo	1983
16528	Stone, Frank Evertt	1998
9998	Stone, Frank H.	1986
10348	Stone, Frederock Jesse	1986
8830	Stone, Glen Boulton	1984
12030	Stone, Harvey	1990
3411	Stone, L. E.	1965
1744	Stone, Lila Ella	1953
5981	Stone, Lisle E.	1976
10498	Stone, Roger	1987
3680	Stone, Susan Frances	1967
2002	Stone, W. L.	1956

File	Deceased	Year
1750	Stone, Walter C.	1953
1708	Stone, Walter Corey Sr.	1953
3753	Stone, Zeddie Claud	1967
16420	Stopke, Edward Leo	1997
17860	Storey, Mary F.	2000
17034	Storey, Mildred L.	1998
17836	Storey/Story, Myra Deal	2000
3788	Storey, Pearl L.	1967
11696	Storey, Vivian Walter	1989
9928	Storey, Walter Bruce	1986
3307	Storms, Brock	1965
417	Storms, Gilbert	1917
18654	Storms, Herod Hardin	2001
13692	Storms, Julia	1993
7438	Storms, Melba O.	1980
280.5	Storms, Sallie A.	1909
2987	Storms, Virgil	1963
13992	Storto, Nicholas John	1993
7862	Stotts, Joseph Lee	1981
5955	Stotzner, Walter Eugene	1976
18248	Stoughton, Marilyn R.	2001
14816	Stoughton, Ralph Eugene	1995
13406	Stoughton, Ruby M.	1992
3287	Stout, Warren M.	1965
5908	Stovall, Florence Eliz.	1976
4926	Stovall, Peter Franklin	1972
13764	Stover, Lewis E.	1993
13638	Strader, Eugene W.	1992
545	Strain, Troy Allen	----
3519	Stratton, Bess Hutchings	1966
5890	Stratton, Margaret J.	1976
11152	Straub, Edward C.	1988
8436	Straube, Josephine	1983
17116	Straube, Olinray C.	1999

File	Deceased	Year
17116	Straube, Olinray C.	1999
1213	Strauch, Anton	1944
16570	Strawn, Arthur J.	1997
14670	Street, James Wayne	1994
12636	Strickland, Ellis Howard	1991
9246	Strickland, Grace W.	1984
14272	Strickland, Viola	1994
2599	Stringham, Emerson	1960
2110	Strohacker, Dora	1957
8748	Strom, Edward G.	1983
2729	Strombeck, Lois Adele	1961
5398	Strong, Jessie B.	1974
4907	Stroud, Herbert W.	1972
16172	Stroud, Lucile R.	1997
11250	Stroup, Alta Prichard	1988
5062	Stroup, Guy Jacobs	1973
1566	Strube, Fritz	1951
9982	Stromberg, Edward H.	1986
16640	Strunk, Madison E.	1998
6855	Stuart, Clarence Eugene	1979
7974	Stubbins, William J.	1981
8823	Stubblefield, Evelyn Doveine	1984
2176	Stubblefield, James E.	1957
13670	Stubblefield, Mary Patricia	1993
3596	Stubblefield, Sadie Bess	1966
SE70	Stubbs, Lee H.	1982
8893	Stuckey, Daniel B.	1984
4047	Sturdivant, J. R.	1968
6471	Sublett, Audrey Jane	1977
10200	Sublett, Burkett Jordan	1986
5847	Sublett, Effie A.	1976

File	Deceased	Year
12128	Sublett, Herman L.	1990
14998	Sudbury, John Woodson	1995
14136	Sudbury, Martha Harville	1993
19242	Suhr, Edmund G.	2002
13700	Sullivan, Charles Henry	1993
7684	Sullivan, Gertrude Heath	1981
5136	Sullivan, Mabel C.	1973
5477	Sullivan, William A.	1974
13164	Summers, Benjamin Franklin	1992
2059	Summers, Frederic Gordon	1956
16694	Summers, Jeam Audet	1998
17824	Summers, Norman Lee Jr.	2000
1062	Summers, T. O.	1941
10840	Sumner, Jimmie E.	1987
9518	Sumner, Joe D.	1985
10652	Sumner, Peggy J.	1987
15522	Sumner, Robert P.	1996
17906	Sunstrom, Elsie H.	2000
6457	Surber, Charles E.	1977
751	Surber, J. F.	1931
573	Surber, Mary Anna	1925
3182	Surber, Q. C.	1964
1425	Surber, Mrs. S. E.	1949
11254	Surles, Edgar Wendell	1988
10146	Sublett, Jesse J.	1986
7245	Surhart, Rolf C.	1980
3695	Sutch, Vincent J.	1967
2438	Sutherland, G. C.	1959
4525	Sutherland, Joe	----
5539	Sutherland, Lelia	1974
15736	Sutherland, Mildred L.	1996

File	Deceased	Year
5081	Suttle, Earl L.	1973
7826	Suttle, William	1981
18748	Sutton, Alvin Lloyd	2001
18568	Sutton, Callie Brink	2001
14524	Sutton, Dorothy C.	1994
13702	Sutton, Lillian Grace	1993
9224	Sutton, Mabel Crawford	1984
6268	Sutton, Marguerite B.	1976
4767	Sutton, Neville	1971
6363	Sutton, Robert S.	1977
18172	Swafford, Lamoine E.	2000
12638	Swan, Herman A.	1991
13562	Swan, Hubert M.	1992
8783	Swanson, Alfred Adolph	1983
8492	Swanson, Allan R.	1983
9398	Swanson, Genevieve	1985
7667	Swanson, Jeanne Austin	1981
6478	Swasey, Mabel C.	1977
12600	Swayze, Douglas A.	1991
6079	Swayze, J. P.	1976
2652	Swayze, Jennie Jelka	1961
5489	Swayze, Lorine K.	1974
4207	Swayze, P. E.	1969
2585	Swaze, George A.	1960
1185	Swearengen, Hamp F.	1944
SE97-7	Sweeney, Charlotte C.	1997
SE11654	Sweeney, Joseph Berchman	1989
12318	Sweeney, Sally Walker	1990
16980	Sweeney, Thomas A.	1998
15930	Sweeney, William John	1997
1945	Swindle, John B.	1955
17640	Swinford, Keith Raymond	2000
4009	Swing, Mary E.	1968
4244	Swing, R. P.	1969

File	Deceased	Year
13488	Swinney, Bessie M.	1992
3091	Swisher, Warren C.	1964
SE99-3	Switzer, Alvis Loyd	1999
8074	Syfan, Helen Edwards	1982
5325	Sykes, Willie Sr.	1974
6104	Sylvester, Sybil L.	1976
10160	Synder, Katherine	1986
8457	Szekely, Barbara	1983
17356	Szekely, Charles Sr.	1999

T

File	Deceased	Year
17256	Tabares, Raymond C. Sr.	1999
7872	Tait, Robert R.	1981
14788	Talbert, Anita Basse	1994
17330	Talbert, B. N.	1999
13974	Talbert, William Curtis	1993
2125	Talley, Arthur Thurman Sr.	1957
SE12082	Talley, Mary C.	1990
3537	Tallman, David O.	1966
5599	Tally, Fred H.	1974
9292	Tank, Herbert Frederick	1984
6763	Tannehill, Francis A.	1978
4860	Tanner, Carl Clayton	1972
16466	Tanner, Kyle L.	1998
12360	Tanner, Mary F.	1990
7382	Tanner, Mary Grabawa	1980
5436	Tarr, Bessie Reed	1974
13482	Tarrant, Tomas Gage	1992
15968	Tarver, Ada Dean	1997
12714	Tasto, Minnie Lee	1991
5881	Tate, Ann Margaret	1975?
1651	Tate, Edward W.	1952

File	Deceased	Year
1093	Tatom, Granville	1941
1591	Tatsch, Apolonnia	1951
3320	Tatsch, Ferdinand	
	(Fred)	1965
13	Tatum, Henry	1872/80
10504	Taylor, A. B.	1987
11256	Taylor, Aileen Taylor	1989
165	Taylor, Alice	----
9724	Taylor, Alice J.	1985
17982	Taylor, Dorothy F.	2000
7017	Taylor, Edna	1970
7299	Taylor, Elizabeth	
	Atwood	1980
4025	Taylor, Ernest E.	1968
8538	Taylor, Ernest Marvin	1983
7076	Taylor, Eva Mae	1979
19310	Taylor, Frances K.	2002
9396	Taylor, Francis E.	1985
742	Taylor, George L.	1931
16088	Taylor, Harold Otho	1997
763	Taylor, Harry B.	1932
321	Taylor, J. W.	1911
17358	Taylor, Jack L.	1999
1243	Taylor, Leslie Thomas	1945
13614	Taylor, Mary Catherine	1992
10062	Taylor, Mary Christian	1986
6678	Taylor, Max E.	1978
800	Taylor, Myrtle	1933
4776	Taylor, Myrtle	1972
8010	Taylor, Neva Elizabeth	1982
1165	Taylor, P. B.	1942
7920	Taylor, Raymond Autie	1981
18132	Taylor, Sam H.	2000
3969	Taylor, Theron R.	1968
6415	Taylor, William W.	1977?

File	Deceased	Year
18484	Teague, Doris Lee	2001
3388	Teague, T. Dean	1965
18532	Teel, Minnie	2001
13048	Teele, Arthur J.	1991
3242	Telford, Edward J.	1964
-----	Tell, Fritz	----
16178	Teltschik, Avie K.	1997
16480	Temple, Theo Lewis Latane III	1998
11374	Templeton, Mary Eliz.	1988
7608	Tenberg, Johanna M.	1981
9710	Tenneson, Henry W.	1985
10878	Tenneson, Mellie	1987
10612	Terrell, Jerry William	1987
14934	Terrell, Josephine Johnnie Burns	1995
17124	Terrell, Thomas H.	1999
11704	Terry, Clarence Howard	1989
372	Terry, Henry	1915
12052	Terry, James Clarence	1990
5633	Terry, James Rodney	1975?
16194	Terry, Mary Kathryne	1997
6795	Terry, Maude Elizabeth	1978
4015	Terry, William James	1968
17200	Teten, Naomi Helen	1999
3559	Teter, William Henry	1966
9338	Tewksbury, Emma B.	1985
13722	Tewksbury, Robert T.	1993
15160	Thalman, Ernest H.	1995
9860	Tharp, Robert Calvin	1986
3686	Theodore, Ernst	1969
8455	Theodore, Hilda Webber	1983
14614	Thiel, Darwin Frederick	1994
15010	Thies, Raymond J.	1994
16886	Thigpen, George R.	1998

File	Deceased	Year
9810	Thomas, August Lafayette	1985
18726	Thomas, Clare Houghton	2001
6062	Thomas, Elizabeth	1976
5405	Thomas, Fred Carl	1974
17626	Thomas, Freda S.	2000
13066	Thomas, Garwood V.	1992
13202	Thomas, Gerda	1992
12336	Thomas, Harold Happel	1990
519	Thomas, James	----
50	Thomas, Jane S.	----
3249	Thomas, Johanna	1964
7808	Thomas, John M.	1981
7981	Thomas, John Mabry	1981
7227	Thomas, Kate Brewer	1980
15570	Thomas, Mary Jeter	1996
5133	Thomas, Maxwell J.	1973
7287	Thomas, Nellie Arie (Marie??)	1980
7161	Thomas, William Harris	1979
7997	Thomason, Frank	1982
9874	Thomason, Mildred L.	1986
2941	Thompson, Annie Lee	1963
7103	Thompson, Arthur Roy	1979
13890	Thompson, Clement C. C.	1993
8604	Thompson, Edward	1983
2489	Thompson, Francis Scott	1960
16486	Thompson, Garland Brown	1998
8337	Thompson, Glenn Russell	1982
5107	Thompson, Grover C.	1973
15840	Thompson, Hal K.	1996
11368	Thompson, Harlow M.	1988
6382	Thompson, Harvey Lee	----
3930	Thompson, Herbert L.	1968
8943	Thompson, Hilma Marion	1984

File	Deceased	Year
16580	Thompson, Jack	1998
11674	Thompson, James Edward	1989
16982	Thompson, James W.	1998
10218	Thompson, Jewel Olivia	1986
10246	Thompson, Jim R.	1986
14718	Thompson, Juanita Mae	1993
6076	Thompson, Lillian	1976
5106	Thompson, Loa L.	1973
15168	Thompson, Lois L.	1995
19108	Thompson, Luke	2002
16530	Thompson, May J.	1998
6954	Thompson, Misty Dawn	1979
2524	Thompson, O. H.	1960
8659	Thompson, Robert L. Jr.	1983
10804	Thompson, Rosemary Lillian	1987
1985	Thompson, S. E.	1956
7127	Thompson, Todd Stuart	1979
13966	Thompson, Viola Belle	1993
3431	Thompson, W. Elizabeth	1965
15352	Thompson, Willie Jr.	1995
108	Thomton, P. T.	----
8081	Thorn, Faye M.	1982
5976	Thorn, Francis Harold	1976
9434	Thorn, H. A.	1985
13730	Thorne, Harry H.	1993
3254	Thorson, Swan Conrad	1964
18446	Thrash, Ava Tuttle	2001
7403	Threadgill, Phil	1980
7129	Threadgill, Sedonia	1979
4137	Thurman, J. E.	1969
8427	Thurman, Lucille S.	1983
11354	Thurmon, Emmett	1988
CV920035	Thurmon, Emmett	1988

File	Deceased	Year
19034	Thurmond, Robert Hyler Jr.	2002
12890	Tidemann, Fred E.	1991
12118	Tidwell, W. R.	1990
15734	Till, Edmund J.	1996
15684	Till, Ily Jean	1996
8991	Timberlake, Herman Wesley	1984
14788	Timm, Vesta Winond	1994
18038	Tinley, Marian Edna	2000
11732	Tinley, Robert Emmet	1989
8525	Tippit, Ray R.	1983
SE10	Tipton, Donald Lee	1973
2525	Tirey, James D.	1960
12708	Tiritilli, Fred C.	1991
10170	Tittle, Loyd	1986
121	Tivy, J. A.	1892
3641	Tobin, Minnie Thronton	1966
1734	Todd, F. E.	1953
17654	Todd, Leslie Fay	2000
5997	Toepperwein, Herman W.	1976
12808	Tokaz, Albert John	1991
8132	Toler, Cedric R.	1982
18082	Toliver, Billy Joe	2000
4463	Tolle, Lela Gladys	1970
4775	Tolle, Leroy	1972
7724	Tomberlin, Thomas M.	1981
15672	Tomlin, Mae J.	1996
2395	Tomlin, William T.	1959
17064	Tomlinson, Dorothy Lee	1999
4679	Tomlinson, Frank S.	1971
10994	Tomlinson, Mary Clare	1988
3617	Tooley, Richard H.	1966
11732	Tooley, Teddy Ray	1989
3993	Toone, Robert T.	1968

File	Deceased	Year
17920	Tope, Howard Otis	2000
16240	Torgerson, Jeralde L.	1997
3416	Torres, Mrs. A. D.	1965
8506	Torres, Jesus C.	1983
506	Torres, Margo	----
7662	Totter, Othel	1981
16922	Towell, Harold Vernon	1998
18846	Towns, Eugenia Davis Turner	2002
3588	Townsend, A. L.	1966
12822	Townsend, Claude Ross	1991
1495	Townsend, Donald Fisher	1950
7552	Townsend, John H.	1981
15712	Traegel, Edna Earle Cook	1996
1030	Trahan, Henry	1939
18708	Trantham, Mary Madilene	2001
15542	Trapp, Howard Claud	1996
4968	Trapp, Howard Orlan	1972/73
17996	Trapp, Lanara F.	2000
SE107	Traudt, Nathaniel	1986
SE108	Traudt, Pearl	1986
18316	Traver, Jack O.	2001
16612	Travis, Alice Sigmund	1998
13856	Travis, Dorothy Louise	1993
3074	Travis, E. P.	1964
2411	Travis, Guy	1959
8234	Travis, Jewel	1982
12880	Travis, Ramon R.	1991
15090	Traweek, B. B.	1995
13708	Traweek, Robert T.	1993
8437	Traweek, Ruth Marie	1983
14050	Traylor, Bobbie Jo	1993
15590	Traylor, Robert Archer	1996
16190	Treiber, Ada Mae	1997

File	Deceased	Year
16192	Treiber, Albert Anton	1997
4030	Treiber, Callie J.	1968
7225	Treiber, G. H.	1980
15034	Treiber, Joe F.	1995
1576	Treiber, M. C.	1951
4660	Treiber, Mary A.	1971
12282	Trejo, Albert Loya	1990
16470	Trejo, Mary Arredondo	1998
512	Tremmel, John Thomas	----
15672	Tremor, Charles Wilbur	1996
18606	Tremor, Edna M.	2001
5032	Tressler, Dwight L.	1973
17516	Trevino, Candelario Espenoza	1999
4817	Trevino, Juan	1972
8490	Trice, Mary A.	1983
16986	Trinker, Frances Merritt	1998
10394	Triplett, Oscar Lee	1986
4078	Triplett, Willie Edna	1969
6640	Trolinger, John Shelby	1978
10054	Trolinger, W. C.	1986
18178	Trosper, Claude F.	2000
18008	Trott, Stephen Eric	2000
4882	Trotter, C. B.	1972
9886	Trotter, Dorothy W.	1986
7064	Trotter, Frederick James	1979
2231	Trotter, Leona M.	1958
4374	Trotter, Ralph	1970
SE107	Troudt, Nathaniel	1986
SE108	Troudt, Pearl	1986
4565	Troutner, Mary A.	1971
7150	Troutner, Roy E.	1979
18232	Trueblood, Ronald E.	2001

File	Deceased	Year
17384	Truesdale, Paul H.	1999
16972	Truitt, Lola Diehl	1998
2683	Trushel, Alfred	1961
8803	Trushel, Emma	1984
16322	Tschirhart, Ernst Spencer	1997
5479	Tubbs, Luther Hank	1974
14568	Tuck, Joseph Grady Jr.	1994
18342	Tucker, Cullom Owen	2001
12986	Tucker, Elbridge A.	1991
11422	Tucker, Ivan	1988
15288	Tucker, M. T. Jr.	1995
17834	Tucker, Maxine Ellison	2000
7716	Tufton, Beatrice	1981
17188	Tull, Delores M.	1999
4499	Tullis, Lena	1970
3482	Tullis, Richard E.	1966
18927	Tune, Robert L.	2002
2782	Tunstall, John R.	1962
2181	Turley, George E.	1957
11924	Turley, Mary F.	1989
16140	Turley, Roy Donald	1997
7773	Turner, Adriel L.	1981
1233	Turner, Alveda E.	1945
9856	Turner, Ben Tilman	1986
6901	Turner, Bess I.	1978
11330	Turner, Blanche B.	1988
7167	Turner, Clarice	1979
1191	Turner, E. H.	1944
15086	Turner, Edd R.	1995
9546	Turner, Effie Lucille	1985
2564	Turner, Helen A.	1960
8666	Turner, Howard De Witt	1983
12932	Turner, Iria Dean C.	1991
6940	Turner, J. C.	1978

File	Deceased	Year
750	Turner, J. R.	1931/32
16806	Turner, James R.	1998
3810	Turner, Jasper G.	1967
18094	Turner, John Junius	2000
101	Turner, L.	----
7374	Turner, Leo Dalton	1980
16146	Turner, Leon R.	1997
16538	Turner, May B.	1998
10610	Turner, Merrill E.	1987
13648	Turner, Stafford E.	1992
102	Turner, W.	----
6467	Turnpaugh, Laura Lena Lauterback	1978
6475	Turnpaugh, Walter Scott	1978
10184	Turremtine, Gordon H.	1986
14108	Turrentine, Margie T.	----
88	Tuten, A. J.	----
7479	Tuttle, Alexander Gregg	1980
7766	Tuttle, Alma Bales	1981
3122	Tuttle, Alvin Elmer	1964
10114	Tuttle, Ida A.	1986
696	Tuttle, Mrs. Sam	1929
11122	Twilligear, Verne Leith	1988
2262	Tyer, Grace H.	1958
2261	Tyer, Walter A.	1958
11272	Tyler, Injun A.	1988
12818	Tyson, Floy M.	1991
11136	Tyson, Howard E.	1988

U

File	Deceased	Year
372	Udden, Svante	1967
17998	Uglow, May L.	2000
12772	Uli, Margaret V.	1991

File	Deceased	Year
14146	Umberfield, Alton	1993
8142	Unnasch, Alfred	1982
13010	Unnasch, Ella R.	1991
15950	Unnasch, Estella	1997
8770	Underhill, Irene K	1983
13516	Upchurch, Nancy Brown	1992
8465	Uppling, Bernice T.	1982
15974	Uppling, John G. Sr.	1997
7135	Ussery, B. F.	1979

V

File	Deceased	Year
15610	Vadnais, Frank Eugene	1996
17084	Vale, Charlotte Ray Schaeffer	1999
13466	Valentine, Donald	1992
6694	Vallier, Kenneth	1978
9620	Vallier, Lucille C.	1985
9772	Vallier, Virgil J.	1985
17264	Van Aken, Gerald Robert	1999
9007	Van Alstyne, Pierce J.	1984
12312	Vanarsdale, Fred	1990
14290	Van Beysterveldt, Anthony	1994
14860	Van De Meer, Wybe J.	1995
16250	Vandenakker, Nicolas Jozefus	1997
2421	Vanderford, Mildred L. B.	1959
17312	Vandervoort, Chadwick Roddy	1999
19380	Vanek, Gustav Vladimer	2002
13668	Vanham, Joe William	1992
14716	Van Hoozer, Dorothy Mae	1994

File	Deceased	Year
5817	Van Hoozer, F. R.	1975
1532	Vann, Agnes G.	1951
2012	Vann, Baxter E.	1956
977	Vann, Charles C.	1938
17448	Vann, Elizabeth Marie	1999
2400	Vann, Henry Joseph	1959
3069	Vann, W. W.	1963
7183	Van Ostrand, E. D.	1980
10284	Van Pelt, Dan F.	1986
14232	Van Pelt, Virginia	1994
11642	Vansant, Evelyn Bell	1989
SE99	Van Sant, John W.	1982
9184	Vansant, Lester W.	1984
7520	Van Scoy, Elaine Faith	1980
5379	Van Scoy, Roscoe C.	1977
17880	Van Winkle, Cheryl	2000
13512	Van Winkle, Juanita	1992
7850	Van Winkle, Wilson W.	1981
17662	Vargas, Edmund O	2000
10016	Vargas, Frank A.	1986
13594	Vargas, Jesusa Ayale	1992
4188	Vargas, Marcelina	1969
11110	Varner, Chester A.	1988
12106	Varner, Elizabeth	1990
17612	Varner, Gus Noel	1999
11574	Varner, Pina Ann	1989
10624	Varner, Stephen E.	1987
SE11634	Vasquez, Valentina Quiroz	1989
13916	Vaughan, Betty Sue	1993
579	Vaughn, R. H.	1925
9754	Vaux, Elizabeth Gladys	1985
14400	Veatch, James Russell	1994
15126	Vega, Phillip	1995
1211	Vellenga, Charles	1944

File	Deceased	Year
8401	Vellemans, Claude J.	1982
1548	Verble, Lillie	1951
3569	Vest, Anna Scott	1966
3827	Vest, Walter L.	1967
6785	Vetter, Gustav	1978
6784	Vetter, Margaretha	1978
4758	Via, Prudie E.	1972
11104	Vick, Clemmie A.	1988
13280	Vickers, O. R.	1992
7086	Vickery, James Albert	1979
8114	Vickroy, Clemmie D.	1982
11388	Viles, Eunice	1988
2265	Villareal, Rogelio Ibarra	1958
14072	Villanueva, Leandro O.	1993
18280	Villanueva, Paula	2001
11864	Vinas, Elmo M. Sr.	1989
4621	Vincent, Fred A.	1971
13362	Vincett, Agnes W.	1992
15886	Vinson, Beatrice C.	1975
11490	Virdell, Velma Lena	1989
15558	Virgen, Theodore Jr.	1996
7886	Vlasek, Joe C.	1980
1770	Voelkel, Otto	1853/54
10688	Vogel, James J.	1997
18890	Voges, Harry W.	2002
18204	Voges, Marguerite Alberta	2000
8434	Voges, William O.	1983
5954	Vogues, Jeanette E.	1976
15186	Vohl, William H.	1995
6697	Voight, Leroy Henry	1978
867	Voight, Paul	1935
1158	Voight, Robert	1939/43
6040	Voight, Rudy	1976

File	Deceased	Year
6049	Volentine, Donald	1976
SE13466	Volentine, Donald	1992
1254	Volentine, Paul	1945
13662	Volentine, Ruth	1992
17686	Vollmer, Thelma	2000
4729	Volz, Henrietta	----
2218	Von Roeder, R. O.	1958
6465	Voorhees, Irving R.	1977
11634	Vosques, Valentine Quiroz	1989
6413	Voss, George E.	1977
16058	Voss, Julia M.	1997
SE51	Vugtinovich, Martin	1980

W

File	Deceased	Year
209	Wachter, C.	----
1381	Wachter, I. J.	1948
3206	Wachter, Lillie	1964
5920	Wachter, Ren (Leon)	1975
16008	Waddell, William Andrew	1997
12630	Wade, Doris	1991
881	Wade, Louis D.	1936
7761	Wagenfuehr, Charlie E.	1981
9410	Wagenfuehr, Millie	1985
12992	Wagenfuhr, Emil F.	1991
16342	Wagenfuhr, Grace	1997
5232	Wages, Margaret	1973
5028	Waggoner, Ernest	1973
12842	Wagner, Alfred B.	1991
9392	Wagner, Edith	1985
6140	Wagner, Elmer Edward	1976
1546	Wagner, J. Joe	1951
SE98	Wagner, Theodore G.	1982

File	Deceased	Year
SE98	Wagner, Theodore G.	1984
5587	Wagner, Vina L.	1974
6414	Wagoner, Edna Harrison	1977
6577	Wagoner, Edna Harrison	1978
13486	Wagoner, George Elmer	1992
15314	Wagoner, Mary C.	1995
13250	Wahrmund, Gloria E.	1992
8864	Wahrmund, Robert C.	1984
15956	Waibel, George J.	1997
14764	Wait, Edith Hanner	1994
10908	Wait, Eugene	1987
4505	Wait, J. Russell	1970
12962	Waite, Richard	1991
12252	Waldow, Louis A.	1990
12972	Waldrop, Curtis E.	1991
5820	Walenta, Ann M.	1975
4788	Walker, Dr. Allen H.	1972
12552	Walker, Berry Dee	1991
17164	Walker, Carrie Mae	1999
812	Walker, Charlissa G.	1934
2232	Walker, Charlotte G.	1958
6833	Walker, Charlotte T.	1978
7671	Walker, Dewey A.	1981
17940	Walker, Elsie B.	2000
5950	Walker, Forrest D.	1976
1862	Walker, George P.	1954
11146	Walker, George P.	1988
13710	Walker, George W.	1993
7147	Walker, Gerald Melvin	1979
12978	Walker, Helen Griffith	1991
7390	Walker, James Grady	1980
6738	Walker, James Watt	1978
13822	Walker, John Martin	1993
15444	Walker, Merle D.	1996
10452	Walker, Myrtle Page	1987

File	Deceased	Year
9228	Walker, Olin Bryan	1984
454	Walker, R. S.	----
9700	Walker, Reseda A.	1985
18834	Walker, Robert Dennis	2002
1705	Walker, Russell G.	1953
13982	Walker, Thelma Louise	1993
17586	Walker, Uzell D.	1999
15330	Walker, Weldon C.	1995
17772	Wall, Caroline M.	2000
15202	Wall, Robert Frazier	1995
7344	Wallace, Amy	1980
16220	Wllace, Clarence W.	1997
2691	Wallace, Frank	1961
3113	Wallace, Gertrude	1964
9018	Wallace, H. C.	1984
2405	Wallace, Henry	1959
1728	Wallace, Lee	1953
7146	Wallace, Malcolm C.	1979
9708	Wallace, Plessie R.	1985
9127	Waller, Clinton Henderson	1984
6661	Wallingford, Julia Ann	1978
3944	Wallis, Helene E.	1968
4957	Wallis, Virgil V.	1972
13100	Walsh, David Connel Jr.	1992
1036	Walsh, F. C.	1940
11064	Walsh, Justa Zierlein	1988
12474	Walthall, Carl Moten	1990
722	Walther, George W.	1931
1037	Walther, Geraldine S.	1940
17128	Walters, Dorothy Schraer	1999
3243	Walters, Vada	1964
13878	Walton, Emma Barnett	1993
11478	Walton, Frances A.	1989

File	Deceased	Year
8806	Walton, Mildred D.	1984
10602	Walton, William Dewey	1987
6804	Walton, William J.	1978
6450	Wansley, Mattie D.	1977
13634	Wappler, Froeda	1992
9964	Wappler, Willy Runhold	1986
18452	Ward, Agnes G.	2001
CV010192	Ward, Agnes G.	2001
15534	Ward, Charles V.	1996
11502	Ward, Doris H.	1989
9452	Ward, Ethel Burk	1985
7177	Ward, Frances Mary	1979
1370	Ward, Georgealice S.	1948
10332	Ward, J. B.	1986
690	Ward, John H.	1930
6138	Ward, Lizzie	1976
13456	Ward, Marcus L.	1992
17280	Ward, Mattie W.	1999
12462	Ward, N. S.	1990
4071	Ward, O. W.	1968
17010	Ward, Rose Marie	1998
11500	Ward, Roy A.	1989
6588	Ward, Tracy Marguerite	1978
3125	Ward, William	1964
4525	Ware, J. H.	1969
4051	Ware, Lina	1968
6787	Warhurst, Glenn E.	1978
11628	Warmbier, Edward William Sr.	1989
13504	Warner, Alma F.	1992
16756	Warner, Marjorie H.	1998
9850	Warner, Wilmot F.	1986
3123	Warren, James P.	1964
6532	Warren, Jody Lynn	1977
SE78	Warren, Joe A.	1982

File	Deceased	Year
13434	Warren, Raymond L.	1992
17254	Warren, Stanford Robert	1999
10644	Warwick, George Clarke	1987
1541	Washburn, Geneva	1951
1496	Washburn, Pat	1950
17546	Washburn, William Mack Neil	1999
3982	Washer, Anna	1968
3336	Washer, Charles F.	1965
11054	Washington, Charlie Bernice	1988
9696	Washington, Elmer Collins	1985
1565	Washington, Gilbert	1951
10116	Washington, Helen C.	1986
5542	Washington, Hershel L.	1974
13420	Washington, Lucilla	1992
10852	Washington, Sandy Jr.	1987
6971	Wasson, Glen C.	1979
14452	Water, William Berry	1994
12078	Waters, David Eugene	1990
6945	Waterstreet, Mae H.	1979
11460	Watkins, Vera G.	1989
12338	Watson, Alleene Williams	1990
5522	Watson, Alva C.	1974
6544	Watson, Carolyn E.	1978
1471	Watson, Daniel R.A.	1950
13158	Watson, Floyd A.	1992
12782	Watson, James Lewis	----
2578	Watson, Lucy Knight	1960
SE13550	Watson, Nannie Belle	1992
557	Watson, Mrs. O. E.	----
6473	Watson, Verlie E.	1977
6540	Watson, Verlie E.	1978

File	Deceased	Year
2579	Watson, William Arthur	1950
8421	Watt, Zena R.	1983
1881	Watts, Annie Laurie	1955
11274	Watts, Marjorie F.	1988
7738	Waxcler, Adolph A.	1981
9318	Weatherby, Jim W.	1985
6366	Weatherby, Talmadge	1977
14856	Weaver, Clyde Wiggins	1995
19396	Weaver, Delta V.	2002
5531	Weaver, Earnest P.	1974
15264	Weaver, Edna Earle	1995
8026	Weaver, Eula I.	1982
6950	Weaver, Julie	1979
3625	Webb, Ethel S.	1966
3201	Webb, Grover C.	1964
688	Webb, J. M.	1930
8255	Webb, Jessie M.	1982
1181	Webb, Mary L.	1944
16004	Webb, Philip A.	1997
13438	Webb, Rachel	1992
12930	Webb, Thomas Dean	1991
10366	Webber, Noel	1986
14000	Webeler, Lois Carpenter	1993
11322	Webeler, Ray W. E.	1988
3705	Weber, Frank H.	1967
13652	Weber, James William	1992
16588	Weber, Martha	1998
14404	Weber, Melvin George	1994
15776	Weber, Peter G.	1996
2046	Webster, Harvey L.	1956
3593	Wedekind, Etta Roberts	1966
7601	Weeks, Laurence John	1981
17336	Weeks, Lea Belle	1999
5527	Wehe, Milton F.	1974
4944	Wehmeyer, Alvin Arthur	1972

File	Deceased	Year
6245	Wehmeyer, Annie Lois	1977
4942	Wehmeyer, Elgin	1972
3105	Wehmeyer, Emil G.	1964
4892	Wehmeyer, Frieda E.	1972
15050	Wehmeyer, Karl L.	1995
CV950101	Wehmeyer, Karl L.	1995
17854	Wehmeyer, Ruby Alene	2000
14820	Weiner, A. D.	1995
18878	Weinert, Estelle S.	2002
13470	Weinheimer, Jacob	1992
13308	Weinheimer, Mary Margaret	1992
6177	Weir, Alfred Moore	1976
SE63	Weir, Carlton R.	1982
4824	Weir, Helen Downard	1972
4825	Weir, William Calvin	1972
5417	Weis, H. M.	1973/74
8471	Weiss, Bertha	1983
6340	Weiss, Frank	1977
18436	Weiss, Florence	2001
1992	Weiss, Henry	1956
SE30	Weiss, Lillian	----
3718	Weiss, Marie	1967
SE94-1	Weiss, Ralph Lee	1994
10850	Weiss, Rudolph H.	1987
17876	Weissman, Ruth G.	2000
351	Welborn, S. H.	1913
11088	Welch, Carlisle E.	1988
8674	Welch, Dannie Francis	1983
5716	Welch, Elizabeth	1975
12796	Welch, William Alton	1991
370	Welge, Conrad	1915
10052	Wellborn, Ernest	1986
8542	Wellborn, Helen B.	1983
5608	Wellborn, Henry	1974

File	Deceased	Year
305	Wellborn, Ida	----
1866	Wellborn, Norma V.	1954
492/501	Wellborn, Shallum P.	1921
1108	Wellborn, Tom	1942
8725	Wellmer, Jennette Marie	1983
17914	Wells, Christine L.	2000
11362	Wells, Daisy E.	1988
14642	Wells, Dorothy Amanda	1994
8913	Wells, Elisabeth Wilbur	1984
8779	Wells, Erwin C.	1983
1390	Wells, Eva Mae	1948
6701	Wells, Gretch Schrieber	1978
10186	Wells, Irving Dearborn	1986
18418	Wells, James E.	2001
16650	Wells, John Amos Sr.	1999
13126	Wells, John P.	1992
12824	Wells, Kenneth	1991
12848	Wells, Lloyd K.	1991
15696	Wells, Lucille M.	1996
1810	Wells, Mrs. M. M.	1954
14434	Wells, R. A.	1994
2799	Wells, Roscoe Ward	1962
2227	Wemple, J. D.	1958
1847	Wemple, Josephine H.	1954
17538	Wentworth, Evelyn J.	1999
6294	Wenzel, Walter A.	1977
17986	Werner, Irene De Masters	2000
17120	Wesby, Margie Campanella	1999
19118	Wesseling, John M.	2002
SE20	West, Arthur	1933
126	West, E. W.	----
7045	West, Elsie K.	1979
5525	West, Frederick A. M.	1974

File	Deceased	Year
5588	West, Frederick Christopher	1974
13658	West, George	1992
SE99-1	West, Horace Edwin	1999
8059	West, Kathleen Kemper	1982
18804	West, Ona Grace Smith	2001
16514	West, Wofford Randle	1998
2555	Westerman, John W.	1960
5057	Westervelt, Harold Pope	1973
8777	Westervelt, Julia Spencer	1983
13350	Westbrook, Louise M.	1992
6539	Westbrook, Olen Leon	1978
2578	Westfall, Ralph Lea	1960
12780	Westmorland, Claude W.	1991
2385	Weston, Alice	1959
11068	Weston, Bessie V,	1988
557	Weston, Caroline	1924
823	Weston, Charles	1934
1022	Weston, Emma F.	1939
2750	Weston, M. F.	1962
1904	Wetterling, Leah	1955
9190	Wetz, Mary S.	1984
15640	Wetzel, Joyzella L.	1996
17380	Wever, Bernard M.	1999
5989	Wharton, Ayleene	1976
996	Wharton, David N.	1938
892	Wharton, Lucia Ann	1936
385	Wharton, W. C.	1915
9728	Whatley, Ralph Carter	1985
17328	Whayne, Trevor R.	1999
4627	Wheat, Pearl	1971
11934	Wheatley, Marie Aileene Barrington	

File	Deceased	Year
	aka Marie Aileene	
	Heimann	1989
9228	Wheeler, Clarence A.	1984
16842	Wheeler, Gary Lee	1998
18392	Wheeler, Harvey B.	2001
12434	Wheeler, John Quintin	1990
16122	Wheeler, Wilma Marie	1997
SE11286	Wheelock, Inez	1988
SE13584	Wheelock, William L.	1992
4098	Wheelus, Cleveland B.	1969
13116	Whelan, Bernard J.	1992
17954	Whelan, James T. Jr.	2000
3157	Whelan, Jim	1964
4842	Whelan, Joe	1972
3383	Whelan, Kate Charlier	1965
5438	Wheless, Ada Nance	1974
2546	Wheless, Bertha W.	1960
1006	Wheless, J. S.	1939
9183	Wherry, Clara Julia	1984
17028	Whigham, Charlie B.	1998
15844	Whipple, Thelma E.	1996
17278	Whitacre, Mary M.	1999
17620	White, Adele	1999
16534	White, Adele Wilson	1997
7345	White, Alice Jackson	1980
7567	White, Alice Jackson	1980
3137	White, Carrie Harper	1964
8671	White, Charles O.	1983
12510	White, Clara Howell	1991
4548	White, Clarence Morris	1970
13400	White, Constance	1992
15080	White, Donald Craig	1995
8919	White, Edward A.	1984
17078	White, E. B. Jr.	
	/Edward E. Jr.	1999

File	Deceased	Year
12588	White, Gerald A.	1991
15174	White, Horace E.	1995
5148	White, Hugh	1973
7526	White, James N.	1980
6231	White, Jep	1977
2289	White, John Edward	1958
18144	White, John W.	2000
10130	White, Juliet Rodriguez	1986
10430	White, Lettie	1987
3555	White, R. Clyde	1966
15664	White, Robert Elton	----
298	White, Rebecca	1910
9884	White, Robert A.	1986
8623	White, Rudolph D.	1983
14382	White, Stanford	1994
17760	White, Virginia M.	2000
1885	Whitehouse, J. L.	1955
12042	Whitehurst, Frank Elonore	1990
4065	Whitfield, Edwin C.	1968
11874	Whitley, Helen Louise	1989
14056	Whitley, Noble E.	1993
19312	Whitman, Beverley E.	2002
19056	Whitman, Mildred Gaston	2002
15276	Whitmire, John L.	1995
18336	Whitney, Meta Darlene	2001
11900	Whittall, Betty Jean	1989
9932	Whittleman, John W.	1986
19022	Whittleman, Mary Elizabeth S.	2002
12092	Whitten, Owen Alden	1990
13576	Whitton, Jewell	1992
488	Whitworth, Mrs. H. I.	----
5474	Whitworth, N. H.	1974

File	Deceased	Year
8120	Whitworth, Vera Cornelia	1982
13834	Whorton, Frank Benton	1993
19328	Whorton, Melba Verlynne	2002
11130	Wiard, Leon A.	1988
4100	Wiechmann, Veronah	1969
10112	Wicklund, Opal	1986
12370	Wickson, Elvin Thomas	1990
10106	Wickson, Prentice Deward	----
1064	Wickson, T. D.	1941
12906	Wied, Henry Henke	1991
4839	Wiedenfeld, Albert	1972
6317	Wiedenfeld, Benno L.	1977
16244	Wiedenfeld, Bodo	1997
7325	Wiedenfeld, Clarice	----
8303	Wieland, Carl J.	1982
11405	Wiemers, Pearl A. M.	1988
SE104	Wienecke, Otto	1985
7240	Wienke, L. R.	1980
-----	Wiep, Franz	----
18166	Wiese, Hazel Brandes	2000
3473	Wiggins, Addean	1966
5185	Wiggins, Brack J.	1973
12540	Wiggins, Frances T.	1991
3658	Wiggins, John B.	1966
8884	Wiggins, Lena Mae	1984
10346	Wiggins, Platt K.	1986
10514	Wiggins, Stephen Lamar	1987
12276	Wilbar, Helen	1990
19	Wilburn, A. L.	----
6600	Wildman, Edward L.	1978
16732	Wilder, William Briscoe	1998
13806	Wiley, Gordon Young	1993
15670	Wilhoit, Marvin M.	1996

File	Deceased	Year
13006	Wilhoit, Sarah Eliz.	1991
3339	Wilke, C. S.	1965
4898	Wilke, Eugene M.	1972
4996	Wilke, Kenneth F.	1972
8087	Wilkens, Robert	1982
5920	Wilkerson, Alice	1974
1268	Wilkerson, Emily D.	1946
17382	Wilkerson, Lena J.	1999
7142	Wilkes, Orby A.	1979
2734	Wilkins, Joe G.	1961
850	Wilkins, Oscar L.	1935
3493	Wilkinson, Sam G.	1966
16574	Wilkinson, Willis W.	1998
8555	Willard, John H.	1983
17324	Willard, Mildred Wilder	----
2837	Willard, Walter W.	1962
10324	Willemsen, Libern Vincent	1986
12496	Willensen, Bettye Mae Morris	1990
18254	Williford, Hazel	2001
1570	Williford, L. O.	1951
9286	Williams, A. J.	1984
8547	Williams, Annie Laurie	1983
10938	Williams, Barney N.	1988
18268	Williams, Barney K.	2001
16790	Williams, C. Glenn	1998
18024	Williams, Carl E. Jr.	2000
5664	Williams, D. S. Jr.	1974
15836	Williams, David P.	1996
15388	Williams, Earl P.	1996
10450	Williams, Edna	1987
15392	Williams, Edward Ray	1996
17416	Williams, Ellerie	1999
6896	Williams, Ethel	1979

File	Deceased	Year
8609	Williams, Frances Mc Collom	1983
SE15	Williams, Frank E.	1944
12786	Williams, Glenn Thomas	1991
14802	Williams, Grace E.	1995
1017	Williams, Harry	1939
3477	Williams, Henry O.	1966
11622	Williams, Harold Augustus	1989
5889	Williams, James Mauden	1975
578	Williams, James P. T.	1925
3676	Williams, Jennie	1967
141	Williams, John	----
10350	Williams, Lee E.	1986
19334	Williams, Lee Robert	2002
8235	Williams, Lela	1982
2166	Williams, Leonard	1957
5749	Williams, Lester	1975
14446	Williams, Linda Eliz. Lilly	1994
CV990045	Williams, Lloyd George	1999
16564	Williams, Marion Phyllis	1998
11730	Williams, Mary Boone	1989
15916	Williams, Mary C.	1997
3300	Williams, Mary E.	1965
9478	Williams, Melinda	1985
15386	Williams, Mildred Patricia	1996
14842	Williams, Ouida May	1995
113518	Williams, Patricia Mae	1992
2483	Williams, Paul R.	1960
2885	Williams, Rayburn Dan	1962
SE12750	Williams, Robert Bruce	1993

File	Deceased	Year
409	Williams, Roberta	1918
2200	Williams, S. J.	1958
7307	Williams, Thurman J.	1980
17728	Williams, Vivian Louise Walton	2000
14760	Williams, Vivian V.	1994
1683	Williams, Walter B. H. Sr.	1953
15784	Williams, Walter Scott	1996
1362	Williamson, A. B.	1948
14142	Williamson, Clarice Mildred	1993
2461	Williamson, Eron A.	1959
8095	Williamson, F. J.	1982
15204	Williamson, Fraces T.	1995
12190	Williamson, George H.	1990
8974	Williamson, W. B.	1984
448	Williford, J. B.	----
12648	Williford, Helen J.	1991
7812	Williford, James Alsfred	1981
3179	Willis, William W.	1964
SE32	Willman, Natlie Margaret	----
13604	Willoughby, Nadine R.	1992
13888	Willoughby, Pauline E.	1993
11066	Willoughby, Russell W.	1988
2480	Wills, Harry P.	1960
4744	Wills, Inda Bella	1971
1183	Wills, Minnie L.	1944
1098	Wills, Myrtle L.	1942
3133	Wilmoth, Lenore Fern	1964
18572	Wilowski, Palma L.	2001
3294	Wilson, Adam Jr.	1965
1732	Wilson, Adam III	1953

File	Deceased	Year
3383	Wilson, Alfred H.	1965
7613	Wilson, Annie Laurie	1981
9752	Wilson, Bertha M.	1985
18646	Wilson, Burtrust T. Jr.	2001
10042	Wilson, Della E.	1986
4766	Wilson, Dora B.	1971
6293	Wilson, Edward T.	1977
9440	Wilson, Elmo	1985
12064	Wilson, Ethel M.	1990
5468	Wilson, Glenn	1974
3894	Wilson, H. M.	1968
6317	Wilson, Hamilton	1977
3642	Wilson, Harriet	1966
5537	Wilson, Howard G.	1974
6039	Wilson, Howard G. Jr.	1976
3988	Wilson, Ira Oscar	1968
4043	Wilson, Jack D.	1968
13096	Wilson, James Oakley	1992
12114	Wilson, James W.	1990
19174	Wilson, Jean Roberta	2002
16600	Wilson, John Clennie	1998
16660	Wilson, John Clennie	1998
9002	Wilson, Joseph A.	1984
15962	Wilson, Josephine Woods	1997
12110	Wilson, L. A.	1990
4781	Wilson, Laura White	1971
10696	Wilson, Lela	1987
11214	Wilson, Lena Marie Jackson	1988
7945	Wilson, Louis John	1981
SE11292	Wilson, Louis Robert	1988
2298	Wilson, Mary A.	1958
3782	Wilson, Maurice C.	1967
9556	Wilson, Mildred	1985
784	Wilson, Mozel	1933

File	Deceased	Year
16032	Wilson, Myrtle	1997
17712	Wilson, Raymond E.	2000
5683	Wilson, Robert I.	1975
3135	Wilson, Ruth	1964
7763	Wilson, Ruth Hicks	1981
5312	Wilson, Vera G.	1973
5638	Wilson, Wallace W.	1975
1886	Wilson, Walter W.	1955
11750	Wilson, Wesley H.	1989
8836	Wilson, William E.	1984
15440	Wilt, Raymond Charles	1996
8180	Wilton, Loretta Jane	1982
13460	Wiltshire, Donald F.	1992
16968	Windham, Carlie M.	1998
2404	Windsor, Aona L.	1959
18742	Windsor, Clarence Dalton	2001
18766	Windsor, Covey	2001
1070	Winkey, Francis L.	1948
17880	Winkle, Cheryl Van	2000
15228	Winkle, Earnest T.	1995
5024	Winn, John Henry	1973
10088	Winn, Mary E.	1986
18974	Winslow, Barbara Nell	2002
6033	Winter, Annis O.	1976
SE41	Winters, Ruben Thomas	1980
14432	Wise, Charles Morria	1994
12402	Wise, Robert Myers	1990
13390	Wise, Winifred Ann	1992
15446	Wiseman, Ed M.	1996
12248	Wiseman, Nannie D. aka Nan D.	1990
16902	Wisman, William W.	1998
1563	Wisner, Mary	1951
5465	Wisseman, C. L.	1974

File	Deceased	Year
5453	Wisseman, Helen Mae	1974
8649	Wist, Edward B,	1983
6948	Wist, Lorraine L.	1979
6717	Withers, Ned	1978
6626	Wither, William P.	1978
14042	Witherel, Allen W.	1993
14542	Withers, Kathleen Craig	1994
18488	Witt, Betty June	2001
599	Witt, Carrie A.	1926
169	Witt, E.	----
13618	Witt, H. L. Sr.	1992
3181	Witt, Hulda O.	1964
606	Witt, Isaac	----
854	Witt, J. D.	1935
1139	Witt, J. D.	1943
1666	Witt, J. D.	1952
8038	Witt, Minnie Mae	1982
12606	Witt, Morris	1991
3250	Witt, Prentice	1964
2527	Witt, Woodrow W.	1960
16648	Wittlinger, H. Virginia	1998
532	Wittman, John	----
14630	Woerner, Cecelia Amanda	1994
15810	Wofford, Mary Leona	1996
7288	Wofford, Ralph W.	1980
1061	Wolcott, Emma N.	1940
5487	Wolf, C. H.	1974
11326	Wolf, Pearl B.	1988
11702	Wolfe, Lloyd R.	1989
18694	Wolfe, Worthy West Jr.	2001
13682	Wolfmueller, Albert C.	1993
18702	Wolfmueller, G. Charlotte	2001
5054	Wolfmueller, Martha	1973
7703	Wolfmueller, Robert M.	1981

File	Deceased	Year
11662	Wolz, Anne Meyer	1989
13330	Womack, Berta Lee Lewis	1992
14378	Womack, Dorothy Faye	1994
10622	Womack, L. F.	1987
14380	Womack, Louis Carr	1994
6295	Womack, Steven P.	1977
2952	Womack, T. R.	1963
5449	Wood, Forrest Farwell	1974
11458	Wood, J. R.	1988
7512	Wood, Julia Clarice	1980
3950	Wood, Julia E.	1968
15936	Wood, Leola Meyer	1997
3831	Wood, Louise B.	1967
6409	Wood, Marcha Jane	1977
8384	Wood, Orville Wallace	1982
3868	Wood, Ralph E.	1967
6410	Wood, Sidney C.	1977
11186	Wood, Virginia Hamill	1988
783/785	Wood/Woods, William H.	1933
1008	Woodall, Elenore	1939
6156	Woodall, Felix G.	1976
17450	Woodall, Regenald O.	1999
5295	Woodard, Rachel	1973
13716	Woodbury, Jovita L.	1993
18612	Woodbury, Roma Jean Tom	2001
8279	Woodland, Sully S.	1982
6982	Woodrome, Charles Ruey	1979
16512	Woods, Clemmie E.	1998
11606	Woods, Dwight H.	1989
14078	Woods, Elmar L.	1993
1123	Woodward, Carrie	1942
13684	Woodward, Charles Day	1993
16062	Woodward, Grace	1997
17562	Woodward, John M.	1999
16258	Woodward, Katherine H.	1997

File	Deceased	Year
18490	Woodward, Louise K.	2001
14070	Woodward, Royce A.	1993
2750	Woody, L. W.	1961
19102	Woolbright, Melvin C.	2002
61	Woolls, G. W.	----
748	Woosey, Allen M.	1931
10046	Wootton, Charles Richard	1986
1170	Wootton, J. W.	1943
18330	Wootton, Lillian Marie	2001
3649	Wootton, Mattie Lloyd	1966
5097	Wootton, Minnie L.	1973
4551	Wootton, Virgil E.	1970
4848	Wopat, George W.	1972
1146	Worcester, Roy G.	1943
4071	Word, Alice O.	1969
3933	Word, H. K.	1968
14570	Worden, John M.	1993
19234	Worden, Richard C.	2002
9340	Work, Buford F.	1985
7970	Workman, Fred L.	1981
16602	Workman, Ursala G.	1998
11728	Works, Mildred P.	1989
SE52	Works, Richard C.	1981
14990	Works, Roy C.	1995
11258	Wothe, Phyllis M.	1988
5434	Worthen, Bamma Zella	1974
1457	Worthen, William Roy	1949
1926	Worthington, Blanche	1955
11636	Worthington, Clyde H.	1989
4905	Worthington, Joseph A.	1972
1383	Worthington, William P.	1948
16782	Wortman, Rosa Lee Grant	1998
9528	Wothe, George D.	1985
433	Wottrice, Alfred	----

File	Deceased	Year
2198	Wray, Alita Clark	1958
3980	Wray, Jay	1968
406/407	Wray, Mrs. S. E.	----
17292	Wrede, Janeen I.	1999
707	Wren, Ross E.	1930
2596	Wren, Mrs. Ross	1960
4191	Wren, Thomas W.	1970
1965	Wren, Walter	1955
17182	Wright, Alfred P.	1999
8620	Wright, Austin E.	1983
11824	Wright, Carrie K.	1989
17618	Wright, Chester	1999
3919	Wright, Clarence H.	1968
1302	Wright, D. M.	1946
18964	Wright, Dorlene W.	2002
3486	Wright, Ed	1966
3668	Wright, Eugene F.	1967
10894	Wright, Eugene W.	1987
6521	Wright, Francis	1977
10928	Wright, Frankie Mae	1987
5511	Wright, Gladys Mae	1974
18024	Wright, Gladys P.	2000
16188	Wright, Grace T.	1997
16462	Wright, Harriet F.	1998
174	Wright, J. W.	1899
1357	Wright, Jessie	1948
4677	Wright, Laurene Nairn	1971
19008	Wright, Mildred	2002
236	Wright, N. E.	----
7633	Wright, Paul E.	1981
5354	Wright, R. M.	1973
SE9	Wright, Raymond E.	1973
12692	Wright, Stanley G.	1992
15650	Wright, Thorold Waldon	1996
7275	Wright, William Guy	1980

File	Deceased	Year
4523	Wright, William J.	1970
14890	Wright, William Vernon	1995
17078	Wrobel, Gerald C.	1999
10706	Wuest, Edgar James Jr.	1987
17040	Wulf, Irving	1998
11450	Wulfman, Gladys S.	1989
9604	Wyatt, Beatrice T.	1985
2746	Wyatt, Charles E.	1961
12518	Wyatt, Rose Mitchell	1991
11540	Wylie, Sherrell W.	1989
6153	Wymer, Otto U.	1976
7002	Wynne, Clark F.	1979
7655	Wynne, John	1981
6914	Wynne, Mayme Grace	1979
16392	Wynne, Lsvonnr	1997
10032	Wynne, W. E.	1986

X

None

Y

File	Deceased	Year
15394	Yancey, Robert A.	1996
6187	Yantis, Boyd Dixon	1975?
6849	Yarborough, Ruth Owen	1979
8845	Yarbrough, George D.	1987
4605	Yarbrough, John W.	1968
8845	Yarbrough, Lillie H.	1984
7079	Yarbrough, Lois Pettigrew	----
2448	Yarbrough, Mattie B.	1959
5909	Yarbrough, Mattie Lee	1975?

File	Deceased	Year
3440	Yarbrought, Nelson	1965
2693	Yariger, E. H.	1961
11822	Yaswanawong, Noi	1989
1547	Yates, Bessie	1951
16882	Yates, David L.	1998
13780	Yates, Emily Gard	1993
12278	Yates, Grace H.	1990
4000	Yates, Henry H.	1968
6319	Yates, Irene G.	1975
13962	Yates, Richard O.	1993
1652	Yates, W. H.	1952
17044	Ybarra, Rogelio	1998
11646	Yeargan, Fay Knight	1989
11984	Yeargan, Roy A.	1990
6467	Yingling, Howard R.	1975
13816	Yocum, Janet S.	1993
8416	Yoder, Austin F.	1983
9662	Yoder, Helen Hudelson	1984
3442	Yokley, Otto O.	1965
9078	York, Allie B. Jr.	1984
4067	York, C. Frank	1968
4169	York, C. Frank	1968
2943	York, L. W.	1963
2433	York, Leatie A.	1959
14466	Yost, George S.	1994
5113	Youle, Joseph B.	1973
12506	Youmans, Franklin D.	1991
3458	Young, Ara Dee	1966
3863	Young, Carlton E.	1967
5849	Young, Charles M.	1975
5310	Young, Clarence F.	1975
6189	Young, Cyril	1975
618	Young, Edna	1926
11248	Young, Francis Theodore	1988
4169	Young, Fred E.	1969

File	Deceased	Year
541	Young, George T.	1960
9270	Young, Gertrude S.	1984
SE79	Young, Harry	1982
2993	Young, Hazel M.	1963
4432	Young, Henry O.	1970
2705	Young, J. B.	1961
1712	Young, J. Estle	1953
15462	Young, J. Wells Jr.	1996
4683	Young, James B.	1970
1553	Young, John P.	1951
18160	Young, John S, Jr.	2000
3295	Young, Kate	1965
10744	Young, Kenneth Edgar	1987
5246	Young, Lynn O.	1973
11486	Young, Mary Agnes	1989
2706	Young, Mattie	1961
2297	Young, Mollie Black	1958
9416	Young, Naomi E.	1985
18542	Young, Noble	2001
8467	Young, Phillis Ann	1983
8479	Young, Ronald D.	1983
11868	Young, Ruby Sutton	1989
6743	Young, Ruth Anderson	1976
17362	Young, Ruth Marie	1999
18148	Youngberg, Eric G.	2000
10780	Youngblood, Floyd Andrew	1987
624	Youngblood, J. H.	1926
4966	Younger, Ellen Mae Odom	1972
4234	Youngs, Helen Mc Bride	1969/70
2015	Youngs, William H. W.	1954/56
16632	Youngstedt, Etelka R.	1998
13422	Younts, Ethel Shane	1992

File	Deceased	Year

File	Deceased	Year
15752	Zuber, Minnie Marion	1996
18732	Zuercher, Ella	2001
10550	Zuercher, Louis W.	1987
19044	Zuniga, Leonor	2002
9576	Zunis, Rachel A.	1985
2710	Zwanzig, Charles D.	1961
7006	Zwamzig, Sara	1984